Teaching for Apocalypse

Teaching for Apocalypse

COVID-19's Message to Educators
and Those They Serve

MEG GORZYCKI

RESOURCE *Publications* • Eugene, Oregon

TEACHING FOR APOCALYPSE
COVID-19's Message to Educators and Those They Serve

Resource Publications
An Imprint of Wipf and Stock Publishers
199 W. 8th Ave., Suite 3
Eugene, OR 97401

www.wipfandstock.com

PAPERBACK ISBN: 978-1-7252-8511-8
HARDCOVER ISBN: 978-1-7252-8512-5
EBOOK ISBN: 978-1-7252-8513-2

Manufactured in the U.S.A.   11/30/20

This book is dedicated to the memory of Dr. Li Wenliang, the physician in Wuhan, China, who lost his life in the fight for professional integrity, truth, and public safety. It is also dedicated to every teacher, educational administrator, and public policy-maker who are not yet disturbed by achievement gaps in student learning and holes in the general public's knowledge about the world. Arguably, it is time to be disturbed. This is for readers who are ready to think about what ignorance does to individuals and society, and to consider what the failure to cultivate compassion and the commitment to live for causes higher than one's own self does to civilization.

Contents

Acknowledgments

There are those who help us find the appropriate words because they help us find an appropriate way of thinking. There are those who help us find the courage to articulate what we have learned. These scholars and prophets often speak to us through great literary works of the past, and they also speak to us in the present, face to face, if we listen carefully. Special thanks to Don McLeod, Sondra Arnsdorf, Ben Owens, Pamela Howard, Geoffrey Desa, Greg Vanderheiden, Debbie Dean, Diane Allen, and Stasia Fisher.

Preface

Getting to apocalypse takes a lot of effort from a lot of people, but somehow, we made it look easy. We made it to the precipice of our own extinction by way of global warming, disease, and war for so many reasons, that it is difficult to say which has had the greatest impact. Was it corporate corruption? Greed? Bigotry? Entitlement in all class levels? Bad parenting? Rotten education? Scandals in our houses of worship? The refusal to love as Jesus loved? Buffoonery in high office? Partisan news media? Junk food? Disrespect for ecosystems? Egos gone wild? There are so many choices. Undoubtedly, however, ignorance plays a huge role in our plight.

The apocalypse here addressed is a planet-wide catastrophe characterized by the collapse of economic systems, global environmental ruin, and non-cooperation. Nobody should be surprised by a candid discussion of death and doom. We are as human as other civilizations before us who were annihilated by plagues, war, and environmental change. Unlike many who have gone before us, however, we have the science to predict and prevent many disasters. Yet, it appears that we do not always want to dodge the inevitable bullet.

During the COVID-19 crisis in the United States, I wondered whether my vocation, education, contributed the chaos, irrationality, and suffering that attended the pandemic. While schools and colleges are not to blame for the outbreak, I believe that they helped to create a society that is vulnerable to crises and does not mind creating them. If we think about knowledge, ethical judgment, and epistemological sophistication as society's defense against lies, propaganda, and hatred, then in medical terms, we have a "compromised immune system." Teachers and administrators at all levels have tolerated mediocrity or worse in our schools and universities for so long, that many Americans were intellectually unable to tell the difference between credibility and hogwash. I realized during the pandemic that educators on the whole believe in making the world a better place, but have often compromised the quality of education and pursued misguided trends at great cost to our intelligence, well-being, and sustainability. I cannot speak for all in the ministry of education, but I offer the following letter to Americans with both sincerity and exasperation.

Dear America,

I am sorry about the gaping holes in what we Americans know about the natural environment, biology, world cultures, geography, economics, and our own constitution. It was my profession's job to keep you well-informed and your minds fit and ready to put assertions to the test of reason, fairness, and accuracy. We dropped the ball lots of times.

I imagine that as the COVID-19 pandemic swept across the nation, many of you said to your selves, "My God, are we really that stupid!" I know that it is politically incorrect to use the word "stupid," but I heard it a lot during the crisis. Some say that the word "uninformed" is better. That works up to a point, but many Americans were not just uninformed, they clung to their opinions despite what scientists said, and were openly hostile to information that contradicted their personal beliefs. Teachers are supposed to foster respect for science, patience for complex problem-solving, and open-mindedness. Clearly, we were not 100 percent successful.

I apologize for being intimidated by accusations of elitism when I stood for high standards. In a world where high standards have been code words for bigotry, I get why people do not like the term. I also see why high standards of learning are urgently needed across privileged and vulnerable populations. I sometimes confused community satisfaction with exemplary teaching and learning. I am sorry for tolerating the idea that self-esteem is more important intellectual and character development. Such tolerance helped to create a society in which we have many who are proudly confident in their knowledge and reasoning, but who in fact have little knowledge and do not reason well. I am sorry that I was not more active in helping the community create safe schools wherein students learned to love learning.

I apologize for being afraid to tell parents and school boards that it is very difficult for even the best teachers to teach children who were never taught by their parents how to delay gratification, clean up their messes, how to be courteous, and how to take responsibility for learning. I also feel shame in not having taken a bolder stand against tenure protocols that have allowed incompetent teachers to teach, and against the ghastly bloating of administrative costs.

I am sorry that I did not more effectively protest the pressure put upon professors to improve persistence and graduation rates that rewarded them for making atrocious compromises in their work. With every inflated grade and every lowered standard the integrity of my profession takes another hit. I am sorry for tolerating post-secondary teaching that retreated from teaching students how to think critically, read deeply and analytically, and write proficiently because instructors "lacked training," or "did not have time." In too many instances, students did not learn how to grapple intelligently and compassionately with vagueness, paradox, irony, and the complexities of the human condition. Too many college graduates do not understand the difference between the expert and the novice, and lack humility in the face of their own ignorance.

I am sorry for not being a bolder advocate of studies in religion, spirituality, and sacred wisdom traditions. Such knowledge represents a universal yearning for meaning in life, and a desire for moral paradigms that respect human dignity. Without understanding these things, it is easier for us to hit the default button on our conscience, and let popular opinion, egoism, ignorance, and prejudice be the four corners of our moral compasses, and to mock the existential journey of others.

I regret being selfish with praise and gratitude for instructors and administrators who are "top shelf" humanitarians and educators. I appreciate the many patient, wise, and compassionate people who generously illuminated my path.

Sincerely.

This book uses the COVID-19 crisis as a graphic illustration of why our educational system needs an overhaul. It is a manifesto against ignorance, partisanship, and self-interest that creeps into all of our institutions. I believe that education has the potential to make us wiser, slower to judge, more empathetic, and more effective problem-solvers. I also know that even when our educational system is at its best, it will never ensure—100 percent—that people will drop their egos and join hands for a tender Kumbaya. The will to hate and hurt cannot be purged by learning alone. Our values and attitudes matter. We all need education to do a better job of helping us recognize soul-savaging monsters, what is at stake in empowering them, and how to avoid becoming one.

Chapter 1

Introduction

THE BIG BUG

After discovering that a parent of a student had contracted the COVID-19 virus, a high school near the campus of the public four-year university where I work cancelled classes on March 5, 2020. The high school's administrators closed the campus without word of when classes would resume. Word spread quickly through the corridors and offices of the university. My unit was especially attentive to developments, as it provides faculty with instruction on how to design and facilitate remote instruction. We understood the implications of a campus closure.

At that time in March, about 6,000 people in the United States were infected with COVID-19, and 12 people had died from the disease: eleven in Washington and one in California.[1] At the university, effective March 9, 2020, faculty and staff were directed to move instruction and certain operations to remote venues. On March 16, 2020, employees, faculty, and students were informed that only the most essential administration and staff would be permitted on campus, with the possibility that this arrangement could be in place until the semester's end. The announcement signaled an "all hands on deck" for my unit. With nearly 30,000 students enrolled, and about 1,700 faculty to serve, my united braced for high impact. We expected and received waves of petitions for individual consultations and assistance with

1. "WHO Urges Nations," para. 3–4.

technical operations. We knew that not all students had access to computers and laptops at home. We knew that many students did not have reliable internet service in their homes. We knew that many instructors had never used a digital, internet-supported learning management system (LMS) for teaching. Like millions of students and teachers all over the country, we faced the question of how to maintain the continuity and integrity of teaching and learning as it was suddenly forced into online venues.

My unit was fortunate as our directors had been proactive about increasing the number of instructors who were proficient with our LMS. For years prior to the COVID-19 outbreak, the team developed workshops, mentoring opportunities, and "help documents" related to remote instruction. As the nation braced itself for school closures, our unit anticipated a deluge of requests for consultations and technical support. We experienced a spike in webinar attendance and Zoom® meetings initially, but the swells were not overwhelming. We rode the waves with relative ease, in part because the tsunami we expected was diverted by peer support. As the urgency of getting courses online intensified, instructors seemed to pop up in every department to help colleagues in distress. It was impressive. The threat of COVID-19 managed to accomplish what years of small grants and administrative encouragement had failed to do: it motivated instructors en masse to become proficient with remote instruction.

By the end of March, 2020, my unit had developed and facilitated several webinars devoted to remote instruction and LMS tools. It provided consultation and guidance for over 300 faculty members in 21 days, posted new digital resources for faculty seeking pedagogical insights to online teaching and learning, and participated in frequent meetings to access progress and plan for subsequent faculty support. The team was especially focused on acquainting faculty with the basic tools and options in the LMS. There were many faculty already proficient with the LMS who wanted to learn more about how to use the technology for teaching in ways they had never dreamed they would need to know. The team grounded their work in the principles of best practices for remote and face-to-face instruction:

- Communicate frequently with students
- Create lessons that require student interaction and engagement in meaningful activity
- Be explicit and precise about expectations, directions, grading criteria, and standards
- Provide help documents, such as glossaries, examples of work, or links to data banks and reports

- Provide information about where students can get tutoring or psychological services
- Exhibit empathy
- Be mindful of student behavior that might indicate that they are adversely impacted by trauma
- Be flexible with the pace of lessons and deadlines.

We "had it wired." We helped faculty resolve problems related to accessibility, academic integrity, humanizing remote instruction, and how to maintain equity in education.

On the whole, faculty and staff leaned into the challenge of radically altering the mode of instruction with confidence that we were not "salvaging" a semester, but instead were sustaining the semester's work—going ahead with pedagogical principles that were already in place for face-to-face classes, as if the only thing we did was to change lanes on a freeway. That is how it was for most students and teachers. For others, however, the freeway abruptly ended, potholes the size of volcanic craters opened up, and fog as dense as gelatin settled across the landscape. Despite the team's success with training faculty in how to use the LMS and assisting them in making critical decisions about lessons and teaching strategies, there remained questions about the quality of instruction, many of which predated the COVID-19 pandemic.

This book is not about how to save education with remote instruction, or how to build faculty proficiency with technology. Yes, my unit performed efficiently and effectively as the university shifted from face-to-face courses to remote instruction. If the story here were about how a single team rose to the occasion of adversity, I could end here with much sincere praise for the pedagogical expertise, technical skills, industriousness and compassion of the staff. However, that is not what this book is all about. This book is about our limited expectations for education, and how gaps in learning contribute to our crises and suffering.

This book is about the big picture that COVID-19 forced me to think about. This book is about disparate puzzle pieces of practice, social expectations, and educational politics that crashed into my mind as I thought about how Americans reacted to the crisis. The crisis placed the quality of our national preparedness and leadership in the spotlight. It made me think about how the United States, one of the most powerful, technologically and scientifically advanced, and wealthiest of nations in modern history, could have become the pandemic's epicenter. Throughout the ordeal, it was nearly impossible for me not to think about what went wrong. Questions begat questions. Why did the federal government delay executive actions to shelter in place? Why were there shortages of medical supplies, such as ventilators, masks, gloves, and sanitizers?[2] Why did the president say the epidemic was a hoax?[3] Why did so many people not take seriously the warnings about COVID-19 when there was time to mobilize resources? Why did so many journalists, elected officials, and citizens devote endless hours of discussion to getting the country back to business to revive the stock market, and spend so little time talking about how our values and way of life were contributing factors to crisis?

MY KALEIDOSCOPE

We all see the COVID-19 crisis through the lens of our own experiences and convictions. My lens is a kaleidoscope. I look with the eyes of an educator, historian, baby boomer, social critic, and woman on a spiritual journey. I look with beliefs in my heart that get challenged every day. Chief among my beliefs is that creation and all of us exist for a sacred purpose, which is to learn to love and serve causes greater than ourselves. I believe that people are more important than wealth, power, and popularity, despite relentless propaganda to the contrary. I also believe people are not only diminished and debased by corporate exploitation, but that people diminish and debase themselves when they neglect the development of their own knowledge and intelligence, when they expect others to clean up their messes, and when they deny their own ignorance even when the evidence for it is overwhelming. Ignorance knows no class distinction. Both the pauper and the prince suffer and cause suffering when they inflict their ignorance on others.

Through my lens, I saw the COVID crisis as the logical consequence of human interaction with nature. Viruses and other pathogens, after all, pre-date the existence of human beings by millions of years, and they are designed to survive under harsh conditions. For pandemics to occur, bugs have to have access to, and learn to live inside human beings. Human beings help these tiny critters along by coming into contact with animals already on the microbe's menu, or by invading the pathogen's once isolated home turf.

The minute human behavior becomes a factor in any crisis, I think about the responsibility of people in my profession. I think about what is essential to know. I think about whether our own ignorance is inching us ever closer to apocalypse, and if so, are we obligated to do something about that? The overarching question driving this composition is: "Is it possible

2. Ranney et al., "Critical Supply Shortages," para. 1–4.

3. Egan, "Trump Calls Coronavirus," para. 1–5.

for schools, colleges, and universities in the United States to do a better job of educating the public, so that we are able to, and committed to reducing the likelihood of extinction, and the messes we have made that produce so much suffering, death, and destruction?"

I take the question seriously because our messes are serious. COVID-19 is not the first epidemic to appear in the U.S. in my lifetime. Polio made the rounds in the 1950s, London Flu (H3N2) toured the country in 1972–73. HIV/AIDS ravaged the U.S. in the 1980s and beyond. Measles, always had a place in the American 20th century and annually in the 1950s, case numbers averaged 550,000 with nearly 500 deaths.[4] Despite the introduction of a vaccine for Measles in 1963, epidemics that killed over 165 individuals erupted in the 1980s and 1990s, largely due to the unwillingness of people to get vaccinated or vaccinate their children. In 2009, the N1H1 or "Swine Flu" infected over 60 million and killed nearly 12,500 Americans.[5]

One might bristle at the notion that an epidemic could be a manmade mess. It is easier to believe that the pandemic is an organic phenomenon that occurs independent of human activity. "Not so," says Mother Nature. Many outbreaks have erupted across the planet because human beings are disrupting wild habitats that have had no human contact for generations. Moreover, once a pathogen makes its way into a community, human activity often accelerates infection and mortality. Such activities include: insufficient stockpiling of medical supplies; limited access to clinics and hospitals; failure to teach our children good health habits; failure to fund research aimed at preventing pandemics; refusal of our national commitment to cooperate with other countries in the tasks of disease prevention, reporting, and intervention; acting with indifference toward the appalling conditions of care facilities for our elders and vulnerable populations; failures to prohibit hunting of and consumption of wild animals; and, cutting our way into wilderness not yet commandeered for human profit—every time we do these things, we put ourselves at risk and enable disease.

Pathogens and pandemics, however, are not the only things that disturb me as an educator. Our apocalypse is a puzzle with many pieces, such as global warming, over population, nationalism, and militarism. I am disturbed by chronic poverty and racism, and the visceral feeling that macho demagogues are ready to destroy what cannot they understand and control. There is also the sickening sensation that many of our elected leaders—guardians of the republic and public well-being—are more committed to protecting millionaires and their interests, than they are committed to

4. Gindler et al., "Acute Measles Mortality," para. 1.
5. Centers for Disease Control, "2009 N1H1," para. 2.

protecting democracy and the well-being of people and the environment. Why bring elected officials and corporations into a discussion about CO-VID-19 and American education? The simple answer is that this pandemic and other catastrophes—from economic recession, to chronic poverty, to war, to global warming—are consequences of manmade economic and political policies and practice. In the republic, those we elect regulate production, distribution, taxes, and public support for private and public enterprise. They also decide when to enforce regulations and when to "let things slide," and to what extent the nation will work with others around the world to monitor, prepare for, and avoid all types of catastrophes.

History teaches us that individuals can play pivotal roles in disasters. Think of Napoleon's decision to invade Russia in 1812, and the one million soldiers and civilians who perished because one man lusted for empire. Think of Police Officer Derek Chauvin's decision to pin George Floyd's neck to the asphalt of a Minneapolis street long enough for Floyd to die as witnesses filmed the event. That nine minutes of indiscretion and brutality set off weeks of protest which led to looting and arson in many cities across the U.S.[6] History teaches us that tragedies are also often the result of the common individual's own sense of duty, sense of self, and image of glory. Let us not forget that 650,000 men willingly marched with Napoleon against Czar Alexander's army.[7] Let us not forget that police officers had taken the lives of many African American men and women—even when those suspects were unarmed and already subdued— long before George Floyd cried, "I can't breathe."[8]

The COVID-19 crisis teachers us that leadership matters. It teaches us that unless we learn to be better judges of leadership, we could very well be led to an apocalypse when we think we are headed for Shangri-La. It teaches us that unless we alter our way of life, our ecosystems will become exhausted and unsustainable, and that unless we become more and more cooperative with everyone, including our adversaries, we may very well be headed for extinction.

6. See Maxouris et al., "Cities Extend Curfews."

7. Zamoyski's Moscow 1812 narrates the saga of Napoleon's imperialistic ambitions, how his lack of a naval power strong enough to defeat Britain led to his "Continental System" to cripple Britain's economy, and how the Czar's refusal to play along drove Napoleon to underestimate both the Russian people and the Russian winter.

8. African American men who were killed by white officers include Oscar Grant (Oakland, CA, 2009); Michale Brown (Ferguson, MO, 2014); Tamir Rice (Cleveland, OH, 2014); Eric Garner (New York, NY, 2014); Walter Scott (North Charleston, SC, 2015); Alton Sterling (Baton Rouge, LA, 2016); and Philando Castile (Falcon Heights, MN, 2016).

HOPE AND MINISTRY

A dear friend and colleague listened as I described my thoughts for this essay, and suggested that perhaps I was being too negative. She told me that my assessments were very "dire." I respect my friend immensely and thought about what she said. I agree that my assessments are dire, but as to the point of being "too negative," I am not sure. I know that thousands of educators and public servants are doing wonderful things to teach others and increase access to education so that everyone can improve their lives. Yet, I feel like a passenger on the Titanic: I am very positive about the hard working, kind, and intelligent crew members on board, and although they may inform the captain about imminent threats, they are not in command.

It is very common for educators to feel that they are obligated to always be "sunny side up," and to be cheerful and optimistic regardless of bureaucratic foibles and our own mediocrity. In the U.S., teachers are often perceived as extensions of maternal caring and symbols of unconditional affection and hope. These tropes sometimes interfere with educators' own ability to be objective and critical about what is happening in our institutions.

Teachers with dire observations are often accused of taking a "deficit approach" rather than a "developmental approach" to education. The deficit approach is characterized by the presumption that students are flawed and need to be repaired. Many dislike the word "deficit" because they believe that this approach ultimately crushes students' spirits and their capacity to learn. The developmental model does not presume students are flawed and need to be fixed. Instead, it sees students as individuals who are full of potential to learn, and who are quick to catch on when the right instructional methods are applied. These terms are sometimes abused.

Not everyone who uses the term "deficit" to describe academic achievement believe that deficits are personal flaws. When speaking of deficits, people often have proficiencies in mind, and many of these proficiencies are those of external agencies and employers who will evaluate the graduate's readiness for employment or advanced studies. Many educators gladly adjust their lexicon as to show respect for students all along the learning curve, but problems arise when people tinker with practice. The "developmental" approach to instruction frequently refers to strategies that "work around" gaps in knowledge and skill. They are sometimes not truly developmental because they excuse students from improving their competence in certain academic subjects by assigning work that does not require competence in certain knowledge and skills. Allowing students who cannot write well to create a poster in place of composing an essay is an example off this phenomenon. The poster might illustrate key findings in research, but it will not demonstrate the student's ability to synthesize the literature, organize components of scholarly composition, and articulate complex information in the same way as scholarly writing.

Deep and meaningful hope is a requirement for our well-being. It motivates us to do our best, and sustains us when our troubles seem overwhelming. Deep and meaningful hope, however, is not authentic and enduring when based upon misconceptions about our condition. Hope is legitimate when it is grounded in honest inventories of our failures and our role in creating dire circumstances. Hope needs truth, and truth is known by way vigilance and the courage to see what is there to see. Though educators are widely expected to give people hope, our primary job is to help us overcome ignorance, and fortify our minds with knowledge and thinking skills that enable us to live self-sufficiently and cooperatively among our fellows and in our environment. Admittedly, this perspective of education is rational in its outlook, as it assumes that people want to be self-sufficient, well-informed, and civil for their own, if not everyone's, well-being. Not everyone, however, strives to overcome ignorance, and not everyone reviles ignorance, even when they know it may lead to ruin.

David Schulz, Professor of Political Science, has written prolifically about how ignorance often prevails in government and political decision-making. He observes that political rhetoric is frequently peppered with exaggerations, lies, distortions, and fabrications, because voters are aroused by the spectacle and the dramatic, and because they gravitate towards leaders who share their own personal biases and myths about the way the world works. Schultz notes that political agendas and priorities are often pushed in irrational or irresponsible directions because voters and politicians *do not seek* nor *believe* what scientists and social scientists have to say about our problems and potential solutions. He wrote:

> It [ignorance] refers to the fact that often times specific ideas such as the building of sports stadiums for economic development, or tax cuts to encourage relocations, have been repeatedly employed or tried in the past, with little evidence of their success being demonstrated. Ignorance refers also to the adoption of proposals or legislative ideas despite the fact that the best evidence available suggests that they will not be successful in securing their stated aim.[9]

Schultz recognizes the power of myths in marshaling public support for bad ideas, which underscores the importance of education that helps us decode and expose the myths that perpetuate the exploitation of taxpayers and the

9. Schultz, *American Politics*, 13.

suffering of the poor.[10] Ultimately, the COIVD-19 crisis exposed not only gaps in American's knowledge about the world, disease, and governance, it also exposed America's stubborn refusal to learn and face facts.

Education is more than a systematic means of imparting declarative knowledge. It is about fostering respect for the how knowledge is constructed and tested against high standards of credibility. It is about the transformative processes whereby individuals move away from uncritical, dualistic, and superficial thinking to critical, deep, and analytical thinking. Education is also formative as it is concerned with the development of personal character, values, attitudes, and moral outlook. The COVID-19 pandemic raised questions about whether our schools, colleges, and universities have been doing their best in the area of character formation.

IS THERE A DOCTRINE IN THE HOUSE?

Talk of character formation at all levels of education makes people nervous, because there is always the potential for formation to be a vehicle of indoctrination. Such anxieties make sense, but they often slide over two critical points. First, educational institutions have been indoctrinating people for generations. We have taught our children, for example, that democracy is the best form of government, that capitalism is the best economic system, and that the American way of live is superior to all other ways of life. Second, it is imperative for large, diverse, and complex societies to indoctrinate their people, because such societies are unlikely to thrive without a strong consensus about what individuals owe to each other, and which norms and values ought to guide legislation, law enforcement, and institutional practices.

Indoctrination is not moral or immoral by definition. It can, however, be abused. It can be based on superstitions and erroneous assumptions. It can be imposed not for the sake of facilitating enlightenment or individual actualization, but to concentrate power and wealth in the hands of the few. Indoctrination can be so thorough that it becomes impervious to scientific evidence that contradicts its assertions. Indoctrination can project the notion that rational ideas are infallible ideas. The doctrine that capitalism is the best economic system, for example, is so deeply entrenched in our minds that we frequently do not question authorities who justify economic policies and initiatives that threaten the environment or community's well-being. We are so well-indoctrinated that many reflexively accuse capitalism's critics of being socialists, even when they do not understand socialism. In the magic of our own myths, we the people sometimes hurt ourselves by

10. Schultz, *American Politics*, 22.

believing that we know what we do not know. What local governments have done to leverage public money for private profit in the world of professional sports provides but one example.

Between 1992 and 2012, taxpayers in various cities across the U.S. paid an average of 73 percent of the cost for building football and baseball stadiums, and between 1992 and 2004, that added up to $10 billion. Team owners who benefit from picking the public's pocket claimed that they did not have enough money to build stadiums, and boasted that new stadiums would create jobs and increase revenue in local and state coffers. Research indicates, however, that the wealth per capita in cities that built such facilities did not increase significantly, and that these enterprises account for less than one percent of the local economy.[11] In the case of the stadium, despite knowing that jobs were seasonal and paid minimum wages, many taxpayers happily opened their wallets to billionaires because of their sentimental attachments to the home team.

What has all this chat about stadiums have to do with indoctrination and the formation of character in our schools and universities? First, indoctrination is implicit in education at all levels. What we are required to know, what perspectives dominate our lessons, and what is unimportant to the academy shapes the narratives by which we live. The question society faces is not whether schools and universities should indoctrinate students—because they already do that—the question is what doctrines may serve us well.

Second, the culture in our schools and universities often champion and mirror popular culture, and scorn those who criticize it. In the matter of big sports, most of us grew up cheering for the home team and developed an affinity to the rituals associated with sports. We readily allow sentimentality to influence our decision-making, but only rarely undertake a rigorous academic analysis and critique of the consequences of such behavior, and where sentiment often clashes with our own espoused values and moral convictions. That taxpayers are willing to give money to the super rich so that they can build stadiums, while local populations are expected to thrive on minimum wage jobs and send their children to dilapidated and dysfunctional schools, signals a need to cross examine our values.

Arguably, there is a need for formal education to increase inquiries into and conversations about morality, ethics, spirituality, and humanitarianism in public policy. The purpose of this is twofold. First, it would enrich students' cultural competency by introducing them to the philosophies and sacred teachings that have shaped and continue to shape our world, and deepen their understanding of the role that philosophical and religious

11. Schultz, *American Politics*, 47—53.

ideas play in the formation of public morality. Second, it would encourage students' to see that our choices, including those regarding public policy and material consumption, have moral implications.

During the COVID-19 crisis, the world witnessed examples of America's courage, generosity, empathy, work ethic, and self-sacrifice. It also saw examples of moral disorientation, inhumanity, lack of integrity, and mean-spiritedness. Is it not possible that we might have done better in the crisis if schools and colleges had helped students understand when and why to be humble, and how to confront the values and attitudes inside of ourselves that prevent us from being empathetic, just, and humanitarian? Might the efforts that schools and universities are already making to refine students' sense of social responsibility and moral reasoning be more effective if curriculum and instruction that addressed these matters were systematically integrated across all levels of all disciplines, rather than representing episodic learning that is often perceived as an amendment to an already complete education?

Many doctrines go unscrutinized, including the claims that Americans have and deserve the best standard of living. Many of us have never been required to study the cost of creating the American empire, who suffers in order to maintain it, and what it has done to the planet. The unspoken bargain that we have struck with our conscience is that the collateral damage resulting from our way of life is justified by the spectacular achievements of the United States and its capacity to generate wealth. At present, the collateral damage of our way of life includes the extinction of animal species, global warming, neglect of our elders, homelessness, pandemics, dysfunctional public services, broken infrastructures, impoverished Native American reservations, urban ghettos, and war.

Our schools and colleges are caught up in the paradox of our plight. On one hand, they are committed to educating for upward mobility and preparing students to succeed in the material world, where "success" is often achieved at great cost to the environment and measured in terms of short-term profit. On the other hand, they also want students to care for the environment, fight for social justice, and mind the global implications of their consumption. The question arises: should we maintain a standard of living for 5 percent of the world's population that consumes about 25 percent of its resources?[12]

One might ask at this point, "Is this book about how education can save the world?" The answer is, resolutely, "No." Social change can be coaxed and informed by education, but educators do not make public policy, nor

12. See Center for Sustainable Systems, "U.S. Environmental Footprint" for details on American consumption.

can they mandate individuals to embrace a particular set of values and habits. Education cannot force people to use knowledge and skills for moral purposes and social improvement, but it can help people understand what could happen if they do not.

AIN'T NOTHIN' NEW

During the COVID-19 crisis, most instructors were not very interested in philosophical conversations about how people learn or what constitutes a proper college liberal arts education. They wanted to just get through the semester. They wanted to know which boxes to click so that they could do what they needed to do with the LMS. They wanted to complete the semester without traumatizing themselves and their students. They flinched when their peers talked about course content, because they associated it with prescriptive teaching. This was nothing new.

As it became clear that remote instruction would likely be mandated for the summer and fall semesters, college instructors who had previously expressed little interest in course design and instructional strategies suddenly became voracious consumers of material that offered tips for teaching. The matter of pedagogy, which so many had dismissed as the concern of K-12 educators, was now center-stage. The demand to learn about outcome-based teaching, student engagement, brain-based instruction, scaffolding, course alignment, and formative assessment was terrific. These were the things that had captivated my colleagues while I was an administrator at the secondary level in the 1990s. It seemed that instantly the works of Ralph Tyler, Robert Marzano, Grant Wiggins, Jay McTighe, Jon Saphier, Robert Gower, and other practitioners in the cognitive developmental and constructivist traditions were in vogue.[13]

What could have been a victory lap for us dinosaurs who have always believed that college professors ought to be trained in pedagogical theories and practice, became in many instances a stroll to the locker room. Instructors wanted to know about teaching strategies, techniques, and methods as they had to adapt their instruction repertoire to the digital platform. That is a good thing. However, the conversations about teaching and learning tended to stall on matters of substance and developmental learning. Professors were interested in how to engage students, for example, but their interest

---

13. Ralph Tyler, *Basic Principles of Curriculum and Instruction* (University of Chicago, 1949); Jon Saphier and Robert Gower, *The Skillful Teacher* (ASCD, 1982), Robert Marzano, *Classrooms that Work* (ASCD, 2001); Grant Wiggins and Jay McTighe, *Understanding by Design*, (ASCD, 2005).

was conditional. They were not always open to certain kinds of engagement, especially critical reading and writing research papers.

The wave of literature that washed over the academic community in 2020 aimed to help instructors use digital strategies, techniques, and methods. Course content was normally addressed in journals dedicated to a specific subject. Professors typically do not like to be urged to integrate developmental instruction that is universal to all disciplines into their courses. They guard their academic freedom, and often believe that only a peer in one's own discipline has anything legitimate to say about course content. This approach to education side-steps the reality that all teaching is by nature developmental, as reading proficiency, epistemological beliefs, rhetorical skills, and moral judgment are all things people learn over a lifetime. Many professors do not think of these things as they "teach their subjects," yet their attitudes towards them is often visible to students. Much of the pedagogical advice instructors received during the crisis focused on using technology, and adjusting lessons to accommodate students. Equity was very much on people's minds. Very few dared to ask whether it was possible to "adjust" and "accommodate" to the point where learning was not "equitable," and had perhaps become inferior. As our current condition suggests, we need education to aggressively confront our ignorance about the world, and to hold us to high standards of critical thinking and moral judgement, because without these things, we may not be able to meet the challenges of living in the 21st century.

Long before COVID-19 showed up, the professoriate was already diverse in its interests and motivations. Some instructors took teaching assignments because they were passionate about fostering intellectual curiosity and growth. Others taught as a way to access research resources. A number liked lengthy summer vacations. Some relished pedagogical studies and learned about course design, while others thought that pedagogical development was beneath them.

Prior to the pandemic, many scholars, policy-makers and leaders of the business community expressed concern that Americans do not always use the right metrics to measure the value and success of schools and universities. In higher education, the value of institutions is frequently measured by how many students persist to degree, how long it took students to persist to degree, and graduation rates of underrepresented minorities. Colleges and universities are not required to administer exit exams. Instead, its administrators and the community at large assume that a professor's grade is a true, accurate, and credible representation of students' achievements. This confidence persists even though the meaning of grades varies not only between institutions, but between departments on the same campus, and between instructors in the same department.

High expectations and high standards in grading policies have often been casualties in the crusade to increase the number of individuals who receive college diplomas, and in the battle for tenure. For hundreds of thousands of students and their families, the college diploma represents a ticket into the middle class and a means of overcoming poverty. Policy-makers, instructors, and post-secondary administrators all know this. The idea that the highest purpose of a college degree is to propel upward mobility has led some institutions to admit greater numbers of students who are ill-prepared for post-secondary studies, and has increased the pressure many instructors feel to inflate grades and lower standards. As one professor of over 25 years told me, "I admit it. . .I am not proud of it, but I admit that I inflate grades. . .I don't' want to be the guy that gets blamed for holding somebody back from the American dream."

The commitment to help students who are underprepared for college, challenged by poverty, and struggling with motivation is noble. Nobility, however, evaporates when the means to an end radically alters the end itself. Grade inflation and lowering of standards pre-dates COVID-19, but the crisis raised the question of whether it is time to end such practices. Can civilization proceed wisely during pandemics and manmade disasters if it is populated by people who believe that they are very intelligent and informed when they are not? Is it not perplexing and problematic that we have so much poverty, bigotry, corruption, and disregard for the dignity of life in the U.S., where 65 percent of the population believe that they are smarter than the average person?[14]

COVID-19 is not responsible for the state of education in the United States. It is not responsible for curriculum, teacher training, tenure, or instruction. It has not determined the purpose for which teachers and professors teach. The COVID crisis, however, raises many serious questions for educators, including:

1. What do Americans know about themselves and the world?

2. Why do Americans know or not know certain things?

3. Is the knowledge Americans possess sufficient for solving the problems humanity faces in the 21st century?

4. Has American education done a good job with cultivating virtues becoming of a benevolent and responsible nation?

14. Heck et al., "65% of Americans," para. 1.

5. Has American education done enough to cultivate personal judgement that is empathetic, broad in regard for others, modest in want, humble, and respectful of the dignity of humanity and the natural environment?

The COVID-19 crisis illuminated the reality that many Americans, including elected officials, have serious gaps in their scientific knowledge and understanding of the law. It revealed that many Americans are willing to believe and disseminate myths and falsehoods about disease, health care, and national preparedness for pandemics. It also showed us that many people are willing to lie and maliciously attack those who speak truth to power. The COVID-19 crisis exposed the nation's vulnerability to ignorance and propaganda.

America has many educators who want reform. COVID-19 invites them and all of us to decide whether we want to make robust changes in curriculum and instruction for the purpose of steering the Titanic away from the ice field, or dispense with substantial reforms and hope that the ice field magically moves out of our way.

PURPOSE AND ORGANIZATION

The purposes of this book is to confront the limitations of our current educational paradigm, explain why it should be changed, and offer ideas and strategies for change. This book expresses a sense of urgency for educators, citizens, and policy-makers to discuss topics that are extremely difficult and complex. The urgency is owed to increasing scientific evidence that human behavior is getting in the way of human existence.

This essay is based on four premises. Frist: formal education contributes to our collective ability to make wise choices about how we live. Second: society has a moral obligation to see that ignorance and incivility are overcome and discouraged. Third: parents are our children's first teachers, and as such are responsible for stimulating their children's love of learning, and teaching their children how to delay gratification, play nice with others, and take responsibility for their actions. Fourth: in its current state, formal education leaves too many people ignorant of the world around them, and too many lacking in critical thinking and problem-solving skills.

Chapter two introduces key notions about American education, and examines the democratization of higher education and its consequences. Chapter three explains why our response to the pandemic and other serious problems is not as effective as it could be. Chapter four chronicles the COVID-19 crisis, which is the backdrop of this discussion, as assertions about education and educational reforms are mapped to specific COVID-19 crisis events. Chapter five addresses what the pandemic teaches us about our ignorance of the natural world, governance, propaganda, and cultural competency, and why such ignorance matters. Chapters six and seven examine prevailing priorities in education and their limited ability to provide essential knowledge and skills. Chapter eight presents ideas about reforming curriculum and instruction, while chapter nine addresses reforms in institutional structure and culture.

In this text, spirituality refers to the aspect of the human experience which is intangible and transcendent, and which is associated with the sense that human beings are part of a sacred creation and created for a sacred purpose that is higher than one's material survival and well-being. In this text, spirituality is not the sole property of any religion, rather it is a universal phenomenon that articulates universal yearning for connectedness, love, and reverence for human dignity, humility, and respect for all creation. Biblical references in this text are from the *New Oxford Annotated Bible with the Apocrypha* (Oxford University Press, 1977).

GLOSSARY

Apocalypse in the biblical sense refers to the end of the world, a summative destruction of the Earth. It also regards events with enormous catastrophic outcomes. This text uses the term to refer to disastrous events, and not the end of the world.

AT stands for academic technology. AT units exist to help students and instructors learn how to use learning management systems (LMS), software, and various media for teaching and learning.

BARDA (Biomedical Advanced Research and Development Authority) is a special unit in the U.S. Department of Health and Human Services (HSS). Its job is to distribute federal money to researchers studying pathogens and potential cures. BARDA also advises government officials about which drugs to stockpile, and how and when to distribute them in a medical emergency.

Bloom's Taxonomy is a classification of cognitive tasks. Lower levels contain cognitive tasks such as recalling and explaining, and higher levels contain analysis, synthesis, and evaluation.[15]

---

15. See Anderson and Krathwohl, *A Taxonomy for Learning, Teaching, and Assessing.*

Coronavirus is a virus that differs from influenza in its structure and effects. Like influenza, coronaviruses are spread by inhaling microbes or having contact with infected surfaces. They cause respiratory distress and symptoms of flu. Coronaviruses incubate longer than flu viruses. The mortality rate for the flu is about 0.1 percent. The mortality rate varies by location and efficacy of diagnoses. Some say the mortality rate for the coronavirus it is about 30 percent,[16] while others say it is roughly 6 percent.[17]

Declarative knowledge refers to facts and information that functions largely to identify or explain things. Declarative knowledge differs from procedural knowledge which regards steps and processes, and contextual knowledge, which regards knowing when to apply specific knowledge.

Dunning-Kruger Effect: The belief that we know more than what we actually know.[18]

Ecological systems are communities of living and inorganic things that share a particular habitat, and interact with each other in unique ways that contribute to mutual well-being.

Epidemiology is the study of disease incidents, epidemics, and pandemics, to discover variables that might limit or prevent outbreaks, or to contain them when they have occurred.

Epistemology is the study of the nature of knowledge, and how knowledge is acquired and created. Those with less epistemological development tend to rely heavily and unquestioningly on authorities as their source of truth and see truth a dualistic way, and those with greater development routinely question authority, and see truth as complex and the product of many perspectives.[19]

Fallacy refers to a mistaken belief or assertion. It is often the product of faulty logic, invalid reasoning, or assumptions. Fallacies include the claim that because everyone is doing something it must be right, and the assertion that probability makes something absolutely true or false.

---

16. Christenbury-Emory, "Study in ICU," para. 3. Rettner, "How Does the New Coronavirus," para. 1–3; 14.

17. Roser et al., "Morbidity Risk of COVUD-19," see figure "Case Fatality Rate."

18. Dunning, "Dunning-Kruger Effect," pp. 259–262.

19. Perry, *Forms of Intellectual and Ethical Development*, pp. 64–65.

Learning management system (LMS) is digital software that provides a platform for remote instruction. They typically include tools for assigning and grading work and posting videos.

Moral development refers to the refinement of judgment and one's understanding of right and wrong. Moral judgement may or may not have theological foundations and implications.

Morbidity and mortality are indicators used by scientists to describe effects of a disease or condition. Morbidity refers to the distribution of the effects of a disease or condition. Mortality refers to the number in a given population that die as a result of the disease or condition.

Pathogens are microorganisms that can causes disease, and include bacteria, viruses, and fungi.

Pedagogy refers to teaching and concerns methods and strategies. It also refers to the semantics instruction, the scope of inquiry, and the attitude of the instruction, which can determine whether it reinforces or challenges society's distribution of power and opportunity.[20]

Social Darwinism is the theory that human societies thrive when the "fittest" prevail. It holds that the weak diminish the well-being of society by using resources that could have been given to those who are "stronger," "more intelligent," and more likely to "contribute" to society.

STEM refers to science, technology, engineering and mathematics.

World Health Organization is an agency of the United Nations that monitors global health risks and coordinates global responses to health emergencies. It operates with support from the World Bank and scientists who contribute their research and consultation.

---

20. Freire's seminal work, *Pedagogy of the Oppressed* illuminates how education has been used to perpetuate poverty, hopelessness, and exploitation.

Chapter 2

The Set Up

PART I: COMMITMENT TO LIBERAL ARTS

Even before the U.S. Constitution existed, Americans placed faith in a collective effort to educate children and provide for advanced studies necessary to produce sufficient numbers of clerics and civic leaders. Dozens of colonial schools and universities that pre-date the American Revolution testified to Americans' resolve to secure social order, prosperity, and public morality by way of secular and religious education.[1]

The evolution of American education is not a monolithic procession whereby all institutions marched in unison towards a single target. Some institutions diverged from the pack. There are, however, a few themes that have dominated the way Americans have conceptualized and designed education. Traditional themes include: faith in liberal arts education to civilize society and prepare students for citizenship in a democracy; the desire to articulate faith-based values; and, an aspiration to see that individuals become self-sufficient. In modern times, themes include: the commercialization of education; faith in science to advance national security and interests; and, determination to increase persistence to degree for the sake of global dominance. A look at these themes brings us closer to understanding the state of education at present.

---

1. McClellan, *Moral Education in America*, 1–14.

Liberal arts education in the U.S. is predicated on the notion that democracy is doomed when citizens are ignorant of the world and the human circumstance. Liberal arts in the U.S. instruct people in the arts of liberty, civic duty, and civil conduct. To study history, philosophy, science, and literature is to learn about the human experience and the ideas that lifted human beings out of feudalism and "savagery."[2] It is also to learn what nefarious conditions might threaten democracy and the public's well-being. As he departed the presidency, George Washington urged the nation to create institutions for the dissemination of knowledge, and stated that since democracy had endowed citizens with a unique role in their own governance, it was essential that public opinion be enlightened.[3]

Washington and his peers understood that the young republic was vulnerable to partisanship, foreign entanglements, and domestic demagoguery. They knew that ideals of the Enlightenment—beliefs that natural law endows humanity with liberty and certain inalienable rights—was forever at war with its unshakable nemesis: human nature. They understood that the success of the American experiment relied on leaders who rose above the volatile masses and puny men driven by self-interest. Schools and universities of the 17th and 18th centuries taught piety and morality from the Bible, and turned to the classics, the Greek and Latin essays, speeches, and histories of antiquity, for insights about governance and civic virtues.

As the U.S. became a modern, industrial, global superpower, its faith in the liberal arts to produce individuals worthy of their liberty and leadership remained strong. William Charles Elliot, former president of Harvard University (1869–1909) stated in his inaugural address, that unless a great many individuals are acquainted with "many branches of knowledge," there can be "no such thing as an intelligent public opinion" and thus no social progress.[4] Nearly 80 years later, President Harry Truman's commission on higher education was tasked with evaluating the merits of general education and asserted:

> A society whose members lack a body of community knowledge is a society without a fundamental culture; it tends to disintegrate into a mere aggregation of individuals. Some community of values, ideas, and attitudes is essential as a cohesive force in this age of minute division of labor and intense conflict of special interests.[5]

2. See Association of American Colleges and Universities, "Joint Statement."
3. Washington, "Farewell Address," para. 29.
4. Elliot, "Inaugural Address," 32.
5. President's Commission on Higher Education, *Higher Education*, 47–48.

By 1977, the concept of liberal education had evolved so much, that the Carnegie Institution for the Advancement of Teaching declared liberal arts education a "disaster area." It charged that general education, the basic liberal arts requirements in four-year institutions, was so packed with electives and so specialized in content that there was no real program at all.[6] The institute complained that general education had drifted from education that was supposed to empower "individuals with broad knowledge and transferable skills. . . that cultivates social responsibility and a strong sense of ethics and values."[7] It lamented that many high school and college students did not know what was meant by a "liberal" education, and that many employers presumed liberal education had nothing to do with getting students ready for the work force.

How did higher education's concept of liberal arts change to the point where many educators came to question the value of general education and liberal arts themselves?

Education historians often point to Clark Kerr, President of the University of California, Berkeley (1958–1963) as the man who reinvented the American university by wedding university research to the cause of nationalism. Prior to Kerr's theories, universities had already demonstrated their capacity to support government research and programs for the sake of national security. Many colleges and universities welcomed Reserve Officers Training Corps (ROTC) to their campuses during World War One, and some—as did the Universities of Chicago and California, Berkeley— lent a hand to create the atomic bomb. Kerr's essay, *The Many Uses of the University*, captured public imagination and announced a brave and bright new role for higher education.[8] His vision for the university was in step with the spirit of the time, as Americans dreamed of going to the moon, delivering "third world" nations from disease and hunger, and defending democracy around the world. Kerr's vision was a "multiversity," an institution that served many interests and functioned in a variety of ways. In many instances, it ultimately became an academy sponsored by "corporations and the military," and sometimes "clandestine agencies" with opaque agendas.[9]

Military and corporate contracts and institutes in higher education proliferated all over the country, as universities competed for funding and resources. With these things, universities could secure the best and the brightest researchers who would undertake research in nuclear energy,

6. Carnegie Foundation for the Advancement of Teaching, *Missions*, 184.

7. Humphreys, *Making the Case*, 3.

8. See Kerr, *Use of the University*.

9. Hacker and Dreifus, *Higher Education*, pp. 35–36.

medicine, agriculture, weapons, and engineering.[10] Many institutions won very lucrative contracts with the Department of Defense. At present, more than 300 colleges and universities get at least half of the Department of Defense budget for research and development.[11]

Many were skeptical of the multiversity. They saw it as a threat to intellectual development, with its creeping limitations of academic autonomy wherever universities made contracts with private industries and the Pentagon. Others saw it as a perversion of the liberal arts, as it amplified the mantra that education was primarily materialistic and technical in its purpose. Many objected to the notion that education was purely materialistic in its utility. Professor of Law at Yale University, Anthony Kronman argued that, "a college or university is not just a place for the transmission of knowledge, but a forum for the exploration of life's mystery and meaning through the careful but critical reading of the great works of literary and philosophical imagination that we have inherited from the past."[12] Kronman elevates inquiries of life's meaning above other academic pursuits, as it urges us to consider what is valuable, noble, right, wrong, just, virtuous, and worthy of our effort and lives.

In some respects, the American university of the 21st century has answered the question of education's value, as it increasingly sees its primary purpose as the "production" of college graduates, especially in the STEM fields, not only for the purpose of stimulating upward mobility, but securing national interests. In some ways it has already answered the question of what is worthy of our consideration by rebuking studies of what Kronman called "great works of literary and philosophical imagination that we have inherited from the past," because so much of that literature was penned by dead white men who, for many, represent a culture of oppression and exploitation. In some institutions, studies of "great works" has been replaced by studies of diversity, multi-culturalism, and social critiques that some believe focus too narrowly on identity politics and not enough on timeless ideals that have unified people and made civilizations great.

Liberal arts remain central to undergraduate education, but it is far from the 19th century education that once required students to read classical literature and refine their rhetorical skills in oral exams and formal debates. Educators and tax-payers continue to argue about undergraduate requirements. Some say that if the university exists primarily to train the workforce, then we are wasting our time on liberal arts and general

10. See Etzkowitz et al., "Evolution of Entrepreneurial University."

11. Turse, *Complex*, pp. 32–39.

12. Kronman, *Education's End*, 6.

education. Praise for liberal arts was loud and strong in 1960, but within a decade, as "democratizing" reforms swept through higher education, students' demands for making education more relevant and user-friendly led to reductions in general education requirements.

PART II: DEMOCRATIZING HIGHER EDUCATION

While Kerr re-conceptualized the uses of higher education, society at large orchestrated an educational revolution of its own. As the 20th century unfolded, greater numbers of Americans sought a college education. In 1949, about 2.4 million students attended college, and by 1990 that number tipped 14 million.[13] By 2019, 21.9 million Americans were enrolled in college.[14]

Access to a college education became synonymous democratic rights, and that left colleges and universities open to criticism for being "too" selective in their admissions. Many institutions adopted open enrollment or variations of open enrollment. The purpose of this was to ensure that every American, regardless of ethnicity, income, race, gender, or SAT/ACT score had an opportunity to earn a college degree. Open enrollment diversified the student population as greater numbers of nontraditional students, ethnic minorities, first-generation college students, and students with disabilities enrolled. Open enrolment also increased the demand for remedial courses, tutoring, and special programs, as many students were ill-prepared for college studies. With that demand came controversy.[15]

Ultimately, remediation did little to ensure that under-prepared students would persist to degree. After 40 years of investing in remedial courses and developmental programs, researchers found that nearly 50 percent of students in two-year colleges and about 20 percent of students in four-year institutions required remediation. Getting students ready for undergraduate studies cost states and students around $3 billion a year, and graduation rates were dismal. In 2011, only 10 percent of those who took remedial courses in community colleges graduated, and just above one third of those who took remedial courses in four-year institutions graduated.[16]

Democratizing college admissions did not necessarily produce consistency in student achievement. The acquisition of a college degree, for example, did not guarantee that graduates were ready for the workforce, or had significantly improved their critical thinking, and ability to locate and

13. Snyder, *120 Years of American Education*, pp. 65–66.
14. Bustamante, "College Enrollment," General Statistics.
15. Arendale, "Then and Now," 5.
16. Complete College America, *Remediation*, 2–3.

use knowledge. Corporate executives and business managers have reported that many college graduates lack proficiency in critical thinking, communication, problem-solving, and adaptability, and also have a poor work ethic.[17] Research also indicates that many college graduates are ill-prepared for graduate studies, as they lack information literacy and research skills.[18] Moreover, while 96 percent of academic officers at colleges and universities believe that their institutions are "very" or "somewhat effective" at preparing students for the workforce, just 33 percent of business leaders agree.[19]

Whether democratization of higher education proceeded in a reasonable way is debatable. Some hold that since cognitive abilities are not evenly distributed in the human population, a traditional college education may not be right for everyone. Others argue that such assertions are wrong, as they believe that cognitive abilities are evenly distributed in the human population, and therefore dismal graduation rates are the result of poor instruction and poor institutional support. People complain that college graduates are not ready for the real world, but they do not always complain for the same reasons. The prevailing arguments tend to land on whether graduates have the knowledge, skills, and habits that make them valuable employees who are likely to contribute to the nation's economic prowess at the global level. This complaint is very different from the complaint that our college graduates do not know much about the world, governance, economics, and how to make fair, well-informed, and intelligent moral judgements.

By some accounts, the democratization of higher education did not do much to increase the intellect of the general population, because Americans are largely anti-intellectual. In his book, *Anti-Intellectualism in American Life* (1963), historian Richard Hofstadter addressed America's preference for education dedicated to "life adjustment" and practical, economic activity. He argued that by enlarging educational opportunities for the masses, education became more utilitarian, less philosophical, more mechanical, and less cerebral. Educators, he argued, neglected the gifted learner in an effort to purge elitism from schools.[20] Hofstadter determined that, though this approach to education appeared to be progressive and liberal, it was essentially conservative, inasmuch as educators adjusted their expectations and practice to meet the needs of students who exhibited no particular pleasure and interest in intellectual activity.[21]

---

17. Hart Research Associates, *Fulfilling the American Dream*, pp. 12–15.

18. Harris, "Case for Partnering," 599–603.

19. Sidhu and Calderon, "Many Business Leaders," para. 1–6.

20. Hofstadter, *Anti-Intellectualism in American Life*, 353.

21. Ibid, 356.

Jacques Barzun, historian and educational philosopher, saw other consequences of the democratization of education and observed that, "Education in the United States is a passion and a paradox. . . . Millions want it and commend it, and are busy about it, at the same time they are willing to degrade it by trying to get it free of charge and free of work." He also believed that American education had become a "duty and a diversion" that managed to "elude intellectual control so completely that it became an empty ritual without arousing protest."[22] The statement implies that intellectuals are not in control of education, and that if they were in control, they would not indulge the fallacy that high academic standards are the enemy of democracy.

Derek Bok, former President of Harvard University, asserted that the status of liberal arts is uncertain in America because the rationale for the university is uncertain.[23] He surmises that colleges and universities are not providing the best education possible in part because institutions are not singular in their vision and purpose, and in part because there is not enough rigor applied to the development of the intellect. Professors of education, Wilson Smith and Thomas Bender noted that during the 1980s, education lost much of its intrinsic value as it was judged against market criteria whereby education was an investment in human capital, and that "This change produced the student as consumer, too often more interested in certification than in inquiry."[24] The "consumerization" of students was not only a consequence of democratizing higher education, it was also brought about by waning public support for education.

During the 1980s and beyond, states decreased funding for public colleges and universities. In 1986, the average state expenditure per student in a four-year institution was about $10,726, and by 2009 that amount had dropped to $8,655. This trend sent tuitions skyward. Between 2000 and 2011, tuition for a four-year institution increased by 67 percent.[25] By decreasing funding for the increasingly democratized university, the state essentially "de-democratized" higher education as college tuitions put college education out of reach for many. Further, high tuition does not motivate students to linger long on campus to soak up curricula for personal enrichment. Instead, it motivates them to get in and out of college as quickly as possible, and to spend money only on courses that are essential for their degree. With government decreases in funding for post-secondary education, campuses had to find alternative sources of capital just to keep the

22. Barzun, *House of Intellect*, p. 89.
23. Bok, *Our Underachieving Colleges*, 58–60.
24. Smith and Bender, "Introduction," 9.
25. Department of the Treasury, *Economics of Higher Education*, 21–22.

doors open and the lights on. The corporate model of business offered an alternative. Many snarl that this alternative is a Faustian affair.

PART III: CONSUMER STUDENTS

To maintain solvency as states decreased funding, colleges and universities enriched amenities offered to students and welcomed corporate sponsorship.[26] Corporate logos popped up on campus, corporations assumed control of campus bookstores, and institutions undertook branding campaigns that placed school logos on everything from accessories to zip drives. To maintain high enrollment, institutions lured students with dormitories supplied with coffee bars, private bathrooms, air conditioning, and dining halls plump with organic and vegan cuisine. Such amenities reinforced the notion that students are consumers.

Treating students as consumers in matters related to campus amenities is one thing, and treating students like consumers in matters related to academic expectations and standards is another. The democratization of education also granted students the power to influence curriculum, course rigor, faculty retention, tenure, and promotion by way of rating instructors and courses. Although many faculty have learned how to improve their work by listening to student feedback, some have been unfairly treated because students rated professors with criteria that differed very little from the criteria they used to rate pizza delivery.[27]

Students' evaluations have ominous implications as they are widely used in administrative decisions concerning retention, tenure and promotion. Students know this. They also know that their critiques have the potential to shape curriculum and instruction. On many occasions, professors have confided to me that they no longer assign dense scholarly reading or writing, and no longer feel committed to designing courses that dive deeply into their subjects, because they do not want to provoke foul evaluations. They weary of student complaints that translate into difficult conversations with department chairs and tenure committees. Instructors are in a tough spot. They fear that by catering to student demands for "user-friendly courses" students' intellectual, professional, and moral development will be compromised, while at the same they worry about job security.[28]

Many educators are obsessed with students' feedback for the wrong reasons. They sometimes believe that student favor is equal to student

26. Bok, *Universities and the Marketplace*, 8.

27. See Hartman and Hunt, "What RatemyProfessors.com. Reveals"

28. See Bunge, "Students Evaluating,"

learning. Whether they contain glowing recommendations or damning castigations, student evaluations are sometimes tainted by the Dunning-Kruger Effect, the cognitive bias that motivates people to confidently report that they know a great deal about something when in fact they know very little.[29] Contrary to the cliché, the customer is not "always right." Yet, educators continue to revere student evaluations in part because keeping customers happy means keeping a paycheck.

Until the 1960s, it was widely accepted that responsibility for college success was all on the students. Professors lectured and gave exams and students either demonstrated mastery on the instructors' terms, or they did not. Failure was largely seen as the students' lack of intelligence or motivation. Three things came together to shift the paradigm. Frist, the cognitive theory of learning and the constructivist theory of learning gained substantial credibility in the 1960s. Both postulated that leaning is a meaning-making activity that is enhanced and guided by social interaction.[30] Second was growing acceptance that institutions themselves played a key role in college dropout rates.[31] Sociologist Vincent Tinto and his colleagues were early advocates of this notion. They concluded that, in order to be successful in college, students had to feel that they belonged in an academic community and were surrounded by faculty who genuinely cared for them.[32] Third, students and social scientists rebelled against the traditional paradigm because it was often used to justify discrimination in higher education. These three variables spurred interest in student-centered teaching and student evaluations of teaching.[33]

In the 1970s and 1980s, student-centered teaching movement led to important changes in higher education. Colleges gave students a greater say in what topics were addressed, how learning should be assessed, how courses should be paced, and what standards should be applied when grading their work. The effective professor was seen as one who demonstrated the relevance of studies, was flexible with expectations, provided abundant feedback to students, gave students samples of competently completed assignments, accommodated various learning styles and preferences, and awarded credit for experiences and prior knowledge.[34]

29. Dunning, "Dunning-Kruger Effect," 259–262.

30. See Wadsworth, *Piaget's Theory* and Vygotsky, *Society and the Mind*.

31. See Tinto, "Dropout from Higher Education."

32. Engstrom and Tinto, "Access," 47–49.

33. McKeachie, "Research on College," 191.

34. Chickering and Kuh, "Promoting Students," 2–3.

At the dawn of the 21st century, the pedagogical mantra in higher education was "student engagement." Articles and books attesting to the efficacy of engagement strategies and student satisfaction with engagement techniques flowed from the academic press like chocolate in a Wonka factory. Student engagement itself is a complex and dynamic concept. It may refer to students' compliance with rules and directions, asking and answering questions in class, and paying attention in class. Student engagement also refers to the immersion of students in creative projects, problem-solving, community service, and critical analysis of propositions, policies, and events.[35] Student engagement was also at the core of the movement to diversify instruction based on the theory that there existed multiple intelligences, and that effective instruction was characterized by the teacher's ability to craft lessons that were aligned with learning styles associated with these intelligences.[36]

With good intentions, faculty adjusted their curriculum and instruction to accommodate student needs and preferences. Eventually, however, many instructors were confronted with the question of whether or not accommodation had gone go so far as to adulterate college learning so thoroughly that it was not much more than glorified high school studies coupled with vocational training. By allowing students to act like consumers, many institutions quietly decreased requirements and lowered expectations. Further, by making persistence to degree their cardinal priority, many institutions neglected the developmental aspects of learning, and lost sight of whether course content was designed in accordance with the urgent need to improve students' understanding of the world and the need to integrate ethics and sustainability across curricula.

PART IV: PERSISTENCE

The rates at which students persist to degree is a national concern. About 41 percent of students obtain a BA in four years, and roughly 60 percent take six years to earn their degrees. The cost of education motivates colleges to move students through their programs as quickly as possible. To expedite students, many institutions have abolished remedial courses and reduced general education requirements.

35. Van Der Ark, "Learning for a Reason," para. 4.

36. See Garner, *Frames of Mind: The Theory of Multiple Intelligences.* This was the seminal essay that launched the controversial movement of teaching to students' "learning styles."

In 2017, the California State University (CSU) system announced its elimination of remedial course requirements as part of their effort to smooth the road to graduation. For decades, the CSU relied on remedial courses to bolster the reading and math skills of roughly one third of the students' they enrolled.[37] Many complained that remedial courses discouraged students, and forced them to pay for courses that generated no college credit.[38] Each campus was given the freedom to develop courses and resources to "compensate" for the retirement of remedial courses, and to ensure students who need developmental learning got it. The autonomy tacitly sanctioned a variety of proficiency standards. The initiative did not provide a system-wide exist exam that assesses students' reading, writing, and quantitative reasoning proficiencies. The CSU has also suspended SAT testing for admissions, and so without data from the SAT and exit exams, it is very difficult to qualify how the college experience has improved students' literacy, cognitive, and epistemological skills.

For the sake of moving students quickly towards graduation, many universities have reduced the number of general education course requirements. As these courses are traditionally the backbone of liberal arts, tinkering with them arouses bitter controversy. Many dislike general education requirements because they delay students' full immersion in the subjects related to their majors, and force students to "waste money" learning things outside their interests.[39] Where there is consensus on the value of a core curriculum in a liberal arts general education, faculty often squabble over how to distribute required courses across disciplines. In pursuit of job security, instructors engage in "turf wars," as they want requirements to include courses they teach.

General education emerged in the 1920s as a way to ensure that as specialization and research universities proliferated, liberal arts would not be lost. General education requirements typically represented roughly 25 to 35 percent of course work required for a bachelor's degree. Traditionally, it consisted of a fixed set of introductory courses that represented "a unifying element of culture," and it aimed to make students proficient in their understanding of scientific principles, universal moral truths, and the aesthetic and spiritual dimensions of the human experience.[40] During the 1960s and 1970s, students demanded greater choice in the matter of general education courses, and gravitated towards subjects they felt were important but

37. Guzman-Lopez, "More Than a Third of Cal State," para. 3.
38. Koseff, "CSU Eliminates Remdial," 1–7.
39. Jack, "Gen-Ed Revision," 3.
40. O'Banion, "A Brief History of General Education," 327.

ignored, such as the history and literature of women and ethnic minorities, social justice, and labor.

To fill these demands, many institutions took the "smorgasbord" approach, whereby students select courses from disciplinary areas, such as "Quantitative Reasoning," or "Creative and Fine Arts." While students like the options, others are disgruntled. The American Council of Trustees and Alumni complained that colleges "offer unstructured and chaotic curricula," in which courses that have "vague outcomes" too heavily based on self-discovery and personal identity.[41] The council took umbrage with courses that dodged what they believe are core competencies. For example, they objected to the idea that students could fulfill a literature requirement by taking a course on "A History of Comics" or "Game Design for Non-Majors."[42]

With some insights to how higher education evolved in the U.S. and what priorities have steered its course, we may now examine four pre-existing conditions to the pandemic that contributed to public vulnerability to disease and propaganda that emerged during the pandemic: 1) insufficient knowledge about world; 2) low levels of literacy; 3) the digital divide; and, 4) institutional denial of the need to change.

41. American Council of Trustees and Alumni, *What Will They Learn*, 1. Also see American Council of Trustees and Alumni, *No U.S. History* and *Crisis in Civics Education*.

42. American Council of Trustees and Alumni, *What Will They Learn*, 18.

Chapter 3

Pre-Existing Conditions

PRE-EXISTING CONDITION ONE:
THE WORLD WE DON'T KNOW

Nothing says "welcome home" to germs like the failure to practice simple hygiene regiments, and nothing says "we would like greater intimacy with the world's pathogens" than economic activity that is invasive to ecosystems that have been undisturbed for thousands of years. As shelter-in-place became the new norm, people in my neighborhood sneezed without covering their mouths, spat on sidewalks, urinated in public parking lots, and left their garbage on freeway ramps. While the pandemic gripped the world, deforestation of the Amazon region in Brazil proceeded at a brisk pace. Despite warnings from epidemiologists that clear cutting exposes humans to potentially deadly pathogens, Brazil's president, Jair Bolsonaro, had plans to level hundreds of acres of pristine forests to make way for profitable agricultural development.[1]

Undoubtedly, there will always be corporate executives, investors, and government officials eager to build fortunes at the expense of complex ecosystems and sustainability. The odds of their success, however, may be lowered if more people understood what is at stake in business as usual. One of the most dangerous conditions that pre-existed the coronavirus

1. See Borges and Branford, "Rapid Deforestation of Amazon could bring the Next Pandemic."

pandemic is our poor understanding of science and nature. The problem is not just that so many Americans do not know the basics of biology, chemistry, and physics, it is also that they know next to nothing about scientific methods and how to discern the credibility of scientific assertions. It is also problematic that many Americans know little about economics, American government, history, world geography, and international relations. Initiatives to move students quickly through college, the practice of adapting academic standards to please students, the gross limitations in students' literacy, knowledge of the world, and the academy's denial of the need to reform education *all pre-existed COVID-19' arrival*. Institutions are not all brewing in the same cauldron, and so the quality of learning varies from campus to campus. However, even the best of our colleges and universities may find that they have room for growth, and the potential to be national leaders in innovation and meaningful reform.

Science. A 2019 investigation of adult's scientific literacy revealed the dismal reality that lots of folks not understand the world in which they live: about 20 percent did not understand how overuse of antibiotics creates microbial resistance to medicine; 32 percent did not know that oil and gas are fossil fuels; 40 percent did not know that deforestation leads to erosion; 40 percent did not understand the role of a control group in testing new medicines; and, 40 percent could not accurately interpret data in a chart.[2] The same study found that what people believe about climate and energy is split along partisan lines. While 92 percent of Democrats with a high level of education believed that human activity plays a key role in climate change, only 42 percent of Republicans with a high level of education believed the same.

The matter of why we value science education is important. In the U.S., the rationale for STEM studies has reflected both humanitarian and imperialistic agendas. The U.S. has pursued scientific knowledge with the desire eradicate hunger and disease.[3] It has also pursued them to ensure military preeminence and global economic dominance.[4] Arguably, using scientific knowledge for the purpose of advancing the material interests of a single nation produces a world order and quality of life for the masses takes us in a very different direction than using scientific knowledge to advance a sustainable and healthy existence for all. The conversation about the highest purpose of scientific knowledge is one in which many do not participate. Further, many students do not take math and science courses because they

---

2. Kennedy and Hefferon, "What Americans Know," para. 1–5.

3. See: Zachary, *Endless Frontier: Vannevar Bush Engineer of the American Century.*

4. See: National Commission on Excellence in Education, *A Nation at Risk.*

find that they are boring, too difficult, or unrelated to their majors.[5] Many adults do not like learning about science either, and in one study, 68 percent of adults reported that they got their scientific information incidentally from news stories that contained references to science.[6]

Economics. Americans' economic literacy is mediocre. Economic proficiency concerns one's understanding of economic theory and systems, trade, and the roles of entrepreneurs and regulations. Financial literacy is a close cousin of economic literacy, but it is more concerned with one's understanding of personal budgeting, credit use, balancing a checkbook, and managing personal investments. A 2012 study of high school seniors found that 18 percent were below a basic understanding of economics, while 39 percent were at the basic level, 40 percent reached proficiency, and only 3 percent were "advanced."[7] This means that roughly half of the seniors in the study could not relate the consumer price index to inflation, explain how competition stimulates innovation, explain how currency rates affect international trade, and calculate interest rates on loans. Adding to the problem of low economic literacy is the reality that students who are not proficient with math and quantitative reasoning skills are less likely understand even the most basic introduction to economics.[8]

Adults also are limited in their knowledge of economics and finance. A 2012 study found that only one third of American adults aged 25 to 34 and half of adults age 55 to 64 are able to correctly answer questions about interest, inflation, and diversification of investments.[9] Another investigation reported that the average score on a test of the economic knowledge was 57 percent. The test included questions about who benefits when governments pay for services and what results from government spending that exceeds government revenues.[10] Adults who had a college degree did better on the test than those who did not have a college degree, yet, even in prestigious universities, economics is not a universal general education requirement.[11]

It is troubling that so many Americans lack knowledge about fundamental economic concepts, because it portends a limited ability to understand the implications of economic policies and the economic agendas of candidates running for government offices. Imagine the vulnerability of a

5. Monmaney, "How Much Do Americans Know," para. 8–10.

6 Kennedy and Hefferon, para. 13

7. National Center for Educational Statistics, "Economics," 2.

8. Schuhmann et al., "Student Quantitative Literacy," 60.

9. Hastings et al., "Financial Literacy," 41.

10. Cole and Smith, "Using Results," table 2.

11. Czelusniak, "Crisis of Economic Literacy," para. 5.

society in which very few understand inflation, interest rates, taxes loop-holes, subsidies, how lobbyists impact federal spending, the difference between government subsidies and government funding, the difference between bailing out large publically traded corporations and bailing out "mom and pop" shops, and how privatization of military services, prisons, and nursing homes impact the cost of vital services. Without economic literacy, our access to basic necessities is at risk, as we may be bamboozled by leaders who promise access to all and deliver the opposite.

American Government and History. Several years ago, the American Revolution Center published the results of study that inventoried Americans' knowledge of the U.S. Constitution and other matters related civic competency. The study revealed that over 80 percent of adults failed the test, as they could not identify the basic parts of the Constitution, the meaning of the word "republic," the differences between "conservative" and "liberal," and the era in which the Civil War took place.[12] A 2008 study conducted by the Intercollegiate Studies Institute of over 2,500 adults reported that: 25 percent did not know that the First Amendment to the Constitution forbids the establishment of a national religion; less than 50 percent could name all three branches of government; 40 percent believed that the president has the power to declare war; and, about 25 percent believe that Congress shares its power to create foreign policy with the United Nations.[13]

Civics is not a universally required course in high schools. In 2018, 41 states required high school students to take a course on civics, but just 16 required students to take a civics exam to graduate. Of the 41 schools that required students to take a civic course, 31 (75 percent) mandated only one semester of study.[14] In 2016, students who took an advanced placement (AP) course in civics scored an average of 2.65 out of 5.0 points on the AP exam, a score short of the widely accepted 3.0 necessary for college credit.[15]

Some states have very robust standards for civics instruction across K-12 education. Minnesota, which requires high school students to take a course in civics and to take a civics exam before graduation, built its civics curriculum on 12 standards that aim to foster a strong understanding of: the need for a well-informed an engaged citizenry to sustain democracy; seminal documents that articulate democratic principles and U.S. governance; U.S. respect for rule of law, liberty, and popular sovereignty; the responsibilities that come with rights; the duty to respect the law; the organization

---

12. See American Revolution Center, "Who Cares?"

13. Intercollegiate Studies Institute, *Our Fading Heritage*, 9.

14. Shapiro and Brown, "State of Civics," figure 1.

15. Shapiro and Brown, "A Look at Civics," para. 8.

of government branches and their functions; how rules and regulations provide for the well-being of society; how government and nongovernment entities influence policies and political processes; the need for fair and free elections; the nature of U.S. relations with indigenous and international people; the institutions that shape international relations; diversity in world government systems; and, the need to maintain relationships with nations that have political ideologies different from the U.S.[16]

The good news is that Minnesota's standards are exemplary. The bad news is that the state's requirement for high school civics is just one semester, and many students will never take courses on civics again. Even where state standards for civics instruction are substantial and mindful of the impact that personal values have on policy-making and compliance with the law, there may be gaps in students' comprehension of democracy. The extent to which the most outstanding schools address things such as government transparency, corporate media's role in disseminating political propaganda, the scale of clandestine operations and secret deals, and the complexity of conflicts of interest in government and law enforcement is anyone's guess. There is no guessing, however, as to the benefits of understanding these things. By understanding these things, one may perceive the perennial threats to democracy, and develop strategies to combat them.

College requirements for studies in Western Civilization have decreased over the last few decades. This is a critical trend, as studies in Western Civilization traditionally introduces students to the ideologies and principles that are foundational to democracy. In 1964, courses such as "A Survey of Western Civilization" and "A Survey of Great Books in Western Thought" were ubiquitous features on college campuses, and by 2010 just 32 percent of colleges and universities had such courses.[17] Many colleges and universities relaxed requirements in Western history and literature with good intentions. They wanted curriculum to be inclusive of diverse cultural experiences and welcome critiques of Western civilization. Many wonder, however, if the academy has gone too far in allowing college graduates to marginalize—or even demonize—Western achievements. To dismiss the importance of Western Civilization is to dismiss its respect for rule of law, its defense of individual rights, its pursuit of equity under the law, its contributions to technological and scientific knowledge, its development of public education, its provision for amending the law, and its defense of the right to dissent and protest.

16. Minnesota Department of Education, *Minnesota K–12 Academic Standards*, 10–11.

17. Ricketts et al., *Vanishing West*, 1.

For generations, educators and policy-makers have declared that studies in American government and history should be undertaken for the sake of fostering reverence for democracy and wise use of our liberties. At this stage of our republic's evolution, our reverence wanes as our own government is peppered with special interests, corruption, ferocious partisanship, and unproductive bureaucracy.[18] Cynicism baits anarchy and demagoguery alike. The remedy is not to abandon studies in political science and civics, but to require more of it, and to see that studies foster the skills and the will we need to restore and sustain the integrity of our own democracy.

World Geography and International Relations. In a 2016 study of what 1,203 college-aged people in the U.S. knew about world geography, only 29 percent scored 66 percent or better.[19] The encouraging news is that the majority of the participants in the study indicated that world geography was becoming more important to them, and that they understood that human activity is having an adverse impact on the environment. The geographic literacy of Americans, however, is dismal. Less than half correctly identified Iran, Iraq, and Israel on a map. Roughly one third did not known that "Sub-Sahara" refers to land south of the Sahara Desert. Nineteen percent did not identify the Panama Canal as the link between the Atlantic and the Pacific Oceans, and 25 percent could not identify the continents on which Pakistan, Sri Lanka, and the Alps are located.

The study also revealed that Americans do not know much about the world's people and U.S. foreign policy. Less than half of the participants knew which countries the U.S. is obligated to defend if those countries are attacked. Approximately one third were unable to identify issues that currently faced nations around the world, such as Germany's struggle to accommodate refugees and Brazil's struggle against the Zika virus. Only 35 percent were able to correctly rank recent pandemics in order of mortality rates, and less than one third knew that the U.S. has over 3,000 troops stationed in Japan, South Korea, and Germany.

Geographic literacy is a main ingredient in understanding ecosystems, climate change, why the world's cultures are so diversified, why nations go to war, and which nations are vulnerable to which natural disasters. Knowing where natural resources are concentrated helps us understand why nations will assist with the development of some foreign nations while denying assistance to others. World history literacy helps us understand the diversity of the human experience, the source of international animosities,

---

18. Thomas, "Teaching for a Strong Deliberative Democracy," 78.

19. Council on Foreign Relations and National Geographic, "What College-Aged Students Know," 4.

and the source of threats to our human sustainability, including economic paradigms, war, and political ambitions.

Arguably, geographic literacy and knowledge of the world's people and their history breeds tolerance and empathy. Such knowledge helps us strip ethnocentrism and nationalism from our judgement of others, and enables us to see that human beings are essentially the same all over the planet. Though we may pray to different deities and wear different military uniforms, we are all tempted by the same demons and demagogues who want us to believe that the world consists of "us" and "them," and that the "us" must always vanquish the "them" before the "them" vanquishes the "us." Without a sound understanding of the world, it is likely that we will continue to publically espouse world peace and cooperation, while privately living in fear of strangers. Without confronting the limitations of building bridges between nations for the purpose of enriching the few, we may never be able to envision building bridges for the purpose of global well-being and sustainability.

PRE-EXISTING CONDITION TWO:
LAPSING LITERACY

Of all the threats to our sustainability and ability to choose a wise course of human development, few figure more prominently than our low levels literacy. More than just the ability to read and write, literacy is associated with disciplinary expertise, high level cognition, and the ability to apply disciplinary standards of epistemology in the discipline. Reading proficiency in one's discipline is a skill that distinguishes the expert from the novice. Literacy is also foundational to the development of critical thinking.[20] It is a means of learning how to detect lies, biases, sloppy logic, and poorly evidenced assertions in commercial and political rhetoric. It is also vital to our capacity to engage in complex and sophisticated discourse about knowledge in all disciplines. Literacy enables us to interpret what is communicated in print, imagery, and speech, and to distil meaning from what has been articulated.[21]

Literacy skills are developmental in nature.[22] The sophistication of reading skills translates to the sophistication of our comprehension. Knowing how to read a grocery list, for example, is much different than knowing

20. See Intersegmental Committee, *Academic Reading*, and Manarin, "Reading Value."

21. See Brozo et al., "Content Area;" Geisler, "Academic Literacy," 84–92; and Shanahan and Shanahan, "What is Disciplinary Literacy?"

22. Alexander, "Path to Competence," 413–36.

how to read an article on effects drinking water contaminated with per-fluorooctanoic acid (PFOA).[23] A high level of reading proficiency is defined as an individual's ability to: grasp main and peripheral ideas, compare and contrast information, draw inferences, identify implications, detect cause-effect relationships, detect authors' bias and purpose, recognize the significance of assertions, evaluate the logic and quality of evidence for assertions, comprehend the unique lexicon of scholarly text in various disciplines, and understand the meaning of text in a given context.[24] Highly proficient readers are also skilled in the metacognitive tasks involved with reading, such as monitoring one's own comprehension and detecting one's resistance to assertions.[25] People do not automatically know how to do these things. Without explicit instruction that addresses reading skills at all levels of learning, students may develop critical reading and thinking skills that are insufficient to the task of recognizing the complexities and nuances of social issues and political rhetoric.[26]

The vast majority of Americans know how to read, but they do not necessarily read very well or very critically. The U.S. Department of Education found that reading scores from the 2019 *Mathematics and Reading Assessment*, that the average reading score for eighth-graders was 260 out of 500 points, and that these scores had decreased since 2017.[27] The report also noted that the reading scores for the highest scoring ethnic group, Asians, was 50 points higher than the lowest score for ethnic groups, which was for African Americans. The American Institutes for Research reported that, while 38 percent of students in four-year colleges, and 23 percent of students in two-year colleges are proficient with reading pros, about 12 percent of students in two-year institutions, and about 7 percent of students in four-year colleges are at or below the basic level.[28] The same pattern held for students' document reading. Roughly 13 percent of adults in the general population scored at or below the basic level.[29] Data from the National Assessment of Educational Progress reveal that only 37 percent of college students have achieved a level of "college readiness" in their reading skills.[30] In

23. In 2017, DuPont paid $671 million to settle with 3,550 plaintiffs injured by Du-Pont's dumping of PFOA in West Virginia. See Nair, "DuPont Settles Lawsuits."

24. Intersegmental Committee, *Academic Literacy*, 13–17; Manarin et al., *Critical Reading*, 4–5; Paul and Elder, *How to Read*, 1–8.

25. Ryan, "Critical Reading," 159–65.

26. Manarin et al., *Critical Reading*, 65–85.

27. National Center for Educational Statistics, "Results from the 2019," 2.

28. National Institutes for Research, *Literacy of America's College Students*," 24.

29. Ibid.

30. Camera, "High School Seniors," para. 1–4.

one study, college students scored an average of 60 percent on a reading test ranked at the eleventh grade level, and 13 percent scored just 30 percent.[31]

Reading is an indicator of readiness for college level work, but many Americans do not take that seriously. A friend who has been a principal for many years confided that raising standardized tests scores is very difficult in her district because many parents do not care about their child's low scores. She noted that her school raised test scores consistently over the last few years because it administered special support classes for students who were testing below grade level, and because teachers were willing to adjust their instructional strategies to boost students' proficiencies. She confided that when the support classes were offered to parents, some said, "Nope, not my kid; my kid's going to be fine." The parents expected that their child would find a way into one college or the other regardless of their test scores.

My friend also reported that her school's approach to improving proficiency did not arouse the district's interest because some of its administrators were lazy and complacent. Rather than document why certain schools improve test scores for all children and why others do not, and then use that knowledge to create support courses in the low-performing schools, and encourage enrollment in these classes, some supervisors do nothing. As there is no state mandate for support classes, there is little incentive to take on the work.

Once enrolled in college, roughly 30 to 50 percent of students are not compliant with reading assignments, citing lack of time and difficulties with comprehension.[32] Many do not believe that reading is essential for college success. When asked about why they do not read assignments, many students say that they are "irrelevant," and that they can get what they need to pass the class from other sources, such as lectures and class discussions.[33] Students complain that reading is boring, and say that they would be more compliant with reading assignments if instructors reminded them about their assignments, gave them tips about what was important to know, administered reading quizzes, and made reading more interesting.[34]

Instructors typically require students to buy a textbook, but they are often used exclusively as sources of declarative knowledge, and not as tools

31. Gorzycki et al., "Exploration of Academic Reading," 151–54.

32. See Howard et al., "Academic Reading;" Ryan, "Motivating;" Clump, Bauer and Bradley, "Extent," and Baier et al., "College Students' Textbook Reading;" and St. Clair-Thompson et al., "Exploring the Reading Practices."

33. Gorzycki et al., "Reading is Important," 4–6.; Ihara and Del Principe, "I Bought," 236–40.

34. Hoeft, "Why University Students don't Read," 6–9; Vafeas, "Attitudes Towards," 45–58.

for improving students' critical reading skills. Many professors see reading as the processes of getting the gist of the author's meaning and acquiring facts, and so the developmental aspects of critical and disciplinary reading are widely neglected.[35] Most professors never studied pedagogy and reading instruction, and so they lack not only the skills to teach advanced reading skills, but a sound understanding of what reading does to improve disciplinary literacy and epistemological growth.[36] Professors typically teach as they were taught, and most believe that they are above average teachers.[37] Those who understand the need to teach reading skills to undergraduates are often dissuaded by fears of student retaliation in the form of poor course evaluations.[38] Some college instructors do not teach reading is because they believe it is not their job. Reading instruction in post-secondary education is typically associated with remediation and not life-long development.[39] In addition, professors know that their status in the academy rests on their disciplinary expertise, not on their finesse with developmental instruction, and so there is little incentive to become developmental in one's approach to teaching. Many college instructors believe that if students do not know how to read well, then they should not be in college.[40]

The business of higher education goes on despite waning commitment to doing the heavy lifting of teaching and learning. Sociologists Richard Arum and Josipa Roksa found in their study that, despite strong faculty consensus that higher education should improve writing and critical thinking skills, there were "no statistically significant gains in critical thinking, complex reasoning, and writing skills for at least 45 percent of the students" after three years of college studies.[41] The data defy the sterling grade point averages of college students, whereby 85 percent have a B minus average or better.[42] Indeed, students receive remarkably good grades even as 37 percent study for an average of only five hours a week.[43] College students attending highly selective institutions are more likely to be assigned more than 20 pages of writing in classes, and 40 pages or more of reading per week than those

35. Bosley, "I Don't Teach Reading," 290–99.
36. Brost and Bradley, "Student Compliance," 108.
37. Halpern and Hakel, "Applying the Science,"
38. Lei et al., "Resistance,"
39. Desa et al., "Essential but Invisible,"
40. See Nist and Holshuh, "Comprehension Strategies"
41. Arum and Roksa, *Academically Adrift*, 35–36.
42. Ibid, 88.
43. Ibid, 36–37.

who attend less selective institutions.[44] This supports the assertion that there is one kind of higher education for academically high achieving individuals, and a different kind of education for the masses of average and low achieving students. This raises the question of whether institutional complacency with low student achievement is partially to blame for society's limitations in its response to social, economic, political, and epidemiological crises.

PRE-EXISTING CONDITION THREE: "DIGIBILITY"

The sudden conversion of face-to-face courses to remote instruction impacted different institutions in different ways. It revealed the strengths and limitations of institutional provisions for technological training and support, pedagogical guidance, policies unique to the online environment, and accessibility to the Internet, software, and applications. Prior to the pandemic, there was a substantial range of "digibility," the ability to navigate and trouble-shoot digital technology, and to effectively use LMS tools to teach in the online environment. Sadly, for many students at all levels, the spring of 2020 represents a lost semester, as the quality of some instruction faltered when instructors had to teach and learn the technology simultaneously. The digital divide made matters worse.

The digital divide is the gap between those who have access to technology and those who do not. The divide has existed since online courses and programs were introduced in the 1980s. It concerns educators because access to technology is a key variable in who has access to education and educational resources in the 21st century. Households with incomes of $30,000 or less are less likely to have Internet services than those with higher incomes, and school districts in impoverished communities struggle to put courses online.[45]

President of California's State Board of Education, Linda Darling-Hammond, noted during the pandemic that nearly 1.2 million of California's students had no access to the Internet at home.[46] A 2019 study found that 3 million students in the U.S. did not have access to the Internet at home.[47] Data gathered by the National Center for Educational Statistics revealed a much higher number, asserting that 11 million students in K-12 do not have digital resources in their homes. There is a strong correlation between poverty and lack of digital resources, and a strong correlation between poverty

44. Ibid, 72.

45. Samms, "As Cities Face," para. 2–3.

46. Johnson, "California Moves to Close," para. 4.

47. Melia et al., "AP: 3 Million," para. 1–4.

and race, which means that people of color are disproportionately without computers, smart phones, and the internet.[48]

Families that have the highest rates of computer ownership and internet access tend to be affluent and white. Native American colleges and universities have "the worst internet access," and little to no existing online teaching capability and consistent technical support.[49] Rural areas are especially challenging as internet service and technological support are unavailable for both teachers and students.[50] African Americans, Hispanics, Native Americans, and Pacific Islanders are less likely to have multiple electronic devices than Asian and white Americans, which limits access to online courses and educational materials when one device fails. More than a third of students with only one device say the device is not reliable enough to consistently access homework assignments, e-mail instructors, conduct research, or access grades.[51] Prior to the pandemic, only about 30 percent of colleges mandated student orientations to the LMS and remote instruction, or offered only optional orientations. Having access to the technology did not mean one knew how to use it. [52]

Before the pandemic, there existed inconsistencies in instructors' readiness to facilitate remote instruction. Many who sought assistance and support from my unit said that they struggled with adjusting to remote instruction and felt overwhelmed. Several had little to no experience with teaching a hybrid or fully online course. Some reported that when courses were shifted to remote instruction, a number of students stopped submitting assignments and taking the course seriously. They were not alone. According to a 2019 survey conducted by Higher Ed/Gallup, at least half of college faculty had never taught a fully online or hybrid course.[53] During the spring of 2020, many school districts reported that absenteeism increased when courses went digital.[54] At the college level, many students decided that persisting to degree in the online environment was not worth the stress and lack of contact with peers and faculty.[55]

The abrupt shift to remote instruction exposed gaps in pedagogical mastery. Colleges and universities typically do not mandate much in the

48. USA Facts, "More Than 9 Million," para. 1–5.

49. "Tribal Colleges Need Immediate Funding," Para. 2–3.

50. McMurthie, "Students without Laptops," para. 1–6.

51. Moore et al., *Digital Divide*, P. 4–7.

52. Garrett et al., *CHLOE 4*, p. 49

53. Jaschik and Lederman, *2019 Faculty Survey*, p. 7.

54. See Goldstein et al., "As Schools Move," and Kamenetz, "4 in 10 Teens."

55. See Hess, "Some Students."

way of any pedagogical training for instructors, as it is widely assumed that one who has earned a terminal degree, such as a Ph.D., automatically knows how to teach. Normally, tenure-track professors and lectures alike take their place at the podium because they have met the criteria for subject mastery, and not because they have been certified in curriculum development and instruction. Even for those whose pedagogical skills and integration of developmental learning are brilliant and refined, learning how to use digital platforms and tools takes time and effort. Furthermore, beyond the mastery of technology, instructors must learn how to adapt instruction to a remote experience. Not all strategies and experiences translate well from the classroom to the internet.

A study of chief online officers (directors and managers of academic technology units and centers for teaching) found that only 25 percent of institutions require faculty to work with an instructional designer when they create new online courses, and that private four-year institutions are more likely to require this partnership that public four-year institutions.[56] For many instructors, their immersion in learning the LMS has "taught them skills and practices that have improved their teaching."[57] That news is encouraging.

Despite the surge in instructors' technological skills-acquisition during the pandemic, many learned that digital technologies are not ideal for certain subjects and professional formation. Art and cinema instructors could no longer observe students as they painted, sculpted, and created works in animation, video, editing, and sound studios. Nursing instructors were no longer able to supervise students in simulated or actual clinical situations and evaluate the nuances of patient care, communication, adherence to protocols, and clinical judgment. For some, the experience heightened the awareness of what makes face-to-face instruction a categorically different experience that remote instruction.

Many instructors across all disciplines who relied heavily on face-to-face encounters with students to engage them in discussion and activities found the remote classroom a relatively sterile environment. The face-to-face classroom is by comparison a more personal experience, one in which human beings confront new ideas and wrestle with new knowledge in full view of other people. The face-to-face classroom is less forgiving if people are distracted, or show signs of hostility or indifference. In the physical classroom people can read body language and detect tone that is often ambiguous in online forums. Instructors have the advantages in the physical

---

56. Garrett et al., *CHLOE 4*, p. 49.
57. Jaschik and Lederman, p. 7.

classroom that elude them in the "ether zone." They can gauge students' levels of interest, comprehension, irritation, urgency, confusion, frustration, delight, satisfaction, agency, and empathy by reading students' body language. Moreover, in asynchronous remote learning, wherein discussion and debate are often reduced to blogs and forum posts that are not read in "real" time, there is often a lapse in getting feedback on their statements. The lapse removes the intensity of the affective experiences that are important to learning. The shared moments of discomfort, discovery, conflict, and resolution are dulled and may not be as transformative as those same moments experienced in the presence of others.

Instructors are not the only ones who benefit from immediate feedback. Students often work in groups where they may cultivate leadership skills. Immersing students in team projects means that they will have to learn what it is like to work with all kinds of people. They may be challenged to deal with noncooperation, defiance, personality conflicts, apathy, incompetence, and procrastination; and, they may have to learn new communication and management skills. The emotional and psychological experiences of such learning may be blunted as a result of operating in a relatively isolated environment, even when students are regularly invited to share their thoughts and feelings online.

The physical classroom is a place where feedback is immediate, and where spontaneous tangents lead to new synthesis, new insights, and new applications of knowledge. In synchronous digital formats, such spontaneity is possible. Zoom® discussions readily facilitate such things. The remote classroom, however, leans away from the spontaneous. In the first place, many online courses are asynchronous, which means students log onto courses any time, where they might complete their work in isolation. In the second place, many instructors achieve a sense of control over their synchronous online classes by designing them in ways that are so highly structured that they provide little room for deep and spontaneous discussions.

Many instructors hold that online courses are equal to face-to-face courses. Some even say that their use of the Socratic Method as a strategy for student engagement is just as effective in the online environment as it is the physical classroom. I am skeptical. The "method," Socrates' dialectics, generally involved only one or two pupils at a time. To expose flaws in logic, biases, contradictions, and misuses of evidence, Socrates deliberately provoked frustration, discomfort, and embarrassment. The Socratic Method put pupils squarely in the midst of uncertainty, ambiguity, and paradox, where they might be humbled by their own ignorance and the stature of truth. It prohibited collaboration when individuals got stuck. Contrary to many assumptions, the Socratic Method was highly subjective, as Socrates believed that some reasoning was superior to others and that "the good" represented a fixed ideal.[58] He would not have stood for the idea that all opinions are equal in merit. Many today might regard the Socratic Method in its original form as abuse, because it does not reflect contemporary regard for students' self-esteem and does not permit collaboration to think one's way out of ill-reasoned assertions.[59]

The digital divide is more than a matter of who has access to technology. It is a gap between those who have the motivation and self-discipline to be successful in online learning, and those who do not.[60] The digital divide is also a literacy divide. The fact that many college students cannot read academic text proficiently, nor will comply with reading assignments, raises the question of whether remote instruction will trigger a retreat from language proficiency. Reading proficiency impacts the extent to which students can learn autonomously in the online environment, especially when course materials include dense and complex texts.[61]

PRE-EXISTING CONDITION FOUR: DENIAL

There is growing consensus among educators that schools and colleges should make sustainability and justice the centerpieces of instruction. The growing consensus represents a way to think about academic integrity in ways that go beyond plagiarism and cheating. Academic integrity also pertains to institutional integrity. In the context of our commitment to democracy, justice, and the dignity of life, institutional integrity regards the extent to which the academy consistently challenges students to overcome their ignorance, confront their biases, cultivate empathetic judgement, and tread gently on Mother Nature. It regards the institutional humility to acknowledge that some its most treasured curricula is doing very little to equip students with the knowledge and skills required to solve 21st century problems.

Institution integrity invites us to consider the possibility that our traditional veneration of winning athletes and celebrity alumni is of little consequence if our students are short on knowledge and skills, and indifferent to the disasters we face as a result of our way of life. For some educators, institutional integrity has reached intolerable and dangerous lows. Sociologist Christian Smith summarizes this perspective:

58. Fishman, "Counteracting Misconceptions," 185–88.
59. See Stoddard and O'Dell, "Would Socrates."
60. See Hart, "Factors Associated" and Kauffman, Review of Predictive Factors."
61. See Kerr et al., "Student Characteristics."

...[T]he accumulated effects of all the academic BS are contributing to this country's disastrous political condition and, ultimately, putting at risk the very viability and character of decent civilization. What do I mean by BS?

BS is the expectation that a good education can be provided by institutions modeled organizationally on factories, state bureaucracies, and shopping malls — that is, by enormous universities processing hordes of students as if they were livestock, numbers waiting in line, and shopping consumers.

BS is universities hijacked by the relentless pursuit of money and prestige, including chasing rankings that they know are deeply flawed, at the expense of genuine educational excellence...

BS is a tenure system that provides guaranteed lifetime employment to faculty who are lousy teachers and inactive scholars, not because they espouse unpopular viewpoints that need the protection of "academic freedom," but only because years ago they somehow were granted tenure.

BS is the shifting of the "burden" of teaching undergraduate courses from traditional tenure-track faculty to miscellaneous, often-underpaid adjunct faculty and graduate students...

BS is the fantasy that education worthy of the name can be accomplished online through "distance learning..."

BS is second- and third-tier universities running expensive sports programs that do little but drain money away from academics, when some of their ordinary students cannot find the time to prepare for classes because they work two and three part-time jobs to pay their school bills.

BS is the ascendant "culture of offense" that shuts down the open exchange of ideas and mutual accountability to reason and argument. It is university leaders' confused and fearful capitulation to that secular neo-fundamentalist speech-policing.

BS is the invisible self-censorship that results among some students and faculty, and the subtle corrective training aimed at those who occasionally do not self-censor.[62]

Colleges and universities are run by mere mortals, and all the glowing mystique that surrounds their status as society's most intelligent elite fades as we discover that many of the best and brightest are living in denial of the role education plays in the perpetuation of the status quo and social morbidity. The self-censorship of which Smith speaks is real, and it tends to grind reforms to a halt, even as we know that status quo is hurting us.

62. Smith, Christian, "Higher Education," para. 2–3; 5–6; 8–9; 11; 17–19.

The Wrong Direction

About 61 percent of Americans concur that colleges are "headed in the wrong direction," but the rationale for this belief is fractured along party lines. More Democrats than Republicans tend to say colleges are going in the wrong direction because the cost of education is increasing, but more Republicans than Democrats tend to believe that colleges are not providing students with needed job skills, too concerned about protecting students from offensive ideas, and too tolerant of liberal indoctrination.[63] Democrats have been largely positive about higher education over the last several years, while Republicans have grown increasingly negative about it. What's the beef? Republicans are not happy about "low" standards of college admissions, the cost of remedial education, and hostility towards conservatives on campus.[64]

Both parties have a point about the economic aspects of higher education. A college education in 1963, including tuition, room, and board, cost an average of $9,818 a year, and by 2017, the average was $23,091.[65] Today, there are many highly educated individuals without jobs in their field.[66] Many have second thoughts about enrolling in college because the cost is crippling. In 2020, nearly 45 million people held student loan debt that totaled $1.56 trillion, an average of $32,731 per student.[67] The price tag is a whopper, and the money is not always spent wisely.

Many believe that that the common good is best served if all colleges and universities aspired to be powerful research institutions. The belief has led many educators to copy the practices of R-I institutions, and in the end, they often lack the resources to do what R-1 universities do. Roughly 130 out of 5,300 (2.4 percent) colleges and universities in the U.S. hold the Carnegie Classification of R-1, or Research University of the first rank.[68] They are characterized by the number of doctoral programs, the scale of their research, and the sum of their endowments, patents, and publications. They are highly selective in their admissions.

The problem is not that R-1 institutions exist, or that they are selective and expensive. The problem is that an R-1 status does not automatically mean that the institution uses its wealth and advantages to change

63. Brown, "Most Americans Say," para. 1–9.

64. Parker, "Growing Partisan Divide," para. 1–8.

65. Hess, "Here's How Much," para. 4.

66. See Greenstone et al., "Thirteen Economic Facts," and Cohen, "Why Education Isn't."

67. Fields, "Student Loan Debt Statistics," para. 1–4.

68. Carnegie Classification of Institutions of Higher Education, "2018 Update," 9.

paradigms that are killing us. The problem is that others want to replicate their corporate practices for the purpose of keeping the doors open, and not for the purpose of reforming education. The corporate model, as David Schultz observed, generated competition among institutions for applicants and lots of razzle-dazzle that did not translate into meaningful academic achievement. He has this to say about why higher education is failing:

> For years it [higher education] raised tuition at percentages that far outstripped the cost of living and increases in median household incomes, and now many students cannot afford to go to college.
>
> For years it raised tuition to convince people that the more expensive it was the better a school it was. Except the school did not invest the money in academic programs.
>
> For years it played the *U.S. News & World Report* college rankings game. Except all the other schools played too and all it accomplished was elegant dorms and rising tuition. . .
>
> It adopted a corporate, private-sector orientated model for governance, creating high-salaried vice-presidents for every task or problem it encountered. Except when the financial crunch hit it opted to lay off or reduce faculty and cut back on programs that generated revenue instead of trimming back middle and senior management. It also then hired a new vice-president or a consultant to manage the finances. . .
>
> It reduced the percentage of tenured or tenure-track faculty and replaced them with part time contingents. Except it found that the latter, no matter how well meaning, do not have the same time to provide all the advising and other services full time faculty do.
>
> It expanded sports programs as a way to attract attention and recruit students. Except few sports programs provide a positive return on investment.
>
> It experimented with on-line degree completion programs. Except it did so at the same time everyone else did across the country and therefore it faced a new group of schools competing for the same students.
>
> It lowered admissions standards to maintain enrollment but could not then figure out why the retention rates went down.
>
> It cut requirements such as foreign languages, music, or the arts to make it easier for students to get in and graduate into jobs. Except in doing so it undermined its mission as a liberal arts institution and the reason why students should go to it and not a community college. . .

It jumped on buzz words and slogans such as high impact learning or stackable to sell itself, yet it did little to really change course offerings or programs.

It invested heavily in learning technology letting it drive pedagogy, instead of vice versa.

It talked about the reality of a coming new student demographics, but it did little to change its marketing strategy or services to support them. . .

It hired presidents who promised big change but kicked the real tough choices down the road to avoid taking responsibility for what might happen.[69]

All that has been said so far about education could have been said before the coronavirus pandemic began. The crisis merely magnified how ignorance, hubris, and irrationality put us in jeopardy, and amplified humanity's cry for change. What follows is a condensed chronology of events. It frames an appeal for education reform, as subsequent discussion will be mapped to actual events, statements, and behavior that defined our nation's response to the crisis.

---

69. Schultz, "Anatomy of a Failing University," para. 5–7; 12; 14–18; 22–24; 26.

Chapter 4

From Wuhan to Washington

COVID SPRING

A complete and accurate chronology of the COVID-19 pandemic may not be known for some time. The following chronology may require revisions when more is known about COVID-19, and the pandemic. It is believed, however, that the first case of the novel coronavirus was confirmed in China on November 17, 2019.[1] In December, 2019, dozens of people in the Wuhan district of China were stricken with a mysterious pneumonia. On December 30th, Dr. Li Wenliang, a physician at Wuhan Central Hospital, warned his colleagues that a new and deadly virus was active in the region, and was told by police to stop spreading lies.[2] His warning found its way to Chinese social media, but that venue was shut down by authorities who did not want the public to discuss the matter.[3] On January 11, 2020, China reported its first death due to the novel coronavirus. Ten days later, a man who had traveled to the Wuhan district and returned to the state of Washington, became the first reported case of the novel coronavirus in the U.S.[4] Seventeen days later, Dr. Li Wenliang died from complications of the novel coronavirus.

1. Ma, "Coronavirus," para. 1.
2. BBC News, "Li Wenliang," para. 3.
3. Feng, "Critics Say China," para. 1–5.
4. Schumaker, "Timeline," para. 4–8.

On February 11, 2020, the World Health Organization (WHO) introduced a new name for the novel coronavirus: COVID-19 (coronavirus disease identified in 2019). Fifteen days later, a nursing home near Kirkland, Washington reported the first two COVID-19 related deaths in the United States. On March 13, 2020, six weeks after the WHO declared an international health emergency, President Trump declared a national emergency, but did not mandate shelter-in-place. Four days later, officials confirmed that COVID-19 was present in all 50 states.

The month of March brought state-level shelter in place directives, school and business closures, cancellation of public events, including professional sports and theater, and a dramatic spike in global infections and mortality. Millions of Americans filed for unemployment benefits, and food banks were exhausted by sharp demands. Public health officials, physicians, nurses, paramedics, and nursing home staff complained of shortages in protective gear, testing kits, and ventilators. On March 22, COVID-19 appeared on the list of the top 15 causes of death in the U.S., and by March 31, over 4,000 Americans had lost their lives to the virus.[5] By April 4, COVID-19 occupied first place on the list of causes of death in the U.S.[6] In April, the COVID-19 morbidity rate was so severe in New York City that hospitals ran out of space for patients, and local prisons inmates were called upon to dig mass graves for the scores of unclaimed bodies.[7] By April 14, New York City's death toll topped 10,000. Many who died in their homes or in care facilities were not tested for the coronavirus.[8]

The vital months of COVID spring, 2020 were those in which intervention, such as social distancing, would have kept the contagion in check, and in which initiatives, such as increasing the production and distribution of personal protective equipment, would have prevented infections. States where governors ordered shutdowns earlier saw very different outcomes throughout the COVID-19 crisis than did governors who were slow to order social distancing. On March 19, California became the first state to adopt the stay-at-home strategy, as Govern Gavin Newsom (D) issued a state-wide order for social distancing and closure of non-essential businesses. Within four days, eleven more states took similar measures.[9]

---

5. Worldometer. "Coronavirus," chart: "Total Coronavirus Deaths."

6. Raymond, "Rapid Increase," see animated visualization, para. 2.

7. Durkin, "Mass Burials Surge," para. 2–7.

8. Durkin, "NYC Death Toll," para. 1–4.

9. Perper et al., "More than Half," chart: "US States that Have Issued Stay-at-Home Orders.

Several governors waited until after April 1 to declare strident restrictions. Governor Ron DeSantis (R-FL) said on March 31 that he was waiting for directives from the White House before undertaking shutdowns in his state.[10] Governor Tate Reeves (R-MS) indicated that he was reluctant to take measures until hearing form the State Department, and gloated, "Mississippi's never going to be China."[11] Governor Brian Kemp (R-GA) cautioned that mandates may represent government "overreach."[12]

Eventually, all 50 states had directives for shelter-in-place, business closures, and prohibitions on public gatherings. It took the nation weeks to do what the federal government could have done in 24 hours. The lag in consensus about what states should do was caused in part by uncertainties about the risks, conflicting information about public safety and federal jurisdiction, and fears about the economic fallout of state shutdowns. Some officials speculated that governors were reluctant to act because they feared presidential retaliation in the form of limited access to vital medical resources and financial support. Governor Gretchen Whitmer, (D-MI) put it like this: "I can't afford to have a fight with the White House."[13]

Governors had reason to be concerned about the president's willingness to lend hand. Trump had already established a pattern of punishing those who did not support him in the way he felt they ought to support him. His penchant for publically abusing members of his own administration, firing people, and compulsively blaming others for his errors, failures, and decisions are well known.[14] As the crisis unfolded, governors learned the extent to which they would be responsible for making decisions about social distancing, the procurement of medical supplies, and the distribution of vital resources. Many governors and mayors who expected that the federal government would be more proactive and timely with national guidelines and assistance were stunned by what felt like a federal abdication of duty.

Many governors quickly mobilized resources and established protocols to ensure public safety. Some deliberated longer than others, and some were impatient with the disruptions to local and national economies.[15] The situation begged the question of whether the nation had a sound consensus

---

10. Mower, "No State Shutdown for Florida," para. 1.

11. Judin, "Governor Rejects State Lockdown," para. 1–3; 7.

12. Bluestein, "Kemp Rejects Shutdown," para. 11–12.

13. Ronayne and Lemire, "Flatter or Fight?" para. 6.

14. See Lee, *Dangerous Case of Donald Trump*; Newman, *Unhinged*; and Wolf, *Fire and Fury*.

15. See Chertoff, "The Calvary Isn't Coming."

on what ought to be done and why, or whether the nation had 50 different policies, 50 different standards of safety, and 50 different agendas.

The following abridged chronology provides a foundation for subsequent chapters that address educational reform. The chronology contains examples of what was good, bad, and ugly about America's reaction to COVID-19 in the early months of the crisis.

AN ABRIDGED AND ANNOTATED CHRONOLOGY OF PREPAREDNESS FOR AND RESPONSE TO THE COVID-19 PANDEMIC FROM JULY 2003 TO APRIL, 2020

The chronology of the COVID crisis in the U.S. is a catalogue of partisan posturing, scientific activism, human suffering, courage, good will, and the power of leadership. The chronology raises many questions about what Americans want in their leaders, and what they actually need in their leaders. It also raises the question of whether ignorance was a factor in the calamity.

- **July 31, 2003.** An international association of scientists and government agencies created Group on Earth Observations. It tracks and predicts pandemics from space and on the ground. Its aim is to end pandemics by developing sustainable models of human interaction with the environment.

- **April 15, 2009.** A new virus, H1N1, appeared in California. Twelve days later, the government declared a Public Health Emergency of International concern and began distributing stockpiled anti-viral drugs.[16] The outbreak killed about 12,500 Americans.

- **October 21, 2009.** The United States Agency for International Development (USAID) announced the creation of the Emerging Pandemic Threats Program (EPT) to study zoonotic viruses and conditions leading to pandemics, and to train people in effective responses to outbreaks.[17] EPT's units included PREDICT, an international program to identify and track zoonotic viruses. PREDICT has identified over 160 coronaviruses.[18]

16. Centers for Disease Control and Prevention. "2009 N1H1 Timeline," see chronology.

17. USAID Press Office, "USAID Launches," para. 1–4.

18. Milman, "Trump Administration Cut," para. 1–7. See USAID, "Predict."

- **December 18, 2009.** H1N1 vaccine available to the general public.

- **December 2, 2014.** In his remarks about the containment of the Ebola outbreak, President Barack Obama stated: "There may and likely will come a time in which we have both an airborne disease that is deadly. And in order for us to deal with that effectively, we have to put in place an infrastructure—not just here at home, but globally—that allows us to see it quickly, isolate it quickly, respond to it quickly."[19]

- **January 13, 2017.** Seven days before Trump was sworn into office, the Obama administration briefed the incoming administration about the threat of a pandemic and provided strategies for an effective response. Secretary of Commerce, Wilber Ross dozed off during the session, and others complained that the briefing had no basis in reality.[20]

- **February, 2018.** The United States intelligence community (Homeland Security, etc.) reported that population growth, urbanization, and trade patterns have accelerated the incidence of pandemics, and warned that novel strains of viruses could trigger pandemics that could cost 100 million lives, and radically decrease global domestic production.[21]

- **March 9, 2019.** Trump called for budget cuts of 10 percent for the Centers of Disease Control and Prevention (CDC) and 12 percent to the Department of Health and Human Services (HSS).[22]

- **July 25, 2019.** The Federal Emergency Management Agency (FEMA) reported that a severe influenza outbreak would cause serious shortages of medical supplies, health care workers, and hospitals' capacity to care for the sick and dying. It noted that a pandemic could cripple social services, including policing and fire-fighting.[23]

- **September 30, 2019.** Trump's administration ended a $200 million program, PREDICT, that was part of USAID's effort to identify, track, and prevent the spread of novel zoonotic viruses.[24] Federal funding ended just weeks before the novel coronavirus infected people in Wuhan. Six months later, Congress scrambled to restore the funds.[25]

---

19. Obama, "Remarks by the President," para. 20.
20. Collman, "In 2017, Obama Officials Briefed," para. 1–10.
21. Coates, *Worldwide Threat*, P. 17.
22. Krisberg, "President's Budget," para. 3–4.
23. Federal Emergency Management Agency, *2019 National Threat*, pp. 20–21.
24. Baumgartner and Rainey, "Trump Administration Ended," para. 1–4.
25. Rainey and Baumgaertner, "Trump, Congress Scramble," para. 1–5.

- **November 17, 2019.** China reported its first case of novel coronavirus.

- **December 30, 2019.** Dr. Li Wenliang, a physician at Wuhan Central Hospital, warned colleagues to take special care against infection. Four days later, China's Public Security Bureau pressured him to sign a statement saying he had spread false rumors about the disease. Despite this, his warnings circulated in social media.[26]

- **December 31, 2019.** Wuhan Municipal Health Commission identified cluster of pneumonia-like illnesses.

- **January 1, 2020.** WHO created the Incident Management Support Team to plan responses to a potential pandemic. Officials were unclear about human transmission of the virus and whether transmissions occurred without showing symptoms of infection.

- **January 3, 2020.** By this time President Trump had received several briefings about the virus, but officials were uncertain about whether he read them. Trump at the time was preoccupied by a trade deal with China and his impeachment.[27]

- **January 5, 2020.** WHO announced a pneumonia of unknown origins was in Wuhan.

- **January 10, 2020.** WHO issued a package of technical guidance on how to detect, test, and manage potential coronavirus cases. Dr. Rick Bright, Director of the Biomedical Advanced Research and Development Authority (BARDA, overseen by HSS, began urging the HHS to obtain samples of the virus so that the U.S. could develop treatments and vaccines. China shared the genetic sequence of COVID-19.

- **January 13, 2020.** Thailand confirmed the first case of coronavirus outside China.

- **January 14, 2020.** WHO reported that the virus could be transmitted by human contact, and eight days later, evidence confirmed this type of transmission.

- **January 16, 2020.** Germany announced its Center for Infection Research developed the world's first diagnostic test for coronavirus.[28]

- **January 18, 2020.** Bright asked Assistant Secretary of HSS, Dr. Robert Kadlec, to set meetings of the Disaster Leadership Group (DLG) so it

---

26. BBC News, Li Wenliang, para. 9–14.
27. Marcela and M. Smith, "Virus: What Went Wrong," transcript.
28. Global Biodefense, "German Researchers," para. 1.

could prepare the nation for the pending arrival of the novel coronavirus. Kadlec was dismissive and saw no urgency.[29]

- **January 20, 2020.** WHO urged HHS to fund research of coronavirus. Kadlec had not yet called for a meeting of DLG, confident that the virus would not reach the U.S. Later that day, doctors in the state of Washington reported the first case of coronavirus infection in the U.S. and South Korea reported its first case of the novel coronavirus.

- **January 23, 2020.** China quarantined Wuhan.

- **January 24, 2020.** Trump praised China's President Xi Jinping for China's efforts and transparency to fight the virus. Two weeks later, he repeated his praises.[30]

- **January 26, 2020.** Dr. Anthony Fauci, Director of the National Institute of Allergies and Infectious Diseases (NIAID), said U.S. should not be worried about the coronavirus as it seemed localized in China and because the U.S. had ways of screening people.[31]

- **January 27, 2020.** South Korean officials devised plans to mass produce test kits, open 46 testing stations, and dispatch sanitation teams to routinely disinfect public areas and transportation.[32]

- **January 28, 2020.** Alex Azar, Secretary of Health and Human Services announced that after less than two weeks of development, the CDC was ready to roll out its new test kits.

- **January 29, 2020.** Trade advisor, Peter Navarro sent memo to Trump warning that a coronavirus outbreak in the U.S. could infect 30 percent of Americans and kill 500,000 people.[33] Trump announced the President's Coronavirus Task Force. Its original members included Alex Azar, Secretary of HHS, Robert O'Brian, Assistant to the President on National Security, Dr. Robert Redfield, Director of the CDC, and Dr. Anthony Fauci, Director of NIAID. Their task was to monitor, contain and prevent the outbreak, and their reports were urgent about social distancing.[34] Scientists in France sequenced the whole genome of the

---

29. Bright, *Complaint of Personal Practice*, 16.

30. See Peters, "Detailed Timeline."

31. Moreno, "Government Health Agency Official," para. 1–3.

32. Gaviria and Smith, *Virus: What Went Wrong*, Frontline, [documentary film] transcript.

33. Mark, "Trump Learned," para. 2–3.

34. See White House Press Secretary, "Statement."

novel coronavirus, which was named COVID-19. Sequencing is the basis for building tests, developing treatments, and inventing vaccines.

- **January 30, 2020.** WHO issued a public health emergency of international concern due to novel coronavirus.

- **January 31, 2020.** The CDC issued a quarantine of 14 days for 195 Americans who evacuated Wuhan, China and returned to the U.S. President Trump signed an order prohibiting the entry into the U.S. of all foreign nationals who had traveled to China in the previous two weeks. Delta, United, and American airlines suspend flights to China. Secretary of HSS, Alex Azar, declared a public health emergency in the U.S.

- **February 4, 2020.** Carnival Cruise Line's *Diamond Princess* was quarantined off the shore of Yokohama, Japan, after learning that several people among its 3,711 guests and staff were infected with the coronavirus. The company's 18 ships maintained business as usual for another month, despite the loss of port privileges in several countries.[35] After weeks of quarantine, the *Diamond Princess* saw 712 cases of coronavirus and 14 deaths.[36]

- **February 5, 2020.** After the CDC rejected WHO's offer to acquire test kits from Germany for the U.S, the CDC dispatched kits they had in stock, but they did not have reagents (chemicals that reveal the microscopic composition of specimens) that could reliably detect COVID-19.[37] Testing in the U.S. thus had a late start. Representatives Nita Lowey (D-NY) and Rosa DeLauro (D-CT) urged Congress to increase in funding for resources and services related to fighting the coronavirus crisis through screening, vaccine development, and education.[38]

- **February 12, 2020.** Dr. Nancy Messonnier, Director of the CDC's National Center for Immunization and Respiratory Diseases, announced that flaws in the American-made test kits that rendered them ineffective.[39] The US continued to decline test kits developed by other nations that WHO offered to provide.[40]

35. Cachero, "Carnival's CEO Says," para. 4.
36. See Clark, "Inside the Nightmare."
37. Cohen, "United States Badly Bungled," para. 1–10.
38. See House Appropriations Committee, "Lowey, DeLauro Urge Administration."
39. Global Biodefense, "CDC Update," para. 5.
40. Kenen, "How Testing Failures," para. 1–4.

- **February 25, 2020.** Dr. Messonnier reported that there was no question of whether the U.S. would be hit by the pandemic, but a question of when. Rumors circulated that Trump was going to fire her, and she did not appear in press conferences following her statement. Trump was angry about the statement as it caused a dip in the stock market.[41]

- **February 28, 2020.** Trump claimed that the novel coronavirus was a "hoax," and added, "Democrats will always say horrible things. . .Democrats want us to fail so badly."[42]

- **February 29, 2020.** CDC Director, Dr. Robert Redfield, said that the risk of the virus was very low, and told the public to "go on with their normal lives."[43] The U.S. documented its first fatality due to coronavirus.

- **March 3, 2020.** WHO declared that in order to check the pandemic, the manufacturing of masks, shields, ventilators, and other medical supplies must increase by 40 percent.[44]

- **March 4, 2020.** Passengers onboard Carnival's *Grand Princess* received word that COVID-19 clusters were linked to cruise lines. The next day, the 2,422 passengers were ordered to shelter-in-place in their cabins.[45]

- **March 6, 2020.** Worldwide cases of COVID-19 topped 100,000 and global deaths tipped 3,500. Trump signed legislation calling for $8.3 billion to fight the virus. Trump asserted that the coronavirus crisis was "an unforeseen problem."[46] While visiting the CDC, he also announced that, "Anybody who wants a test gets a test."[47] Evidence at that time showed that clinics rationed tests due to shortages of testing kits.[48]

- **March 11, 2020.** Trump announced a 30-day travel ban from Europe, and stated, "We're having to fix a problem that four weeks ago nobody ever thought would be a problem."[49]

41. Moreno, "Trump Threatened to Fire," para. 1–6.
42. Egan, "Trump Calls Coronavirus Democrats' New Hoax," para. 1–5.
43. Dickenson, "Four Men Responsible," para. 2.
44. World Health Organization, "Shortage," para. 11.
45. Car and Palmeri, "Socially Distance This," para. 1–3.
46. Trump, "Remarks by President Trump," para. 7.
47. Hirsch, "Trump Says, 'Anybody Who Wants,'" para. 1.
48. Valverde, "Donald Trump's Wrong Claim," para. 6–12.
49. Allyn and Romo, "Trump Suspends All Travel," para. 1; 29.

- **March 12, 2020.** Trump claimed, "Testing has been smooth," despite Dr. Anthony Facui's assertion that testing was failing.[50]

- **March 13, 2020.** Trump blamed the Obama administration for the lack of testing kits for coronavirus, and said, "I don't take any responsibility at all."[51] The U.S. suspended travel to and from Europe.

- **March 16, 2020.** U.S. stock market suffered a jaw-dropping loss as the Dow Jones Industrial, NASDAQ, and the S & P dropped by an average of 12.6 percent.[52] The Dow Jones Industrial's February high of 29,551 plummeted to just under 20,000.[53]

- **March 19, 2020.** In response to concerns about the economy, Trump exclaimed, "There's never been anything like this in history. . .Nobody's ever seen anything like this."[54] Chaffed by criticism of his performance, he explicitly attacked the *Wall Street Journal* for being "phony," and the *Washington Post* for being "dishonest." Trump dismissed assertions that the federal government should do more to help states obtain medical supplied. He barked, "The federal government is not supposed to be out there buying vast amounts of items and then shipping. You know, were not a shipping clerk."[55]

- **March 20, 2020.** Trump insulted reporter Peter Alexander who expressed concerns about promoting drugs to fight COVID-19 that had not been thoroughly vetted, and asked the executive what he would tell Americans who were frightened. Trump sarcastically called the question "lovely," then told Alexander "I'd say that you're a terrible reporter, that's what I'd say. . .The American people are looking for answers and they're looking for hope, and you're doing sensationalism."[56] Trump defended his use of the term "Chinese virus" as a reference to COVID-19 because he wanted to "be accurate."[57]

- **March 23, 2020.** Carnival Cruise Lines suspended its tours following an advisory of the U.S. State Department for Americans to avoid travel by cruise lines and the CDC's order not to sail. Despite the cruise ships' community swimming pools, crowded buffets, and compact quarters,

50. Fishel et al., "Fact Check: Trump's Coronavirus Response," para. 8.

51. Wilke and Mangan, Trump Blames Obama," para. 4.

52. McCardle, "Markets Suffer Worst Day," para. 1–2.

53. Merrill and Day, "What the Dow's 28% Crash Tells Us," chart;

54. Trump, "Remarks by President Trump and Vice President Pence," para. 39

55. Forgey, "We're Not a Shipping Clerk," para. 3.

56. Bauder, "Trump Uses Daily Briefing," para. 4–7.

57. Subramanian et al., "Trump Uses China," para. 1–3.

Carnival's CEO, Arnold Donald, stated that the ships did not present a threat to passengers because they are so large, social distancing occurs "naturally."[58] In Iran, Ayatollah Ali Khamenei refused U.S. aid and said that the U.S. created COVID-19 with Iranian genetic data as part of an American-Israeli plot to destroy Iran.[59]

- **March 24, 2020.** Amid criticisms about the shortage of testing for COVID-19, Trump stated that the U.S. had done more testing than South Korea. Up that point, the U.S. had conducted 418,810 tests, and South Korea had conducted 358,896 tests, but the ratio of testing differed significantly. South Korea tested one out of 142 South Koreans, while the U.S. had tested 1 out of every 786 Americans.[60] On the matter of his support for governors, Trump reported: "We're doing very well with, I think, almost all the governors for the most part. . .But you know, it's a two-way street. They have to treat us well."[61] He grumbled "Some of these governors take, take, take, and they complain."[62]

- **March 27, 2020.** Trump signed the Coronavirus Aid, Relief, and Economic Security Act (CARES). It earmarked $2 trillion for paycheck protection, small business loans, unemployment benefits, and hospital support.[63] The package provided $500 billion for distressed corporations, but nothing for undocumented workers.[64]

- **March 29, 2020.** Trump reiterated, "Nobody knew that there'd be a pandemic or an epidemic of this proportion."[65]

- **March 31, 2020.** Senate Majority Leader Mitch McConnell (R-KY) blamed impeachment proceedings for slowing Trump's response to the COVID-19 crisis.[66] At that time in the U.S., there were nearly 190,000 cases and over 4,000 fatalities.

- **March 31, 2020.** After de-funding the PREDICT project, USAID gave it emergency funding to provide technical expertise in global efforts to slow infection rates.[67]

58. Cachero, "Carnival's CEO Says," Para. 1–3; 10.

59. Aljazeera, "Iran Leader," para 1–5.

60. Subramaniam and Lybrand, "Fact Check," para. 4–9.

61. Ronayne and Lemire, "Flatter or Fight?," para. 8.

62. Ibid, para. 14.

63. Cochrane and Stolberg, "$2 Trillion," para. 1, 6–7.

64. Simon, "What the Stimulus Package Means," para. 1.

65. Schwartz, "Trump on Coronavirus," para. 13.

66. Cabrera, "McConnell Blames Impeachment," para. 1–4.

67. Burns, "PREDIT Receives Extensions," 1–7.

- **April 2, 2020.** Dr. William Schaffner, Professor of Medicine at Vanderbilt University, said that while the U.S. was daily testing about 100,000 for coronavirus, it was still not enough, and that testing was still restricted in some parts of the country.[68] A plane owned by the New England Patriots' football team landed in Massachusetts. On board were 1.5 million Chinese-manufactured face masks, purchased by Governor, Charles Baker (R-MA) to replace some of the 3 million masks the governor previously ordered, only to have them seized for the federal stockpile by FEMA in the port of New York.[69]

- **April 3, 2020.** Thomas Modly, Secretary of the Navy, fired Captain Brett Crozier of the *U.S.S. Roosevelt* after Crozier send letters to others asking for assistance with an outbreak aboard his ship. More than 650 of the *Roosevelt's* crew tested positive for COVID-19, and about 350 of those individuals showed no symptoms of infection.[70] Senior advisor to the president and son-in-law Jared Kushner, told reporters that, "The notion of the federal stockpile was that it was supposed to be our stockpile—its not supposed to be stockpiles that they then use."[71]

- **April 4, 2020.** Governor Jared Polis (D-CO) reported that FEMA took ventilators that Colorado bought for their own hospitals. Polis expressed frustration to federal officials about their mixed messages on crisis management, stating, "Either be in or out. . .Either you're buying them and providing them to states and you're letting us know what we're going to get and when we're going to get them. Or stay out, and let us buy them."[72]

- **April 6, 2020.** Trump verbally abused ABC reporter Jonathan Karl after he and another reporter asked the president about his response to a federal report issued by Christi Grimm, Inspector General of the U.S. Department of HHS. Trump said the report was wrong about shortages of tests and medical supplies, and then, demanded to know "his" (Inspector General's) name. When Karl identified the Inspector General as a woman who had worked under previous administrations, Trump ridiculed her association with the Obama administration. Trump refused to acknowledge that *he himself* had appointed Grimm.

68. Alltucker, "Labs are Testing," para. 1–3.
69. Rose, "War for Medical Supplies," para. 10–14.
70. Welna, "Navy Not Ruling Out," para. 1, 5, 14.
71. Porter, "Jared Kushner," para 4.
72. Tabachnik, "Either Be In or Out," para. 2.

Trump snarled, "See there's another typical fake news deal. . .You're a third rate reporter, and what you just said is a disgrace."[73]

- **April 7, 2020.** Trump attacked Christi Grimm's federal report that documented shortages of medical supplies and equipment essential to combat COVID-19 and care for the sick. He called the report "another fake dossier."[74]

- **April 13, 2020.** Dr. David Skorton, President and CEO of the Association of American Medical Colleges, petitioned the Coronavirus Task Force to strengthen the federal government's coordination of its response to shortages of testing kits. Skorton noted that the shortages were exacerbated by variations in the testing platforms that were produced by different vendors. Not all kits used the same components and calibrations. Skorton also identified strategies to improve the federal coordination of testing.[75]

- **April 14, 2020.** Trump declared that he alone had the authority to reopen states, and tweeted that resistance to reopening on the part of state governors was "mutiny."[76] He also announced a halt to U.S. funding of WHO, (about $400 million annually). He accused WHO of "severely mismanaging and covering up the spread of coronavirus."[77]

- **April 15, 2000.** Thousands gathered at Michigan's capitol to protest Governor Gretchen Whitmer's mandate to continue sheltering-in-place. Many carried assault rifles, chanted "lock her up," waved Confederate flags, and called Whitmer a Nazi.[78]

- **April 17, 2020.** One month after state initiatives to close down businesses, over 22 million Americans had applied for unemployment benefits. Many went without an income for weeks as gridlock slowed the processing of applications.[79]

- **April 18, 2020.** Governor Andrew Cuomo (D-NY) asked the federal government to coordinate a national supply chain to effectively distribute tests so that states could move quickly towards reopening.[80]

---

73. CNN Politics, "Trump Berates Reporters," video.
74. Samuels, "Trump Decries IG Report," para. 2.
75. David J. Skorton to Deborah Birx, MD, April 13, 2020, para. 6–11.
76. Johnson et al., "Trump Says He'll Speak," para. 1–19.
77. Ollstein, "Trump Halts Funding," para. 3–7.
78. Lenthang, "Protestors Waving MAGA Flags," para. 5.
79. Ordonez, "Pending Unemployment Benefits," para. 5–7.
80. New York State. "Amid COVID-19," para. 1.

At that time, New York led the nation in COVID-19 cases with nearly 237,000 cases, and a total of 18,298 deaths related to the virus—about 45 percent of all COVID-19 related death in the U.S.[81]

- **April 19, 2020.** The number of fatalities in the U.S. due to COVID-19 topped 40,000.

- **April 20, 2020.** Dr. Richard Bright, (BARDA) was transferred to the National Institutes of Health to fill a less impactful role in the crisis. Bright had spoken publically against the use of hydroxychloroquine to combat COVID-19 because of its potential toxic side-effects. Bright maintained he was removed because he contradicted Trump's assertions that hydroxychloroquine could cure people with COVID-19.[82] When asked about this, Trump stated that he did not know Bright and added, "Maybe he was [removed after raising concerns], maybe he wasn't."[83]

- **April 23, 2020.** Trump suggested that the coronavirus could be killed by injecting or ingesting disinfectant or bleach. Disinfectant manufacturers issued warnings to the public that their products are not for human consumption and can cause death.[84]

- **April 24, 2020.** Trump said his suggestion to use disinfectant to kill coronavirus inside the body was said "sarcastically," and "put in the form of a question to a group of extraordinary hostile people. Namely, the fake news media."[85]

- **April 25, 2020.** Despite warnings from health officials, Governor Brian Kemp (R-GA) ordered certain non-essential businesses, such as hair salons, bowling alleys, and gyms to open. Mayors in Atlanta, Augusta, and Savannah objected to the move. Dr. Charles Steele Jr., President of the Southern Christian Leadership Conference, said "We cannot use poor people as sacrificial lambs." Many believe Kemp wanted to alleviate economic disaster as Georgia faced a $4 billion loss in taxes due to business closures.[86]

81. Worldometer, "Coronavirus, United States," table.

82. See Bright, *Complaint of Personal Practice* for a chronology of his transfer and precipitating conflict.

83. Swasey, "Federal Scientist," para. 4.

84. Levin, "Lysol Manufacturer Warns," 1.

85. Fottrell, "Trump Floats Idea," para. 5.

86. Democracy Now! "Nobody Wants to do This," para. 1–9.

- **April 28, 2020.** Trump blamed China for not telling the world about the coronavirus sooner, and indicated he was exploring punitive consequences against Beijing. He stated that China "will do anything they can," to prevent his re-election, and suggested that the pandemic was deliberately unleashed to ruin the U.S. economy and discredit him.[87]

- **April 30, 2020.** Trump blamed Obama for leaving his administration ill-prepared to fight COVID-19, stating, "We had broken tests. We had tests that were obsolete. We had tests that didn't take care of people." The president was unfazed by a reminder that COVID-19 was not a known virus during Obama's terms, and so vaccines and treatments for it could not have possibly been developed.[88] World-wide, there were 3,304,220 cases of COVID-19, and 233,824 deaths. In the U.S., there were 1,095, 023 cases and 63,856 deaths. The U.S. had roughly four times the number of cases as Spain, the nation with the second highest infection cases, and twice the deaths that Italy, the nation with the second highest death rate. Health officials warned that pre-maturely re-opening of the country could trigger a second wave in infections. Dr. Anthony Fauci said that hundreds of millions of COVID-19 vaccines could possibly be ready by January 2021.[89] The number of applications for unemployment relief topped 30 million. By Thanksgiving, 2020, COVID-19 had claimed over 250,000 American lives.

PARTISAN PATHOGENS

Trumps' response to the crisis divided Americans. By mid-April, as tens of thousands of fatalities lay ahead, many Americans were desperate to reopen the country and get back to business. The economy was on everyone's mind. Working class families struggled to pay rent and many were displaced. The demand for food banks doubled in many areas and quadrupled in others, as millions of Americans turned to charitable organizations that were already stressed by food insecurities pre-dating the pandemic.[90] Some lost not only their jobs, but their own businesses. Stores all over the U.S. experienced shortages of dried and canned goods, cleaning supplies, sanitizers, and toilet paper. Those who had money in the stock market trembled in the wake of jarring declines in the value of their investments.

87. Holland, "Exclusive," para. 1–4.
88. Rupar, "Trump is Blaming," para. 2–5.
89. Booker, "Fauci Says Its Doable," para. 1–5.
90. Walker and Schor, "Pandemic Provokes Spike," para. 6–9.

The COVID crisis compelled us to decide which pathway was the lesser of evils. At one end of the spectrum, the pathway called for sheltering-at-home, cancellations of public events, and restrictions on social contact and travel. At the other end of the spectrum, the pathway called for business as usual modified by hygienic requirements. The first path ensured significant disruption to the economy, and additional loss of savings, homes, jobs, and perhaps even pensions. The trade-off for adopting quarantines would be a significant reduction in the morbidity and mortality caused by COVID-19. The second path ensured very high rates of infection and death, but would allow for people to go to work and collect a paycheck. After nearly two months of shelter-in-place, the way forward was not clear. The number of cases and deaths in the U.S. had not leveled off, and testing was not yet universal nor fully reliable.

No matter which way we turned, we always seemed to come back to the economy. We did not want to commit economic suicide, and nobody could say with absolute certainty which outcome would be worse in the long-run. Would we be better off if we went about our lives as usual, or would be better off if we closed the doors to our homes and businesses? The short-term outcomes for millions of Americans were so excruciating that many were willing to take their chances with infection if they could just go back to having a steady income.

Conservative radio personality, Rush Limbaugh, who daily drew about 15 million listeners to his program, said in mid-April that it was time to re-open the country and get back to business. He told his audience that the national shut-down was "absurd," and that he got "suspicious" when people said it was not time to re-open the country. Limbaugh crowed, "I know that the Democratic Party wants to keep this shutdown for as long as they can as a political objective. They know how damaging this is to the president."[91] One who protested shelter-in-place in Michigan snapped, "Governor Gretchen Whitmer [D] will put you out of business before allowing mere citizens to be responsible for their own behavior. That is madness."[92] The critic's confidence in human reason came at a terrible price. As states relaxed social distancing rules, the number of cases and fatalities in the U.S. surged to the point where some governors quickly threw their re-opening plans into neutral or into reverse. An unfortunate lesson of the pandemic is that human beings are not always responsible for their behavior, and not humbled by what experts say about health and safety.

91. Schwartz, "Limbaugh: I Hope," para. 1–5.
92. Bowden, "Demonstrators at Michigan," para. 4.

Throughout the crisis, Americans quietly deliberated about what might be an acceptable threshold of "collateral damage" for keeping our economic engines at full throttle. We were not open and explicit about the matter in public discourse, but it was implicit in them nonetheless. Trump was transparent about swift reopening. On March 24, he told the nation he wanted to reopen the country by Easter, April 12, and said that the country was not built for shut-downs in commerce. He stated that, "I don't want the cure to be worse than the problem itself," and added, "We lose thousands and thousands to the flu each year. We don't turn the country off."[93] Trump was correct in his assertions about deaths due to seasonal flu. The CDC indicates that 30,000 to 60,000 Americans die during flu season every year.[94] That estimate, however, includes people who die of pneumonia and are not tested for any particular virus.[95] We do not shut down the country when the flu season is upon us, because many of viruses lurking about from October to February are known, and are thus somewhat predictable. We also have vaccinations for familiar flu viruses.[96] In the case of COVID-19, we faced an unfamiliar pathogen for which we had no vaccine and killed at a higher rate then that of the known influenza.

Americans were divided along party lines in their opinions about the crisis, and that interfered with Congress' ability to reach consensus about the way forward. A Pew Research Center study reported in March, 2020 that most Americans thought the media greatly or slightly exaggerated the dangers of COVID-19, and nearly half said that they had "seen at least some made up news."[97] The study also revealed that Republicans were more likely than Democrats to give media coverage of the crisis lower ratings, more likely to say they saw fabricated news, and more likely to believe that the COVID-19 virus originated in a lab.

A second Pew study also released in March indicated that 52 percent of Americans felt that Trump did not take the crisis seriously at all or not seriously enough. Opinions split on party lines, with 79 percent of Democrats and 22 percent of Republicans agreed that Trump did not take the crisis seriously enough.[98] The study also found that, "59 percent of Democrats and Democratic-learning independents say the outbreak is a major threat to the health of the nation as a whole," while "only 33 percent of Republicans

---

93. Breuniger, "Trump Wants Packed Churches," para. 31–33.

94. Gillespie, "This is How Many," para. 2.

95. Learner, "Trumps Deadly Mistake," para. 1–4.

96 See Maragakis, "Coronavirus Disease 2019 vs. the Flu."

97. Mitchell and Oliphant, "Americans Immersed," para. 2–3.

98. Pew Research Center, "US Public Sees Multiple Threats," graphic 3.

and Republican leaners say the same."[99] In addition, while 82 percent of Republicans were confident that Trump was doing a good job responding to the crisis, only 12 percent of Democrats concurred.[100] By April, with "cabin fever" gripping the nation, thoughts about re-opening the country varied widely. In one study, 89 percent of Democrats and 72 percent of Republicans still agreed that it would be better to keep sheltering in place until safety could be assured.[101] Approximately 58 percent of respondents to an NBC News/Wall Street Journal poll expressed concerns about reopening the country too quickly. While 77 percent of Democrats expressed concerns about early reopening, 39 percent of Republicans expressed the same.[102]

As Trump declared that he had the authority to force states to reopen, John Yoo, former member of the Department of Justice's Office of Legal Counsel, contradicted the president's assertions, and explained that the U.S. Constitution did not provide the president with authority to force states to conduct business.[103] Governors were also feisty about the president's insistence that he alone could "authorize" states to reopen, as they believed they better understood the needs of their states. Trump astonished the nation as he not only accused governors of being mutinous, but, in a statement that appeared to channel the ghost of Richard Nixon, he declared, "The President of the United States calls the shots. . .When somebody is president of the United States, the authority is total."[104]

As Americans wrestled with their decisions about who to trust and what to believe, it was clear that the trauma might have been dulled had we known more about science, health, our own government, economics, and how to evaluate the accuracy and credibility of non-stop propaganda. With greater knowledge and proficiency with critical thinking, we might have been better able to decipher truth from fiction, and to separate the partisan posturing from erudite visions for managing the crisis. By mapping the rationale for radical reforms in education to the actual events of "Covid Spring," we may see the urgency and direction of educational reforms come into focus.

99. Pew Research Center, "US Public Sees Multiple Threats," para. 9.

100. Ibid, graphic 5.

101. Shepard, "Poll: Don't' Stop Social Distancing," para.

102. Coleman, "Nearly 6 in 10," para. 1–4.

103. Yoo, "No Trump Can't," para. 6–8.

104. Johnson et al., "Trump Says," para. 19. In defending his role in the Watergate burglary, Nixon said of wrong doing, "When the president does it. . . that means it is not illegal." See Nixon, "Transcript," para. 7.

Chapter 5

What COVID-19 Teaches
Us about Knowing

THE TEACHING VIRUS

Truth demands accountability even when people do not. Truth matters not only because it can save our lives, but because it is a vital ingredient to trust. Without trust, society would crumble under the weight of erroneous assumptions, false accusations, and endless suspicions about our neighbors. Throughout the COVID-19 crisis we heard rumors about where the virus originated, which interventions were curative, what obligations the federal government had to the people and to the states, and who was derelict in his or her duty to protect the public. We were all challenged to be patient as the truth was slow to emerge. We were tempted to throw caution to the wind and to believe whatever our favorite partisans told us. Our progress in the ordeal was impeded by our lack of knowledge and limited ability to assess the credibility of assertions.

Apart from the need to explicitly cultivate epistemological development in our children and in ourselves, the pandemic taught us that certain knowledge is essential for everyone if we as a human race are going to achieve a sustainable relationship with the planet and each other. In this instance, it became clear that we needed more knowledge about our world, history, biology, environmental science, governance, civic virtue, leadership, and mass media. What our leaders said and did, and how the public reacted during the crisis often revealed our willingness to make critical decisions based on suppositions and inaccurate representations of reality. If we are to achieve sustainable relationships with nature and each other, we are challenged to acknowledge that many in our society privately do not want certain people to thrive, and hide their festering hatred behind politically correct rhetoric.

OUR WORLD, OUR HISTORY

During the crisis, some elected officials said that they had no idea that a pandemic such as that caused by COVID-19 could occur, and no idea that the pandemic could be as bad as it got. In many cases, those claims were not true. As the chronology suggests, the public records of conferences, meetings minutes, and official reports point to the reality that the president and his advisors were presented with evidence that the U.S. was probably going to experience a dangerous pandemic at some point, and told that it was wise to be prepared.

The claim that, "nothing like this has ever happened before" suggests either a remarkable lapse of memory or a wholly vacuous understanding of history, or both. Plagues are a fixture in human history. They ravaged civilization in antiquity, and in the Middle Ages reduced Europe's population by at least a third. Small pox, tuberculosis, and cholera were constant threats to urban industrial communities in modern times. From 1918 to 1919, influenza swept around the world more than once to claim roughly 50 million lives.[1] Did folks really forget about the AIDS pandemic, which killed nearly 700,000 people in the U.S. between its onset and 2016[2] and the influenza pandemic of 1918–1919 that killed 675,000 Americans?[3]

The traditional approach to history makes it easy to forget plagues and pandemics unless they were record-breaking in morbidity and mortality. History typically focuses on the chronology of a people's progress, their achievements, and pivotal points in their development. In the American narrative, nature is typically cast as backdrop of human activity and not as a living thing with dignity. When nature is mentioned, it is usually the wilderness that must be "tamed," or a desert that must be made to bloom. We personify draughts, floods, and wildfires as the wrath of an adversary. In American history, nature is presented to humanity as an endless bounty of resources that may be consumed on our own terms. Much of what could be learned about sustainable human co-existence with nature has been

1. See Aberth, *Plagues in World History*.

2. Avert, "HIV and AIDS," Para. 4.

3. Centers for Disease Control and Prevention. "1918 Pandemic," para. 1.

marginalized because we do not regard nature as an equal partner with humanity in civilization's story. It is nearly incidental until we desire to possess its treasures, its minerals, vegetation, animals, and waterways.

Knowing history helps people avoid hysteria. It also helps us put things into perspective. Knowing, for example, that hundreds of thousands of scientists, biologists, epidemiologists, anthropologists, veterinarians, geneticists, virologists, immunologists, pathologists, physicians, and statisticians have been studying coronaviruses for decades, neutralizes the assertion that the U.S. went into the COVID-19 crisis without a clue as to what it was facing. Knowing that thousands of scientists have been trying to understand zoonotic viruses with increasing urgency because these viruses are making their way into human populations with greater frequency, tells us that it is no time smug about human invincibility and our dominance over teeny-tiny creatures.

Knowing history also helps us put social events into perspective. The protestors that demanded that their states reopen sometimes accused their local officials of being Nazis and fascists. A society that cannot tell the difference between the genocidal policies of Nazi Germany and the public health policies of people like Governors Andrew Cuomo (D-NY), Charlie Baker (R-MA), Gretchen Whitmer (D-MI), and Tim Walz (D-MN) may lose its democracy because it is unable to perceive the difference between public safety and ethnic cleansing. The people whom governors were trying to protect were often the most vulnerable in pandemics, including the elderly, fragile, sick, and the poor, who are disproportionately ethnic minorities—the very populations that Nazis wanted to exterminate. Nazi ideology held that the purification of the Aryan race required collateral damage, and that weak and non-Aryan populations had to die for the glory and salvation of Germany. Was not the rush to reopen states tainted with just a wee bit of "Nazi" willingness to sacrifice vulnerable minorities for the sake of monetary stability?

BIOLOGY

American ignorance about biology added to confusion and hysteria. The ultimate example of such ignorance was the president's suggestion that perhaps if people were to ingest or inject disinfectants into their bodies, they could kill coronaviruses. Though he later claimed his remarks were not serious, the initial impact of his statement triggered warnings from doctors and disinfectant manufacturers who understood that lots of people did not know that consumption of detergents and bleach could be lethal.

The president was not the only one who bumbled biology. The CEO of Carnival Cruises tried to assure that guests aboard the cruise ships had nothing to fear because the ships were so spacious that people would rarely come into close contact. U.S. Surgeon General Jerome Adams said of COVD-19 that, "You can increase your risk of getting it if you wear a mask if you are not a health care provider."[4] Researchers themselves spoke erroneously as data collection and analysis of COVID-19 was in its infancy. At first, the medical community believed that people without symptoms of the virus could not transmit it, and by February, 2020 that conclusion was overturned by new evidence.[5]

We are vulnerable to disease and to those who manage pandemics because most of us do not have expertise in science sufficient enough to critique their claims about pathogens, pharmacology, and epidemiology. Obviously, there is an incentive to increase our knowledge about the world of microbes, the human immune system, and good hygiene. Our understanding of biology, however, must extend well past declarative knowledge, and the ability to diagram cells or tell the differences between bacteria and viruses. We may panic less and be more reasonable in our expectations for quick remedies to health threats if we better understood the scientific method. This is not to say that we all need to acquire the skills it takes to replicate scientific research, but it helps to understand what it is and why it cannot be rushed.

Scientific literacy is more than the ability to define things such as atoms, ecosystems, and taxonomies, and more than the memorization of certain formulas for solving problems in the chemistry or physics lab. It is also the ability to explain what is meant by the scientific method and to explain why exemplary research meticulously narrows research questions, selects samples from certain populations and not others, conducts double-blind experiments, is imaginative and broad thinking about variables impacting outcomes, and insists on numerous replications of studies before speaking with certainty about scientific truth. Scientific literacy also means understanding the relationship between research and public safety, and knowing when certain scientific inquiries ought to have greater priority than others and why.

---

4. Perrett, "U.S. Surgeon General," para. 1–3.

5. Kupferschmidt, "Study Claiming," para. 1–5.

GOVERNMENT

As noted earlier, many Americans are unable to identify the three branches of government and which branches have which powers. During the crisis, official announcements and speeches often confused the public. It appeared at times that governors and the president himself did not know much about the limits of their authority and which options they had relative to mobilizing resources and enacting policies in response to a public health emergency. Convoluted and contradictory messages irritated individuals who were complying with directives and trying to be patient with the process of reopening. Confusion agitated people and legitimized their violations of safety directives. Some posited that if our government officials did not even know the law and the options they had to move forward, what was the point of obeying the law?

Many Americans did not know the details about the legal reach of the federal government. Yet, they knew enough to be befuddled by Jared Kushner's cheeky remarks that the federal stockpile did not exist for distribution to states, and by Donald Trump's declaration that "when somebody is president of the United States, the authority is total." People do have the sense that the federal government has an obligation to help and not harm the people.

Article II of the U.S Constitution describes the duties of the president, and identifies the ways in which other branches of government may check executive action and hold the executive accountable for wrong-doing. The Constitution does not grant the president "total authority." The Constitution, however, does not specifically say that the president will automatically be removed from office if the president lies, breaks the law, abuses power, or endangers public health. That can only happen when Congress decides to take legal actions when it believes that such action is warranted. Congress often makes decisions about legal action against a president based on partisan objectives and party allegiances. Thus, the law can only protect citizens from dastardly executives if people with the power to enforce the law have the will to enforce it.

Many Americans leave high school without ever studying civics and American governance. The problem is not just that they might not be able to identify their state senators, the problem is that they might not understand all the moving parts of governance and how each part impacts others. The problem is that many voters put people in high office without knowing much about the committees on which they will serve, how they are likely to be targeted by lobbyists, how their background and prior work experiences might create conflicts of interest, and why executive appointments to the courts and cabinet positions are so important.

COVID-19 reminded Americans that racism is still a part of our national dynamics. For decades, the CDC has acknowledged that ethnic minorities and people of color have experienced greater morbidity and mortality in times with and without pandemics. Such morbidity and mortality is associated with poverty, poor education, lack of access to health care, limited access to nutritious food, and social neglect. COVID-19 impacted minority populations with greater ferocity than it impacted whites. In June, 2020, the rate of hospitalization for and death due to COVID-19 in the African American community was about 2.5 times that of Caucasians.[6]

The COVID-19 crisis reminds us that the suffering of people of color, the poor, and the vulnerable is collateral damage for the American dream. People who are left in the margins are not blind to the reality that there is a double standard of government protection in the U.S., whereby corporations, bankers, and affluent whites are shown greater favor than the poor and people of color. It is logical that those who have experienced legal favoritism would want to protect their advantage, and that those who have experienced no favoritism and abuse in the justice system would feel hostile towards the law itself.

Violent and destructive protest against discrimination in our legal system often kindles public interest in demagogues who promise to "drain the swamp" and protect people from fellow citizens whom they believe have robbed them of a decent life. The COVID-19 crisis magnified the reality that Americans can be seduced by autocratic individuals who use our anxieties about race, privilege, and wealth to gain power, and then use power to abuse people at home and abroad. The crisis showed us that the character and moral outlook of our leaders may matter more to our well-being than whether the stock market produces double-digit dividends.

CIVIC VIRTUE

The first person people turn to in a catastrophe is often not the one with the most integrity and intelligence, it is often the one who is loudest and most persuasive. This is human nature. Volume and persuasion, however, are not virtues. They are qualities of presentation and rhetoric, not goodness of character. The COVID-19 crisis taught us that egotistical, short-sighted, and malicious leaders are not very good moral examples to citizens who

6. See Centers for Disease Control and Prevention, "COVID-19 in Racial and Ethnic Minority Groups."

are navigating their way through illness, job loss, the death of loved ones, isolation, and poverty.

Ideally, democratic societies do not tolerate leaders who lack virtue and offer no moral example, and eventually remove them from office, or simply do not vote for them in the first place. However, we do not live in an ideal world. We live in a democracy filled with people of all shades of vice and virtue. Moreover, we ourselves embody our own blends of vice and virtue. The integrity and durability of democracy are not set in stone. They are cultivated crisis by crisis, opportunity by opportunity, character by character. This cultivation does not happen organically as the result of completing a course in civics, political science, or ethics. The integrity and durability of democracy are made possible by a collective suppression of ego, by education that fosters a preference for equity, justice, empathy, and modesty in want, and by zero tolerance for economic and political policies that create special advantages for an elite.

The COVID-19 crisis revealed that Americans are divided about what we want from our leaders, but we knew that before the pandemic showed up. For many people the crisis magnified the difference between leadership that glowed with virtue and compassion and leadership that wallowed in self-pity and indifference to suffering. The crisis taught us that America needs leadership that is humble, far-sighted, empathetic, gracious, honest, and committed to integrity, and we already knew before the pandemic that this is not what all voters want. COVID-19 urged us to integrate into our courses on civics and other social sciences abundant opportunities to explore virtue and its the role in leadership and democracy. During the crisis, two virtues seemed to take on a special aura of urgency and profundity. These were humility and peace.

Humility

Humility is respect for and deference to things that are greater than ourselves. It is modesty and meekness, and it is liberation from ego. It is found in the gratitude we express for the gifts of effort and talent others bring to collective problem-solving. It is found in the open-mindedness we bring to conversations with adversaries and strangers. It is in the way one cooperates with others regardless of whether those individuals have lots of power or have very little, and whether those individuals share or do not share our partisan views. Humility steers us toward public service for the sake of the public good, and away from self-congratulatory prose and partisan posturing. It nourishes us with knowledge that our benevolence is life-giving.

As COVID spring unfolded, the president frequently presented himself as a man who knew more than pathologists, epidemiologists, and physicians. Early in February, 2020, before scientists knew the true mortality rate of COVID-19, and before scientists fully understood the behavior of the new virus, Trump confidently announced the disease would go away all by itself once the weather warmed up.[7] In May, 2020 when Vice-President Pence's press secretary, Katie Miller tested positive for coronavirus, Trump noted that Miller had previously tested negative, and then "out of the blue" she tested positive. The president then stated, "This is why testing isn't necessary. We have the best testing in the world, but testing is not necessarily the answer because they were testing them" [White House staff members].[8] The remark suggested that Trump did not understand that it is precisely because infections can "come out of the blue," even without symptoms, which makes testing an essential intervention in the containment of a disease. The scientifically astute know that an infected person may have no symptoms, yet transmit the virus to others. To grasp this epidemiological principle, one must respect the communal dimensions of disease and that pathogens are constantly seeking opportunities to invade new hosts. One must also be humbled by the phenomenal scientific expertise that is required to discern complex and often elusive aspects pathogenic behavior.

At times the president's remarks sounded bizarre, as if the morbidity and mortality left in the wake of infections were incidental. He did not appear to be genuinely sorrowful about the loss of tens of thousands of people, and he left the impression that his greatest concern was for the market and his own re-election. When the daily fatalities in Trump's home town, New York City, overwhelmed the capacity of municipal government to bury the dead who had no one to claim their bodies, they were interned in mass graves on Hart Island. It would have been charitable for the president to arrange a special ceremony at the site, and to offer prayers for the least of our brothers and sisters. It would have been inspiring to see him express gratitude for those who tried to save their lives. That priority was so low that Trump did not even send his wife or the Vice-President to offer condolences and support.

The humble take responsibility for mistakes and for conditions they helped to create. The humble recognize the folly of personalizing everything. When confronted with questions about the shortage of testing kits, Trump declared on March 13, 2020 that he did "not take any responsibility at all." He regularly blamed the Obama administration for leaving emergency

---

7. Levin, "Trump Claims," para. 2.

8. Gearan et al., "Trump Says Testing," para. 7.

health protocols in disarray and for leaving his administration with "bad tests." His ally, Senator Mitch McConnell (R-KY), blamed the impeachment hearings for interfering with the president's planning and preparedness for mass infections. Instead of putting his ego aside and focusing on helping as many people as possible, and working with others around the world to contain and treat the illness and develop a vaccine, he twisted the narrative of the crisis into a tale of personal persecution. He portrayed the pandemic at first as a hoax perpetuated by Democrats who wanted to get him out of office, and then later as a legitimate health emergency perpetuated by the Chinese to get him out of office.

In contrast to the president's conduct, many reporters during the crisis exhibited astonishing humility, as they politely endured the president's abuse during press conferences. When journalists asked Trump questions he did not like, he publically excoriated them and ridiculed their credentials. Peter Alexander, Jonathan Karl and others generally bore the president's wrath gracefully and did not launch verbal retaliations. They were able to return to their assignments covering the president without permitting whatever personal injury they felt to interfere with the integrity of their work. Many elected officials wearied of repeatedly explaining themselves and their policies, but Trump's agitation signaled something more. He often gave the impression that every probe into his statements and policies was a personal assault, and that he was above accountability to the people.

Humility requires the courage to let go of total control and to be collaborative. This is because the best course of action to take is sometimes obscured from our view, and only comes into focus when there are many perspectives considered in collective assessments. From the onset of the crisis scientific experts found that their knowledge and professional assessments were subordinated to the president's narrative. Doctors, pathologists, and epidemiologists who contradicted the president did so at the risk of losing their jobs or being publically disparaged.

Dr. Rick Bright's abrupt and involuntary transfer out of the Department of HSS where he led the BARDA program, was precipitated by several conflicts between Bright and Dr. Robert Kadlec, Assistant Secretary of HHS. Bright had angered Kadlec and other members of the Trump administration when he publically discouraged the use of chloroquine and hydroxychloroquine to treat COVID-19, stating that the stock of these drugs that the administration wanted to use came from factories in Pakistan and India, and had not been evaluated against the standards of the U.S. Food and Drug Administration (FDA). When Bright's concerns were snubbed by officials in the HHS, he turned to journalists to ensure that the pubic knew that these drugs had potentially lethal side-effects, and were not known to be effective against COVID-19.[9] What journalists learned did not stop there.

Bright complained to journalists that HHS was wasteful, abusive, and fraudulent. He noted that in 2017 he had been pressured by Kadlec to "ignore expert recommendations and instead to award lucrative contracts based on political connections and cronyism."[10] Kadlec's friend, John Clerici, a consultant to pharmaceutical industries, urged Bright to renew federal funding for Aeolus Pharmaceuticals, which had been denied additional grant money by BARDA's In-Process Review committee. Clerici reminded Bright that Aeolus' CEO was a friend of Jared Kushner, son-in-law and special advisor of the president, and that the CEO did not like to be denied. Bright further angered Kadlec by refusing to transfer $40 million to the Strategic National Stockpile fund so that it could purchase Osilamivir, and anti-viral medication used to treat influenza. Bright did this because he believed the drug was inferior to other FDA-approved medications. In 2019, Bright rejected Kadlec's appeal to invest millions in the development of EIDD-2801, a "miracle drug" invented at Emory University by one of Kadlec's buddies. The drug supposedly cured many infections including all types of influenza and Ebola—a claim that was made without any data from clinical testing to back it up.[11]

We depend on whistleblowers to alert us to government corruption and the waste of taxpayers' money because sometimes the watchdogs are themselves the wolves. Teaching people about how government agencies work to protect public health and safety is important, but the lesson is incomplete without helping people understand why individuals are tempted to be corrupt and wasteful and what is at stake when these things are tolerated.

Peace

The COVID-19 crisis teaches us that peaceful intentions are vital to problem-solving. Trump often said of himself that he was a wartime president because he was combating a pandemic.[12] The label "wartime president" conjures images of honorable men battling fascism and tyranny. It is a title bestowed by biographers and historians to remind readers that the executive bore extraordinary burdens and undertook Herculean tasks at a pivotal point in history. Presidents who took the U.S. to war normally assured

9. Bright, *Complaint of Personal Practice*, 2.

10. Ibid, 6.

11. Ibid, 6–7.

12. Oprysko and Luthi, "Trump Labels Himself," para. 1–3.

citizens that unity was vital to victory, and that tremendous undertakings and sacrifices were essential for the sake of peace. Trump's objectives, however, did not resonate with reverence for unity, peace, nor a peaceful vision for the future.

The president was often combative with his own staff, state executives, journalists, and scientists. Whatever war he was fighting, the central causes always seemed to be himself, his re-election, and reinvigorating Wall Street. His combativeness was a condition that pre-existed the coronavirus outbreak. Between January 2017 and November, 2019, over 65 members of the Trump administration left office, and roughly one third of those individuals had been fired, some after only a few weeks of service.[13] The turnover rate in Trump's "A Team," the president's closest advisors and White House directors, was 35 percent in his first year alone, roughly three times the rate of the previous five presidents.[14] By May, 2020, the A Team's turnover rate was 86 percent. Turnover in lower levels of his administration was also high, with many resigning their positions because they found the work environment was untenable, chaotic, and abusive.[15]

High turnover rates in any executive level of organizations is not good for institutions. It can slow work rates, disrupt the flow of information, cause reorganization of duties, derail momentum to resolve serious problems, and decrease trust between staff members and their executives. Turnover decreases the sense of psychological safety in the work environment. It can also breed sycophants and echo chambers, when people adopt lines of thinking for the purpose of pleasing the boss, and not for the purpose of offering the most intelligent and productive ideas possible.[16] Turnovers knock people "off their game." Some people like to keep others off balance because they think it enhances their power and control of the organization.

Despite the Trump administration's implementation of the *National Biodefense Strategy* in 2018, its response to the pandemic was often slow, vague, and chaotic. The *National Biodefense Strategy* acknowledged the threat of "biological incidents," and articulated the government's commitment to "enhance" defenses against pathogens with the help of international partners and private industries that built "cutting edge medical countermeasures" including "diagnostics and biosurveillance."[17] The document specifically committed our government to ensuring that "decision-making

13. Diehm et al., "Who Has Left," see interactive chart.

14. Tenpas, "Tracking Turnover," see chart.

15. See Woodward, *Fear* and Wolf, *Fire and Fury*.

16. Makunda, "Why Staff Turnover," para. 1–5.

17. United States. *National Biodefense Strategy*, 1.

is informed by intelligence, forecasting, and risk-assessment" and to "prompting measures to reduce or prevent the spread of naturally occurring infectious diseases," and to working with international agencies and governments to "strengthen global health securities capacities."[18] The president created a task force in January to fight the pandemic, and he already had strategies at his fingertips. Federal agencies were staffed by experts who had experience fighting pandemics, monitoring potential threats to the U.S., and working with their international counterparts to manage a crisis. So what went wrong?

Though we may never know the full details about every committee meeting, report, phone call, and e-mail, and every mistake made by those who were supposed to implement the national strategy, it is clear that political ambition and partisanship compromised the efficacy of the U.S. response to the crisis. The minute the president framed the crisis as a political hoax and as a diabolical Democratic plot to destroy his presidency, was the minute the crisis was no longer about containing a pathogen, and treating the sick, it was about destroying barriers to one man's ambitions. It was clear when the president expressed desire to cut funding for WHO, that his commitment to international cooperation to fight the disease was contingent upon the extent to which WHO contradicted his assessments of the situation.

We may never know how many lives were lost because of administrative quibbling. We may never know the extent to which taxpayers were gouged as officials purchased goods through middle-men vendors, rather than purchasing items through factory-direct contracts that could have been made by the federal government. We may never know whether those middle-men vendors were friends of people in high places, or whether elected officials used their knowledge of federal contracts to steer their own stock investments.

We do know that the antagonism between the president and governors was exacerbated by chronic shortages of medical supplies and test kits. When the president told governors that they were responsible for obtaining medical supplies and test kits, it sparked a controversy in part because it meant that states would not only have to compete against each other to secure supplies from global and domestic vendors and to secure contracts with laboratories to process tests, it meant that they would also be competing with the federal government for the same things. We may never know the extent to which the quality of products distributed by multiple vendors was impacted by a rush to supply the demand. We do know that key advisor

18. United States. *National Biodefense Strategy*, 9, 12, 13.

to and son-in-law of the president, Jared Kushner told Trump that media coverage of the novel coronavirus was exaggerated and fake news.[19] We also know that his remark about the federal government's right to conserve its stockpile of supplies, left many governors feeling confused and abandoned.

The tussle over whether states or the federal government were responsible for procuring supplies fueled public relations wars that pitted the reputations of governors against the president at a time when there should have been universal bipartisan cooperation among all government officials who shared the task of securing public safety. During the crisis, the president complained that governors just wanted the federal government to fix their problems. In his March 24, 2020 remarks, he said that governors needed to "treat us well," which sounded like he was holding supplies hostage for homage.

Even as Trump told governors that it was their responsibility to locate supplies, governors were "damned if they did, and damned if they did not." Governors who openly criticized the failure of the federal government to obtain and distribute masks, ventilators, and test kits to the states risked a presidential verbal flogging. When Governor Jay Inslee (D-WA) — whose state was the first to experience the full force of COVID-19— criticized the federal response, Trump called him "a snake" who takes advantage of people when people are nice to him, and directed Vice-President Pence not to be "complimentary of him."[20]

When Governor Larry Hogan (R-MD) took initiative to purchase 500,000 test kits from South Korea, Trump chided him publically and scoffed that Hogan made a bad deal. He said, "The governor could have called Mike Pence, could have saved a lot of money. . .I don't think he needed to go to South Korea. . .I think he needed a little knowledge."[21] Governor Jay Robert Prtizker (D-IL) tried for weeks to get federal assistance with obtaining medical supplies, until he finally gave up in despair and concluded that the president was not doing his job. Trump's response to Pritzker's frustration and accusation that the president did not understand the word "federal" was caustic: "There's a governor, I hear him complaining all the time. Pritzker. He's always complaining. In Illinois, the governor couldn't do his job, so we had to help him." Trump's smear came just weeks after he tweeted to governors, "We are there to back you up should you fail, and always will be."[22]

Critics of Governor Hogan have asserted that the president was correct when he said that Hogan could have gotten test kits from the federal

---

19. Levin, "Of Course Jared Kushner," para. 1–5.

20. O'Sullivan, "President Trump Calls Inslee," para. 7.

21. Vasquez and Homes, "Trump Targets Hogan," para. 1–7.

22. Herscowitz, "Timeline," see chronology, March 22, 2020 and April 5, 2020.

government, and paid 20 to 30 percent less of the cost than the South Korean tests. Fairness and Accuracy in Reporting (FAIR), a national media watchdog organization, suggested that Hogan's purchase of South Korean test kits was a publicity stunt aimed at shaming the president. FAIR also claimed that the South Korea test kits did not include ancillary products, such as reagents, the chemicals used to perform tests on specimens.[23] Without reagents that precisely target the presence of specific nucleic acids and antibodies in specimens, tests cannot be performed. Had the federal government been more aggressive early in the spring of 2020 about getting test kits, stockpiling essential ancillaries, mobilizing as many laboratories as possible to process testing, and acting more swiftly to ensure universal state access to these things, it is possible that at least some of the theatrical contests between governors and the president might have been avoided.

Why did so many Americans approve of a president who had trouble finding his way to peaceful collaboration with others? Could it be that our schools and colleges have not done enough to teach people about the dangers of partisan politics? Could it be that Americans are limited in their capacity to teach and pursue peace because our way of life glorifies competition even to the point of predatory behavior and metaphorical cannibalism? Is peace collateral damage for our standard of living?

The COVID-19 crisis taught us that peace is not just the serenity that comes when we have overcome adversity and resolved conflict. Peace is also a mindset, a belief that tranquility is a necessary condition to cooperation and well-being. Peace is both and objective and the way to that objective. The capacity to be peaceful and to be a peace-maker is relative to the capacity to be liberated from chronic want of wealth, power, and fame. The pandemic hit the U.S. hard in part because our understanding of peace is profoundly limited.

Highly effective responses to pandemics and other calamities require peace, which is a state of security free from civil and institutional turbulence, and the condition of harmony and mutual respect among governments, citizens, business communities, and foreign nations. We Americans often characterize ourselves as peaceful people even as our legal and economic systems provoke civil turbulence, class conflict, and mistrust of our own government. As we characterize ourselves as a "peace-loving" society, we forget that we have waged war for regime change and imperialism, entertain our children with gory and graphically violent video games, sustain economic paradigms that ensure the poverty of certain populations, and sells more weapons to the world's consumers—including foreign governments

---

23. Tucker, "Gov. Hogan's Purchase," para 1–6.

notorious for human rights' violations— than any other nation.[24] So great is the profit from selling arms to the world, that America's elected officials, often bend laws that regulate the arms trade, even knowing that tens of thousands of innocent people will lose their lives because they put weapons in the hands of sadistic madmen and autocrats.[25] Arguably, a nation that takes this approach to peace is susceptible to producing and electing leaders who see fellow citizens and global brothers and sisters as objects in a game of thrones and drones.

MASS MEDIA

One of the most astonishing and disturbing things about high school and college education in the U.S. is that it does not require students to study mass media. Mass communication and digital technology beg us to be wise consumers of media for at least two critical reasons. First, because the speed at which we communicate encourages us to be reactionary, impatient, and less deliberative—arguably not very good dispositions for effective reasoning. Second, we need to be wise consumers of media because we are daily exposed to propaganda that is capable of convincing us that what is harmful to us is actually good for us. We are all influenced by what we hear and see in the media, but many of us are not aware of how we are influenced. Many of us only understand that we are being influenced for commercial reasons, but do not understand that we are also being influenced for the purpose of coaxing our compliance with certain norms and commitment to certain values and world views. In short, we are being conditioned to adopt a particular narrative about the world and our place in it.[26]

The COVID-19 crisis reminded us that we may make communication a sacred space for the pursuit of truth and humanity, or we can make it a carnival of the spectacular and vulgar for profit. In the haze of chaos and crisis, news programs generally did what they were doing before the pandemic. Conservative reporters and talk show hosts presented the conservative point of view and featured conservative guest speakers. Liberal reporters and talk show hosts presented the liberal point of view and featured liberal

24. Hartung, "We're Number One," para. 1–2, 7. About 37 percent of arms sold in global market come from the U.S.

25. Feinstein's *Shadow World* provides a brief history of war profiteering. It offers damning evidence that U.S. foreign policy is corrupted by arms trafficking, that U.S. arms dealing makes the U.S. a gross violator of human rights on a global scale, and that most U.S. arms deals are a blend of legal and illegal elements.

26. Herman and Chomsky, *Manufacturing Consent*, analyzes American propaganda and its threat to democracy.

guest speakers. The crisis ignited public interest in the news, and cable news ratings shot through the roof in the spring of 2020.[27] News commentary programs were platforms for outrage that often did little to deepen the public's understanding of the facts. In the safe isolation of echo chambers, officials and experts could express their thoughts with little time devoted to exploring alternative views or legitimate critiques of one's reasoning. Programs that featured guest officials and experts who represented divergent political perspectives often found themselves refereeing a shouting match that reinforced viewers' conclusion that officials and experts were not leaders, but bullies with six-figure incomes and no answers.

At the local level, the news media did many things to help the public understand and navigate the crisis. They alerted viewers to where they could go to access resources, and announced closures of schools, churches, and public events. They also featured human interest stories that showcased extraordinary acts of charity and constancy in the commitment of local organizations to see that their services continued despite shelter-in-place directives. They aired stories about kids and teenagers who produced face masks and shields in their homes to compensate for the shortages in government supplies, and who delivered groceries to elders sheltering in place. Some news corporations produced documentaries that helped viewers grasp the complexity and implications of the pandemic. *Frontline*, a program of the Public Broadcasting Corporation, aired its documentary *Coronavirus Pandemic* in April, 2020, which traced the introduction of the novel coronavirus to the U.S. and the initial reactions of the federal government.[28] In the same month, Netflix presented *Coronavirus, Explained*, a mini-series that introduced viewers to the coronavirus and explained why viruses of this type are particularly dangerous.[29] The programs were so helpful, yet so few and far between.

The news media is a classroom. It might have been interesting and thought provoking to see a series of "mini-docs" or short documentaries that explained some of the more complex aspects of matters in ways that made sense to the average American. A 10-minute documentary on how specimens are tested for pathogens might have helped people understand why test kits and sampling procedures were such a big deal. A mini-doc on what federal law allows the president and governors to do during a pandemic might have quelled some of the argument over the president's actions. A mini-doc about the differences between testing for the presence of virus

27. Steinberg, "TV Ratings," para. 1–5.

28. Miles O'Brian, dir., *Coronavirus Pandemic* (2020, Boston, MA: Frontline WGBH).

29. Grace Wan, dir., *Coronavirus, Explained* (2020, Scotts Valley, CA: Netflix).

and testing for antibodies might have helped. A mini-doc on how other nations managed the crisis might have opened our eyes to the goodness and industriousness of our neighbors. Mini-docs could have been co-produced by foundations and government agencies and embedded into local and national news, where they might have done more good that the sports report.

The COVID-19 crisis invites us to think about the media's proper role and obligations to society. It magnifies the question of when freedom of speech is being abused. Our legal tradition thus far has been very cautious about restrictions on freedom of expression, and has placed faith in the people's ability to use their freedom of speech responsibly. There are laws prohibiting slander, perjury, and contempt of court, yet U.S. courts are generally cautious about censorship and restrictions of expression. In the liberal philosophical tradition, freedom of speech is not based entirely on the notion that individuals must have far reaching liberties to be fully dignified. Instead, it is partially based on skepticism. The skeptical approach to freedom of speech maintains that the truth is often ambiguous or unknown, and that it is often in the exchange of erroneous ideas and open debate that people inch their way towards the truth.[30] Problems arise when the people society relies upon to given them credible information and fair analysis of the news abandon accuracy and fairness in pursuit of profit.

News media play a special role in democratic societies. Ideally, it provides accurate information about the world and the people running it, so that we can make intelligent decisions about policies, candidates, public health, and consumer products. Ideally, they present editorials that are fair, evidence-based, and insightful. Alas, they are not always held accountable for being thorough, objective, fair, or 100 percent accurate. They have incentives to exaggerate, distort, omit, and sensationalize information. The spectacle attracts attention. High viewership attracts corporate sponsors, and corporate sponsors want more than just 30 seconds of time to sell their wares; they also want programing that is favorable to their interests. For example, they want content that reinforces public confidence in what we call "capitalism." News stories that reveal corporate fraud, bribery, malfeasance, tax evasion, and reckless endangerment of public safety can be bad for business. They also threaten prevailing myths that the economic system is not rigged and capitalism is as pure as the driven snow—even if it does get slushy on occasion.[31]

30. See Legal Information Institute, "Freedom of Expression—Speech and Press" for a substantial yet concise presentation of United States legal traditions and court decisions pertaining to the First Amendment.

31. Robert Reich's *The System* explains how corporate and banking deregulations and lack of accountability have led to a massive gap between the rich and everyone else, and how the myths we believe sustain the gap.

Of course, government plays a role in what the news media present to us. Elected officials are often the source of the news as well as featured commentators. They can spin the stories, and bury troublesome details under the rubble of distractions, vacuous rhetoric, or good old fashioned denial. Elected officials rely on good press because it often translates into votes. This is why politicians are selective about which journalists and which news corporations have access to them. Elected officials and news media have a symbiotic relationship that is often characterized by the pursuit of mutual special interests rather than the pursuit of truth or public well-being. As entrepreneur Peter Vanderwicken notes:

> The news media and the government are entwined in a vicious circle of mutual manipulation, mythmaking, and self-interest. Journalists need crises to dramatize news, and government officials need to appear to be responding to crises. Too often, the crises are not really crises but joint fabrications. The two institutions have become so ensnared in a symbiotic web of lies that the news media are unable to tell the public what is true and the government is unable to govern effectively.[32]

In addition, journalists and government officials do more than add artificial coloring and flavors to the news; they decide what is on the menu. Arguably, we are in a perpetual state of crisis that does not get much press. The poor are in constant crisis, but that does not always place their story in the spotlight. Undocumented and documented emigrants are in constant crisis. Ethnic minorities and people of color are in constant crisis, as are the elderly, and poorly educated. Our environment is in constant crisis as global warming and urban encroachment into isolated ecosystems threaten life on the planet. We live daily with the crises of global armament, threats to clean water supplies, militant religiosity, corporate greed, and—perhaps the greatest of all crises—our own denial that we are in trouble, and yet, these things are far from the headlines.

As the fundamental purpose of education is to overcome ignorance, it is necessarily concerned with the ignorance of our own conditions. Schools and universities have often been so preoccupied with preparing the next generation to take their place in the machinery of capitalism and the material world that they neglect to prepare students for the onslaught of propaganda that is aimed at securing their consent to a way of life that is ultimately killing us. Arguably, the way to overcome ignorance is to expose the mechanisms that perpetuate ignorance. These mechanisms include everything from the local news to social media, to entertainment, to Sunday

32. Vanderwicken, "Why the News," para. 2.

sermons, and school curricula. Additionally, to overcome ignorance we need to know how to identify the purpose, biases, meaning, and implications of communication, and how to assess the credibility, accuracy, and relevance of assertions.

During the COVID-19 crisis, there were many narratives competing for our allegiance. Two leap to mind when considering the general tendencies. The first was the narrative of "America: The Superhero." In that story, the U.S. was cast as a mighty and noble warrior combating an enemy that would swiftly be destroyed, leaving the celebrated nation to resume its place as the world's wealthiest entrepreneur and highest example of greatness. In that narrative, crusading field marshals rejected any culpability for the disaster and lashed out against sinister foes across the Pacific and on the home front. The second narrative, "America: The Humble and Wise," cast the country as a nation equal with all others in the struggle for survival. It acknowledged that the enemy might be our way of life and persistent human activity that gave deadly pathogens access to human populations. The field marshals in this scenario welcomed international collaboration not only for the purpose of overcoming disease, but for the purpose of initiating radical changes in economic and cultural paradigms. They were visionary, and saw the need for a new paradigm of existence that is sustainable and just. Our ability to choose wisely between these two narratives is likely to be a matter of life and death, and so we are challenged see the story tellers and narrators for who they are and what they represent.

Chapter 6

These Things are Fragile

WE GOT WHIZ

I have faith that most instructors, administrators, educational researchers librarians, instructional designers, and educational policy-makers want to create and facilitate instruction that will improve society. I believe that most people believe that everyone should be taught how to be civil and how to be responsible for themselves. I also believe that most people have conflicting thoughts on the matter of how much education should focus on character formation, moral development, and serving causes higher than ourselves. The matter is unresolved. There are many people who oppose the idea that education at all levels should groom character and a civic ethos grounded in humility and empathy. Their skepticism is often aroused by fear that others will impose limits on their behaviors, and dictate to them what they ought to believe. Substantial and meaningful educational reform in the U.S. will inevitably confront resistance because we have made individualism into a religion characterized by the belief that we are entitled to all things on our own terms, and that the individual's obligations to society are and ought to be negotiable.

We are often fearful and anxious about education that targets our values and character in part because we are creatures who seek our own advantage in the world. We also prefer homeostasis in our world, and that means once we establish a norm, we want that norm to be predictable and stable. When new elements are introduced to our environment we are uneasy, in part because we might be asked to sacrifice something we treasure. With change comes a rearrangement of priorities and perhaps demands for behaviors we have not yet learned. Change challenges our sense of entitlement as it sometimes upsets profitable "business as usual." Change hurts because many of us have deep sentimental attachments to our ways of doing things. Sometimes those "old fashioned" ways give us the sense that we are carrying on as did loved ones who have gone before us, and we take succor in the notion that we are safe in the "right order" of things.

Sometimes change provokes anger because we anchor our self-esteem and sense of individuality to certain beliefs and ideologies. We might build fortresses around those ideas and be intensely defensive about them, as if injury to them were fatal to us. Many people believe that their tenacious allegiance to their values and ideologies makes them strong, even when these same values and ideologies make them psychologically and emotionally too rigid to walk in someone else's shoes and empathize with others.

No monster is so terrifying to so many teachers and parents as the dreaded beast of brainwashing, especially brainwashing that smacks of piety and religiosity. The irony is that all education—with or without references to sacred scriptures and God—is indoctrinating, and it must be so. Any society that wants to remain a society—a civilization of peaceful and cooperative people living on the same turf, and not a conglomeration of individuals constantly at war with each other— must universally imprint into the hearts and minds of its people the values that make such a society possible. The issue is not whether indoctrination should take place, the question is: Which doctrines should prevail?

Many of the problems we have with education arise as the academy serves two masters. In the extreme, the academy sings its highest praise for teaching social justice, global awareness, sustainability, and ethical thinking on one hand, while beating the drum for its graduates to compete in the marketplace, for its research to produce lucrative outcomes, and for being what the consumer wants it to be. Many teachers want to integrate more personal reflection on personal values into the curriculum, and to introduce students to what theories of ethical thinking, sacred wisdom traditions, and religions have to say about the human condition and morality. They are held in check by others who are convinced that such instruction would inevitably lead to indoctrination and irreconcilable classroom conflict.

The situation is as mindboggling as it is embarrassing. Educators have invested heavily in instruction aimed to make students "culturally competent," or knowledgeable about diverse cultures, their contribution to society, and their unique needs, yet are afraid of helping students understand the

spiritual dimension of the human experience and the role of religion and sacred teachings in society. The practice conveys the notion that these aspects
of our lives are too dangerous to discuss. The COVID-19 crisis punctuated
the ridiculousness of this notion, as we watched our own loved ones and
neighbors struggle with disease, isolation, job loss, and death. We saw the
pain in their eyes, and heard the agony in their voices. With each story of
individual loss came the common refrain: "This made me think about what
is most important in life, and that's your family and the people you love."
Those statements were visceral reminders that the human connection goes
far beyond material transactions, into deep pockets of our sense of self that
cannot be observed or measured. They were reminders that the flesh is connected to things we cannot see, and that those things concern our concepts
of God, eternity, and faith.

Call it spirituality; call it divine essence; call it the soul; it is the thing
that instinctively "knows" that we are all connected to each other and all
forms of life, and are "wired" to receive the same "frequencies" that tell us
love has a great deal to do with why we are here, and how we may be here in
peace. It is this soul, this transcending essence of humanity that is woefully
neglected in our formal education. Students may pick at the periphery of
these things if they study literature and philosophy, or take a course in medical or business ethics to satisfy program requirements. In such courses they
may ponder the virtues of self-sacrifice and self-discipline, or the restorative
properties of compassion as a side show to "real" learning. These incidental
encounters with the stuff of spirit and moral obligation are not the meat and
potatoes of learning, but often perceived as boxes to be checked enroute to
a degree.

As the COVID-19 crisis unfolded, many became aware of flaws and
corruption that were always in our midst, yet went unacknowledged. Many
perceived that common flaws and corruption exist in all sorts of human
institutions, including the criminal justice system, social work, hospital and
health care services, charity foundations, law enforcement, meat-packing,
banking, and technological industries. Could those flaws and corruption
be mitigated by better education? I think so. Could we improve the quality
of our industries, government, and public institutions by integrating ethical
thinking, epistemological development, and character formation across the
curriculum at every level? Yes, I think so. Could we do that without ram-
ming Jesus, Moses, Mohammed, Buddha, or theological creeds down anyone's throat? Yes, I think so. I think such education would be a monumental
undertaking, but I am not afraid of that; I am afraid of what might happen
if we do not find a way to develop our spiritual and humanitarian potential.
We are capable of creating new educational paradigms. We put men on the

moon, split the atom, communicate with the world with silicon chips, transplant hearts, and invented polyester and Cheez Whiz®; anything is possible.

A new educational paradigm begins where all exemplary education and instruction worthy of society's trust and support begins. It starts with a humble, open-minded inventory of what society needs from education in order to protect the dignity of life. In some respects, this is an inventory of the kinds of ignorance that hurt us the most. The answer to that question leads to a clarification of purpose, and purpose inevitably gets us to the question of why we are here on this planet. If we are here by chance, and there is no sacred or existential purpose, education need only exist for the purpose of expunging ignorance that interferes with our capacity to access and create material necessities for life, and our capacity to see that society maintains order sufficient to its own survival. An alternative is to remain neutral on the issue of cosmic origins and sacred purposes, and to construct an educational system that attempts to serve all interests equally, in the name of a "liberal" and "balanced" approach to socialization, as is pleasing to the majority. Another alternative is to believe that we have a divinely ordained purpose, or a natural, humanitarian instinct, which calls us to love others and all of creation, and to use our faith and philosophical convictions to build a just and humanitarian world, rather than using faith and philosophy as weapons against each other.

COVID-19 teaches us that it is time our classrooms created space for the prophetic voice. Rather than representing doom and judgment, the prophetic voice that is vital to our condition is one of hope and renewal. It is a voice that calls us to step back, away from the precipice of disaster. It is unapologetic in its insistence that our values lie at the source of our troubles. It is instructive inasmuch as it helps people see how blind ambition and entitlement have put our existence at risk. It tears down the myths of national superiority and calls us to international cooperation for the sake of peace, feeding the hungry, teaching the uneducated, and healing the sick. The prophetic voice calls on all of us to look at the gap between our espoused humanitarian and/or spiritual ideals and the way we actually behave. It invites all of us to take honest inventories of values, convictions, assumptions, and conduct for the purpose of learning that, by way of making objects of others and savagely consuming nature, we nullify the dignity of life.

Making space in classrooms for the prophetic voice is not the same as mandating prayer and worship. There are laws that prohibit mandatory religious instruction and prayer in public schools.[1] Making space for the prophetic voice and spiritual wisdom is a way to help students understand

---

1. *Engel v. Vitale*, 370 U.S. 421 (1962) and *Abington V. Schemp*, 374 U.S. 203 (1963).

and appreciate the transcendent aspects of the human experience, and to explore the advantages of serving causes greater than ourselves. It invites personal reflection on the moral moorings of one's conscience, and why some moorings may be better than others. It is possible to do all these things without violating the separation of church and state.

The idea that schools and universities should be more explicit in character formation and more committed to teaching students about moral decision-making and spiritual wisdom makes folks nervous. Keeping morality and spiritual wisdom out of the classroom, however, has not expunged indoctrination from our campuses. Our public schools and universities have been indoctrinating people for generations with highly secularized assertions about the way the world works, the purpose of our lives, and what we ought to value.

By way of omitting or marginalizing studies of moral judgment and spirituality, we indoctrinate students to have faith that human institutions and reasoning alone do the work of humanizing society. The secular doctrine is manifest in curricula that reinforces the proposition that our highest purpose on Earth is material in essence, and that human reason and intellect yield the highest and purest truths that can be known. The secular doctrine presents all manner of human problems as dilemmas that can be resolved and overcome with material solutions alone. At its worst, it is manifest in the way instructors ridicule faith and spirituality in the classroom.

From a pedagogical perspective, the omission and marginalization of studies that explore spiritual wisdom, faith-based ethos, and humanitarian philosophical traditions are not offensive to humanity because it robs people of their faith or the salvation of their souls. It is not offensive because it may offend a majority of faith-filled individuals. It is offensive because it robs people of knowledge about a dimension of humanity that has expressed itself since the dawn of civilization, and that has influenced the conduct and motivations of great humanitarians, scholars, artists, composers, scientists, emperors, congressional leaders, and social activists. When students are excused from studying the religious and spiritual experiences of humanity, they are excused from having to understand why human beings cling to rituals, myths, and prayer, and what that teaches us about being human. They are also excused from achieving a holistic sense of cultural competency.

When schools and universities abandon moral development, the vacuum it creates in the development of one's values and ethical thinking is readily filled by the notion that such things are irrelevant in higher education. Derek Bok saw this and voiced grave concerns about higher education's retreat from moral development. After presiding as Harvard University's president, he openly despaired immorality on college campuses that was flagrant and unapologetic, ranging from cheating to sexual assault, to administrative indifference, to abuse and corruption. He wrote:

> Precisely because its community is so diverse, set in a society so divided and confused over its values, a university that pays little attention to moral development may find that many of its students grow bewildered, convinced that ethical dilemmas are simply matter of opinion beyond external judgment or careful analysis. Nothing could be more unfortunate, or more unnecessary.[2]

Former president of the University of Michigan, Harold Shapiro, chimed in noting that:

> The level of anxiety about the nature and role of moral education in the higher education curriculum has been constant ever since the founding of the American republic. Over time educators have struggled with how to balance the tensions between biblical faith and rationalism, between self and community interest, and between individual liberty and communal values. . .In an era in which market forces seem more dominant than ever, we must remind ourselves that even if private property and market competition are the most efficient ways to provide for our material needs, they may or may not produce morally acceptable results.[3]

As the requirement for studies in things associated with moral development, such as philosophy, epistemology, theology, ethics, and the classics have waned, educational leaders have observed that higher education allows for students to be suspended in adolescence. Harry Lewis, former Dean of Harvard College (1995–2003) put it this way:

> The relationship of the student to the college is increasingly that of a consumer to a vendor of expensive goods and services. . .Yet colleges can and once did have a very different view of their role with students, a role in helping them set standards of personal behavior for themselves, of helping them learn to live up to an honorable idea of personal integrity. That role of moral education has withered, conflicting with the imperative to give students and their families what they want for the money they are paying. Under pressure to make students happy so that the all-important survey ratings will stay high, colleges feed students

---

2. Bok, *Universities and the Future*, 100.

3. Shapiro, *Larger Sense of Purpose*, 102.

candy rather than tougher stuff that will strengthen their ethical bones. As a result, we hold students as fledglings rather than push them out of the nest. Simply put, colleges no longer do a good job of helping students grow up.[4]

Bok, Shapiro, and Lewis aver that material interests have squeezed moral instruction out of curricula. The "balance between the tensions of biblical faith and rationalism" and "community and self-interest" to which Shapiro refers is elusive in part because many Americans believe that "balance" is achieved by having all things in "moderation." We generally bristle at the assertion that somethings ought not to be had even in "moderation."

Perhaps the reason why so many educators in our schools and universities dislike the thought of teaching subjects related to ethics, spiritual wisdom, moral judgement, values, personal virtues, and maturation of reasoning is because they can only see these things as an attempt to control people. Perhaps those who are disinterested in such curricula have lost hope in the proposition that we can decrease malfeasance and curb corruption. Maybe rhetoric about morality and spirituality has been so insincere for so long that mockery and skepticism seem to be the only intelligent responses to proposals to teach them. Perhaps the reluctant resent the ways that clerics and gurus fleeced and abused their flocks. Presidents, senators, and representatives have also fleeced, abused, and exploited those in their care, and perhaps this is why many scoff at the proposition that things will change if people understand the U.S. Constitution.

PEDAGOGY OF THE OBSESSED

Paulo Freire, Brazilian philosopher and educator, held that true education was a process of humanizing. Humanization regards the recognition of self in others, overcoming antagonism, and cultivating empathy and reverence for human dignity. The kind of education people got instead, he argued, was largely about keeping them in their place and perpetuating oppression.

During Freire's lifetime, Brazil had been ruled by dictators under the auspices of being a democracy. While the government, military elite, and landlords lived affluently, the masses endured poverty and repression. When communism gained popularity after World War II, the U.S. helped Brazilian officials orchestrate propaganda campaigns that included censorship of the news, distorted cinematic images of Brazil's progress and public happiness, religious admonitions to obey authority, and indoctrination in

4. Lewis, *Excellence Without a Soul*, 5.

schools.[5] Freire envisioned a pedagogy of the oppressed that awakened people to their condition and the inauthenticity of their lives under the dulling influence of illiteracy and ignorance. He also saw the pedagogy of the oppressed as a process for bringing people into a state of permanent liberation from exploitation and subjugation, into a state of full representation in governance.[6]

Education in the U.S. is in many ways a pedagogy of the *obsessed*. We are preoccupied with global dominance and the accumulation of wealth, and so our education is largely concerned with preparing individuals for the workplace, and for producing the number of engineers, scientists, and other white collar professionals who are essential to the maintenance of the American empire. Our education's highest goal is not necessarily to humanize us. Instead, it prepares us to take our place in the material world where human dignity constantly clashes with commercial interests and the agendas of those who own the nation.

One might argue that upward mobility will humanize us because it will give us financial security and with that, people will become kinder, peaceful, and charitable. Middle class status, however, does not automatically humanize us. If that were true, the bankers and investors who caused the 2008 Recession may have been nominated for sainthood instead of being reviled for wrecking the economy. Upward mobility is morally neutral. It is an economic phenomenon. It does not guarantee that we will help our neighbors in times of trouble, obey the law, dedicate our lives to self-improvement, or work in our communities to assist the poor and vulnerable. It also does not mean that we will be wholly self-sufficient and never rely on public resources for our prosperity. Americans spend over $200 billion a year on subsides for agriculture, oil, gas, and other industries owned by people who millionaires several times over.[7]

We like to think of education as the great equalizer. If we mean to say that education helps individuals get out of poverty, then yes, education can do that. Research tells us that the number of undergraduates from poor families increased from 12 percent in 1996 to 20 percent by 2016.[8] Studies indicate that college graduates earn hundreds of thousands of dollars more over their lifetime than what those with only a high school diploma earn over a lifetime. There is, of course, more to the story.

---

5. See Sarzyncki, *Revolution* and Smith, *Brazil and the U.S.*, 130–162.

6. Freire, *Pedagogy of the Oppressed*, 40.

7. Kostigen's *Big Handout* describes how the gravy train works, its adverse impact on our health, and how it leads to global disparities and terrorism.

8. Smith, "Study Finds More Low Income," para. 3.

Not all college majors are equal. In 2013, the entry level salary for majors in a field of health care (therapists, medical technicians, nurses, etc.), for example, was $12,000 greater than the entry level salary for liberal arts professions (education, history, art, etc.).[9] Starting salaries were greatest for petroleum, chemical, mining, and metallurgical engineers, and pharmaceutical sciences, which averaged between $96,000 and $136,000 in 2013. The lowest paid professionals included consumer sciences, elementary school teachers, social workers, and religious ministers, with incomes between $42,000 and $45,000.[10]

Though college degrees are correlated with higher incomes and upward mobility, they do not fundamentally alter the distribution of wealth in society. In the U.S., the richest one percent of the population owns over 40 percent of the nation's wealth, which is far more than the richest one percent commands in other industrial nations such as Japan (11 percent) and Belgium (12 percent).[11] Despite the increase in college enrollment over the last 30 years, the disparity between the rich and everyone else in the U.S. has widened. In California, which has one of the largest economies in the world, income jumped between 2016 and 2018 by an average of 6.4 percent, but for the top 5 percent of households by income, the increase was 18.6 percent, while the bottom 20 percent of households by incomes *fell* by 5.3 percent.[12] Sometimes, having a college degree means that one can tread economic waters in which they can survive, but never invest.

The distribution of wealth in society is a critical variable in society's well-being. Distribution of wealth is not solely determined by one's job or investments. It is also determined by taxes, which in turn determine funding available to the state for public safety, education, health care, and services to the poor and vulnerable. During the COVID-19 crisis, as governors prepared state employees for furloughs and salary cuts, lot of people wondered why there was no immediate effort to impose a special, emergency tax increase on the 7.2 million households with $1 million or more of investable income.[13] In 2008, California placed state employees on furlough and they lost 10 percent of their salaries as they helped the state overcome a $40 billion dollar deficit created by the Recession of 2008. In May, 2020, California's projected deficit due to the COVID-19 pandemic was about $54

9. Carnevale et al., *Economic Value of College Majors*, 4.

10. Carnevale et al., *Economic Value of College Majors*, 8.

11. Inequality (a project of the Institute for Policy Studies), "Global Inequality," figure 9.

12. Hellerstein, "Income Inequality," para.4.

13. Frank, "States with the Most," para. 2.

billion dollars.[14] Furloughs do more than inflict stress on workers and their families. They reduce state and federal revenue generated by income tax and consumer purchasing, and increase the demand for federal and state assistance.[15]

Since the 1980s, corporations have drifted away from the business model in which executives saw themselves as "corporate statesmen" who took responsibility for the well-being of society by caring for workers, local communities, and consumers in what was known as "stakeholder capitalism." Executives have shifted to "shareholder capitalism," which prioritizes the well-being of stockholders and executives at the expense of the workers, consumers, and local communities.[16] To maximize profits for stockholders, companies led by highly educated people suppressed unions, outsourced production, secured government deregulations and tax breaks, and decreased benefits.

Many college graduates in the U.S. have incomes that place them in the top ten percent of the U.S. population by income, which is income over $152,000.[17] Many more earn less than that. There are also thousands of people in the U.S. who have no college degrees, including professional athletes, celebrities, and entrepreneurs who earn millions of dollars a year.

The sale's pitch for a college education oozes with rhetoric about upward mobility. Americans may be obsessed with upward mobility because so many feel the effects of the widening gap between rich and poor, but wanting to be on the rich side of the gap is not the same as wanting sustainability. One of the greatest challenges of higher education at present is how to help the next generation embrace the need for radical changes in our way of life which could require us to sacrifice our dreams of a middle class life as we have known it since the 1950s. Ironically, ethnic minorities, people of color, first-generation students, and students from poor families who sought higher education to secure an American middle-class lifestyle are now tapped to be the leaders of a new crusade, one that does not rally around upward mobility, but sustainability. Whether students will embrace the new crusade depends in part on their sense of entitlement.

---

14. Koseff, "California Coronavirus Budget," para. 1.

15. Jacobs, "High Cost of Furloughs," 2.

16. In *The System*, Robert Reich traces this phenomenon with examples, and addresses how to change it.

17. Kagan, "How Much Income," figure 3.

RESILIENCE

The lexicon of education is very trendy. Certain words capture the imagination of teachers, administrators, and policy-makers for a time until they are replaced by the next "hot button" or catch phrase. The potency of the lexicon is frequently exhausted in its articulation, as inspiration and hope die enroute to some action plan that is never developed or never executed.

Over the last couple of decades, administrators and policy-makers used catchy phrases that told teachers that we needed to "think outside the box," and to prepare students to "own their own minds." Such rhetoric was not always explicitly associated with the need to turn the world away from economic and political paradigms that lead to destruction. The use of phrases were sometimes like the soliloquies of Willie Loman, the feckless protagonist in Arthur Miller's play, *Death of a Salesman*. They sang with tales of great achievement and dauntless vitality, but they were ultimately the delusions of a man who could not face his own mediocrity.

Delusional thinking is common in higher education. Since it is highly aspirational in its purpose, higher education attracts people who are idealistic about their work. At times, college presidents, professors, and district supervisors are so dazzled by their destinations that they are unable to see the distance they have yet to overcome, or that they are standing in quicksand. Among the more popular delusions is that the expense of education can be justified by the number of people who obtain degrees. The fallacy of that delusion is that a degree automatically makes a person more "valuable" and more intellectually skilled than others with no degree.

Over the last few years, governors, chancellors, and university presidents have campaigned vociferously for improvements in graduation rates and students' persistence to degree. At present, persistence to degree is very nearly the sun around which all things orbit, including spending on student services, course design, course requirements, faculty development, and assessment standards. As pressure to increase the number who persist has intensified, the subjects of student resilience and resistance have gained prominence in institutional discourse. The concern is largely whether students can cope with the demands of undergraduate education, and whether campuses need to adjust their expectations if they cannot.

Students are often psychologically ill-equipped to cope with the stress of college life. Data from 196 campuses indicate that between 2007 and 2017, the demand for counseling and psychological services increased from 18.7 percent of students to 33.8 percent.[18] Depression, stress, trauma, and

---

18. Hibbs and Rostain, "Rising Rates," para. 2.

substance abuse figure prominently in the reasons why students seek mental health care services. Some struggle with schizophrenia or bi-polar disorder, and many do not follow through with treatment.[19]

Some of the psychological distress and anxiety students experience is rooted in ambiguity and frustration over their identity and sense of belonging on campus.[20] Many college students are overwhelmed by pressure to fit in with one's peers, assimilate into a dominant culture, and compete with others. Some are especially troubled by the expectations they feel to accomplish something and by an inability to manage the disparate demands of college life.[21]

Efforts to build student resiliency and resistance have increased on many campuses as scholars believe these traits increase the likelihood of persistence to degree. Whereas resistance pertains to the individual's ability to "recognize and resist negative social influences" and "stand up against those who dare to limit who or what you choose to be," resilience regards "a process in which people dynamically and positively adapt within the context of adversity."[22] Colleges and universities recognize that students sometimes face a variety of prejudices on campus, and have dedicated resources to building students' resilience to adversity, life's challenges, stress, psychological assaults on self-esteem, and lack of confidence. Researchers have discovered variations in resilience that correlate with ethnicity and economic status, and that minority college students are at higher risk than white students for experiencing microaggressions, depression, and adverse health outcomes that interfere with college success.[23]

In addition to adopting new policies related to student safety, instructors, counselors, teachers, and faculty developers have pursued various strategies to improve student's resilience. At their best, these strategies help students complete their work and feel confident about their academic abilities. At their worst, they have lowered standards for learning, and have fostered students' dependency on "the system" rather than their own skills and motivation to get them through the college experience.[24]

Studies of resilience assert that it is strongest in individuals who have high self-esteem, strong attachments to parents, and experience with

---

19. Zivin et al., "Persistence of Mental Health Problems," 184–185.

20. See Strayhorn, *College Students*.

21. See Kadison and DiGeronimo, *College of the Overwhelmed*.

22. Ward, "Lessons in Resistance," para. 8–9.

23. Ingram and Wallace, "It Creates Fear," 86–91.

24. Grey, "Declining Student Resilience," para. 5–6.

stressful events.[25] Colleges and universities do not control how families prepared children to be resilient, but they can help students confront failure and stress in constructive and productive ways. Studies indicate that student resilience is in decline, and that greater numbers of students are seeking counseling and support services to cope with what they believe are serious traumas and overwhelming adversity. Some faculty have expressed concerns that as students are increasingly fragile in their ability to cope with stress and trauma, they feel pressured to lower expectations and create conditions wherein high grades do not require extraordinary achievement or mastery. Psychologist Peter Gray met with faculty to gather notes on their experience and wrote:

> Faculty. . . noted that student's fragility has become a serious problem when it comes to grading. Some say that they have grown afraid to give low grades for poor performance, because of the subsequent emotional crisis they would have to deal with in their offices. Many students, they said, now view a C, or sometimes even a B, as failure, and they interpret such "failure" as the end of the world. Faculty also noted an increased tendency for students to blame them (the faculty) for low grades— they weren't explicit enough in telling students just what the test would cover or just what would distinguish a good paper from a bad one. They described an increased tendency to see a poor grade as a reason to complain rather than as a reason to study more, or more effectively. Much of the discussion had to do with the amount of handholding faculty should do versus the degree to which the response should be something like, "Buck up, this is college." Does the first response simply play into and perpetuate student's neediness and unwillingness to take responsibility? Does the second response create the possibility of serious emotional breakdown, or, who knows, maybe even suicide?[26]

Catastrophes such as pandemics, global warming, poverty, civil unrest, war, and government corruption will not be overcome by the fragile. COIVD-19 teaches us that these things will be tackled by those who have the fortitude, patience, and courage to make mistakes, correct mistakes, investigate, read deeply and widely, make studied observations, revise studied observations when evidence compels it, and welcome the sharpest of criticism from experts who know what catastrophes lie in the wake of having poorly educated individuals manage a crisis. The crises we face require not

25. Robbins et al., "Predictors of Student Resilience," 48.

26. Gray, 9.

only higher level thinking, but epistemological beliefs that help individuals comprehend complexity, relativity, dynamism, and applications of scientific methods in multiple disciplines.[27]

Students are not consistently and explicitly introduced to their own epistemological beliefs. Though they may be nudged toward epistemological development obliquely when instructors challenge their thinking, or ask them "have you considered the alternative argument?" or "how does the evidence contradict itself?" they are often not aware of what it is that they are doing when they think or why they are doing it. It is risky to raise such questions because some students see them as disrespect for their opinions. Students learn "the way of knowing" by paying attention to what is important to teachers. When instructors approach learning as a matter of obtaining and reciting objective facts, students tend not to value thinking at the higher end of epistemological development.[28] Some instructors hold that students' capacity to learn is fixed, some have achieved only low levels of epistemological development, and others have never been trained to target epistemological development in their instruction.[29] All these factors are implicated in the failure of higher education to stimulate students' understanding of the complexity of knowledge.

Epistemological development is facilitated by exercises in critical thinking and helping students grapple with ambiguity, paradox, and their own anger and frustration that the world is so complicated and that truth is hard to find. Like the Socratic Method, it questions students' ways of understanding and representing knowledge, and invites students to respect the reality that problems that seem simple may not be simple.[30] The COVID-19 crisis made very clear that when people did not understand the problem or see its complexity, they were ready to blame innocent people, demand unreasonable actions, and assume facts not in evidence.

Months into the pandemic, scientists still did not have definitive information about why COVID-19 had different effects on different people, whether reinfections were possible and if so under what conditions, what immunity required, and what vaccine could be used to protect the public. However, there were lots of folks who were sure they knew more than the virologists, epidemiologists, doctors, and pathologists working around the clock to understand these things. As people around the country demanded

---

27. Fazey, "Resilience and Higher Order Thinking."

28. Magolda, "Students' Epistemologies," 117–19.

29. See Maggioni and Parkinson, "Role of Teacher Epistemic Cognition."

30 See Hofer, "Personal Epistemology."

that their states re-open, the experts warned the public that, given all the unknowns, reopening was a huge risk.[31]

When the quality of our thinking is not explicitly and consistently groomed, we naturally ease into our "default mode," which largely represents the attitudes and behaviors we assimilated in our homes and communities. The default mode is an intellectual wheel of chance: some people had parents who taught them how to reason, judge fairly, listen carefully, and verify assertions. Others had parents who taught them that the intellectual life was for sissies, or role-modeled bigotry in judgment. Some learned the difference between feelings and conscience, others did not.

One of the greatest gifts teachers can give their students is a skill set and a rationale for metacognitive activity. Metacognition is essentially thinking about our thinking. People who have advanced metacognition are very good at knowing when they do not understand something, and detecting their own biases as they consume information.

People who are adept with metacognitive tasks are less likely to maintain an opinion that has clearly been debunked with sound evidence. A study of adults found that people who held radical beliefs (those who were extremely conservative or extremely liberal) are less likely to change their beliefs about something when confronted with tangible evidence that their thinking is erroneous. The adults were shown a picture and asked to determine the number of dots in the image. Those who held moderate beliefs were significantly more receptive to adjusting their conclusions when presented with the actual number of dots, than those with radical views, who insisted that their numbers were right, and that there was something wrong with the test.[32]

What does this have to do with resistance and resilience? Some people believe that it is noble and evidence of a strong sense of self to hold tightly to one's beliefs even though empirical evidence soundly proves the belief is not justified. For some, this is resistance. For others, there is no nobility in such behavior, because resistance that perpetuates false narratives and irrationality is detrimental to oneself and society's well-being. For some, resilience is the same as resistance, and personified by a refusal to accept ideas, evidence, and narratives that differ from one's own. It is a reflexive belief that alternative perspectives are essentially attempts to diminish one's autonomy and disempower people. For them, making adjustments is often the same as "selling out." For others, resilience is a combination of strength and integrity to pursue truth knowing that one might face external obstacles, and aware

31. Wallace-Wells, "We Still Don't Know," para. 1–2.
32. Rollwage, et al., "Metacognitive Failure," 4014–21.

of the fact that internal obstacles, including one's ego and unwillingness to adjust one's thinking, are equally detrimental to one's success.

It seems logical that a society that wishes to run on full tank of high level thinking would want very much for its schools and universities to explicitly and systematically teach students how to think critically, and to teach them why it is important to move beyond the shallow end of the epistemological pool, where thinking is dualistic and unquestioning.[33] The students who are traumatized by average grades and criticisms of their thought processes may be laboring under the assumption that learning should be easy, and will be easy if instructors "do it right." When instructors lower their standards and expectations, they essentially tell students that these assumptions are correct.

Some believe that resilience is not about adapting, adjusting, and persisting; it is about the extent to which students control what is expected of them. Deep and meaningful learning often requires students to leap into the perplexing world of the unknown, where all previously acquired mechanisms for learning and understanding seem useless. This can be traumatic for students who believe that they must be in control of their environment and feel safe at all times. The need for certainty can be so forceful that it paralyzes the capacity to think creatively and take risks. The desire for control may stem form a compulsive need to always be right. The resilient learner is the one who understands that knowledge does not always come in plainly marked packages, and is often not immediate nor attainable.

SALVAGE

Resilience was important to faculty before the pandemic abruptly closed campuses, but it took on a new luster in the crisis. Prior to the crisis, some professors promised automatic As to students who merely showed up for class, or who submitted work, even if that work was insipid and incoherent. As instructors and students were forced into digital classrooms, some instructors radically reduced reading and writing assignments and permitted students to take all of their exams with an open book as many times as they wanted to take them in order to get a perfect grade. Others used Zoom® sessions to soothe and encourage students by inviting them to share a favorite song or introduce their pets to the class. An exuberant professor of psychological sciences wrote during the pandemic that:

33. See Perry, *Forms of Ethical and Intellectual Development* for an introduction into the seminal theory of epistemological development from a cognitive scientist's perspective.

> Perhaps the most important lesson from academe's rapid shift to remote teaching is that there is no wrong way to salvage your courses during a global emergency.
>
> If this semester you (a) made a good-faith effort to identify what was essential for your students, and (b) set up ways for them to keep moving forward, you did great.[34]

This opinion is widely embraced in the academy, but it is debatable.

It is possible to commit mistakes in the process of salvaging courses. It may not be enough to pat ourselves on the back for "identifying what was essential" if what was essential was whatever remained once robust and substantial inquiries, deep thinking, and specialized knowledge were eviscerated from the course. It may not be enough to have "moved forward" with lessons if moving forward was accomplished by leap-frogging over research assignments and extensive scholarly reading. If students leave the "salvaged" courses short of the knowledge and skills they need for the next level of study, what becomes of the next level of study? What if instructors "salvaged" their courses without any consensus among department members, and thus produced very divergent learning outcomes when there was supposed to be uniformity?

The COVID-19 crisis called on teachers to rally resilience, and it presented a golden "teachable moment" to introduce students to how others have dealt with adversity and danger in the past. Much of the literature on instruction during spring semester, 2020 offered strategies that focused largely on self-care. Students were encouraged to wear their favorite shirt and explain why it was special to classmates, eat their favorite foods, take walks, and avoid watching the news. It almost seemed as if there existed a collective, unspoken consensus among instructors that the pandemic was not the appropriate time to teach students about the meaning of resilience, and how others who survived catastrophes tapped their faith, self-discipline, and courage to persevere with their lives. It seemed at times that by resilience, what many instructors meant was the art of self-soothing, and not building psychological frameworks for persistence with difficult tasks under difficult circumstances.

Students could have been reading the work of Eli Wiesel and Anita Lasker-Wallfisch who survived the Nazi concentration camps in Auschwitz and Buchenwald, and wrote extensively on hope, courage, integrity, faith, and endurance of the human spirit.[35] They could have read passages from

34. Miller, "5 Takeaways," para. 1–2.

35. See Wiesel's *Night* (1960), *Dawn* (1961), Lasker-Wallfisch's *Inherit the Truth* (1996) are powerful nonfictional works.

Alexander Solzhenitsyn's *Gulag Archipelago* (1973) to learn about how prisoners in Soviet prison labor camps endured horrific abuse and state-sponsored denial of human dignity.[36] They could have read from the letters and diaries of Japanese-Americans stripped of their possessions, homes, and businesses, and then imprisoned in concentration camps in the western U.S.[37] They could have read from Joseph M. Marshall III's *The Lakota Way of Strength and Courage: Lessons in Resistance from the Bow and Arrow* (2012), or one of the sixty personal accounts of students and teachers who gained wisdom by confronting their depression, anxiety, and hopelessness in Naing Ye Aung's *The Portrait of Resilience* (2018). They could have read from Esyllt Jones' *Influenza, 1918*, an account of the women who shouldered the burden of caring for the sick and impoverished in Canada during the pandemic of 1918.[38]

Conversations about other people's character, inner strength, faith, self-discipline, courage, and vision might have helped students put their experiences into a new perspective. They might have inspired students to see the possibilities of their own autonomy in new ways. With good intentions, many instructors served their students psychological warm milk and cookies. The practice begs the question: If college is not the time to forge self-discipline and muster the strength to adjust and carry on when circumstances are unpleasant, when is that time?

36. Solzhenitsyn was imprisoned from 1945 to 1953 for criticizing Stalin. His works include *Cancer Ward* (1968), which exposed the brutality of the Soviet system.

37. Yoshiko Uchida's *Desert Exile* (1982) and Jeanne Wakatsuki Houston and James D. Houston's *Farewell to Manzanar* (1973) are eye-witness accounts of Japanese internment and deprivation.

38. Jones wrote of women who built collaboration in a city divided by ethnic and labor conflicts, and how those collaborations transformed society and saved lives.

Chapter 7

Let's Get Real

SILICON SIBERIA

Not long into the pandemic, scholars, corporate executives, elected officials, and managers in a broad swath of industries recognized that the world would not be the same in the aftermath of the COVID-19 crisis. The pandemic had upset the flow of manufacturing, distribution, and investment. It disrupted the manner in which social services were facilitated, including various forms of health care, worship, ministries, criminal incarceration, and education. The pandemic had exposed weaknesses in the ability to track sickness, procure medical supplies, and conduct all manner of business and education remotely. For many people, the way forward was greater reliance on technology that would "connect us," bring surveillance into discrete areas of our lives, and result in greater dependency on technology to meet our daily needs.

At the behest of Governor Andrew Cuomo, former Google Chairman Eric Schmidt led a committee in New York that explored the ways and means of using technology to facilitate remote clinical visits, health monitoring, and distance learning. Cuomo also partnered New York with the Bill and Melinda Gates Foundation for the purpose of developing a "smarter education system," one that did not rely on campuses and classrooms for teaching and learning.[1] The writing is on the wall, so fasten your seat belts.

1. Klein, "Screen New Deal," para. 3–4.

Technology is not only the medium of teaching and learning, it could also become "the message."

Schools and universities have been moving towards remote instruction since the 1990s. Incrementally, teachers and administrators required students and instructors to be proficient with computers, and eased online and hybrid forms of courses into their curricula. Educational websites mushroomed and sold their tutorials and online textbooks. Virtual labs proliferated. At the dawn of the 21st century, many post-secondary institutions offered fully online programs that gave students the opportunity earn a college degree without ever leaving the comfort of home. These programs reduced the cost of commuting and parking, but the cost of tuition and fees for an online degree is similar to that of a state college. Tuition for online programs at public institutions averages between $38,496 and $54,183, while tuition for online programs in private institutions averages around $60,593.[2]

The least selective colleges and universities offer a significantly higher number of online courses than the most highly selective institutions.[3] Online colleges tend to have lower selectivity in their admissions than top tier universities, and selectively has traditionally symbolized institutional rigor of instruction. Despite misgivings about online instruction, it is ubiquitously practiced across all tiers of higher education in public and private institutions alike. While half college and university presidents believe that online courses are equal in value to courses taken in the classroom, only 29 percent of the general public agree with this assertion.[4] Most college and university presidents (89 percent) also believe that computers and the internet play a major role in the increase of cheating and plagiarism.[5] These administrators have faith that by offering online courses and programs, they are remaining competitive in the education market, where students routinely make decisions about their education based on convenience and cost, and not on the rigor and quality of instruction.

When asked about whether remote instruction is "as good" as face-to-face instruction, many instructors hesitate to answer immediately. Most seem to accept the idea that remote instruction is sufficient to meet educational needs, but many struggle to articulate exactly what it is that the face-to-face experience provides that online courses do not. While students like the convenience of online courses, studies tell us that the ones who are most likely to succeed in the digital classroom are those who are highly

2. Kerr, "What You'll Pay," para. 2. Data reflects the academic year 2019–2020.

3. Parker et al., *Digital Revolution and Higher Education*, 6.

4. Ibid, 1.

5. Ibid, 16.

organized, self-disciplined, internally motivated, self-efficacious, and goal-oriented.[6] As we sheltered-in-place, teachers and students found that they yearned for the physical presence of others as if it fueled persistence.

During the crisis, technical and pedagogical support teams offered faculty guidance on how to "humanize" remote instruction. Faculty were directed to consider the tone of recorded lectures and Zoom® meetings, the frequency of virtual office hours and group meetings, the ways various projects would facilitate student interaction, and the use of time to share personal stories. Students crave teacher immediacy, and researchers find that many students perform better when teacher immediacy needs are satisfied.[7] For some students, teacher immediacy provides the psychological comfort of knowing one has an audience for one's thoughts. Immediacy also mitigates anxiety about making mistakes or pursuing the wrong line of thinking. Brains do not learn well when they are anxious or sense that the learning environment is hostile. In threatening circumstances, memories do not form well and analytical thinking is disrupted.[8]

The online learning experience differs from the physical experience inasmuch as it does not engage our human senses and affective responses to the world in the same way. Think of watching a wall-sized screen filled with motion pictures of a train ride along the Trans-Siberian Railroad. The surround-sound speakers fill the room with Russian folk music and the jovial voice of a tour guide who narrates the journey. There is a stop at Khabarovsk where passengers disembark the train to purchase pickles, boiled eggs, bread, and sausage from local vendors. There is a three-day stop at Irkutsk, where hearty travelers take a swim in the vast and deep cold waters of Lake Baikal. In Novosibirsk, the capital of Siberia, the tour guide takes you to cathedrals, some with bulky Romanesque forms, and others with modern glistening onion domes. Viewers can hear Russians talking and going about their routines, but the tourists are provided only translations that explain something about local history or natural resources.

One can certainly say that this virtual tour has taught viewers something about Siberia, but viewers never set foot in Siberia. They did not smell the railyards in the rain or open their eyes under water in Lake Baikal to clearly see the outline and color of rocks fifteen feet below them. They did not experience the spontaneous chat with local residents who offered gifts of fruit, books of poetry and whatever they happened to have in their bags when they met them. They did not fear the presence of pick-pockets and

---

6. See Allan and Seaman, "Changing Course," Hart, "Factors Associated."

7. Jones et al., "Students Perspectives on Humanizing."

8. Jensen, *Brain-Based Learning*, 42–52.

hustlers. They did not hear the urgency of questions asked as strangers quizzed each other about their impressions. They did not have to navigate their way through awkward jokes and unfavorable comparisons between cultures. They did not have the chance to embrace someone who made the alien a member of the family. As we recognize the difference between these two experiences, we may sense that some very intangible and unquantifiable aspect of our humanity is aroused and provoked by the environment and sensory experiences. These experiences are vital to what makes us human.

As we seek answers to the question of whether digital instruction will meet society's need to build the kind of education needed to overhaul our way of life for the sake of sustainability and human dignity, we may be bamboozled and befuddled for the following reasons:

1. Judgements about the quality of teaching and learning are often clouded by and subordinated to political agendas

2. The quality of education is a moving target, because what society wants from its "educated" population changes as do national priorities and "political correctness"

3. The quality of teaching and learning varies from institution to institution, as does each institution's monitoring and measurement of its own strengths and limitations

4. Even institutions that enjoy a credible reputation for quality may falter because of changes in administration or departmental faculty

MINDING THE METRICS

To date, many institutions have been content to measure their worth by the wealth of their endowments, the number of superstar researchers they employ, the number of underrepresented minorities they enroll, and the percentage of students who persist to degree. COVID-19 has cast its eye on those indicators and sneered, "this ain't gonna' work anymore." If the new paradigm for education is characterized only by entrenching universal adoption of distance learning, it is likely to perpetuate the sins of the old status quo. As earlier posited, the status quo excuses students from demonstrating mastery of core knowledge that is essential for problem-solving in the 21st century. COVID-19 and all the other natural and manmade crises we face ask us to decide whether we are using the right metrics to measure the success of our schools and universities. In short: "What does it profit the academy if it gives diplomas to a million people if half of those individuals know little about the world and have very little cognitive capital?" There are at least two ways that higher education can avoid replicating a broken system.

First, institutions could require students to pass exams that test their knowledge of the world, the human condition, and cultural competency and that assess their ability think critically and describe the role of the scientific method in solving contemporary problems. Some might say that students already do this when they enroll in and pass courses that address these topics. In this approach, the professor's grades are assumed to be an accurate representation of student mastery. The assumption stands even if professors who teach the courses are varied in their standards and course content. States have known the limitations of this approach for a long time, and to protect various professions against incompetent practitioners, it has required exams for such things as nursing, accounting, and law.

Admittedly, the idea of having students pass standardized tests in general education courses probably arouses the ire and derision of many, many professors, who might argue that such a thing is a violation of academic freedom. I suggest that no public servant is ever completely free because we are responsible for the well-being of others, and, that if one dismisses the opportunity to do greater good because one dislikes making the requisite personal sacrifice of time, convenience, or preference to do, then one compromises his or her capacity to be a public servant. It is no small irony that many may suffer and perish in the world because the most highly educated people in society prefer to teach what they like to teach, and not what is essential to teach.

Second, the new paradigm should increase requirements for all students to demonstrate proficiency with critical and ethical thinking, and to show evidence of epistemological development. Regardless of the professions they pursue, all students stand to benefit from an academic immersion in critical reading, rhetorical development, ethical reasoning, and refinement of judgement. It is possible to test students in their first and fourth years of college to discover the extent of their development. The tests may be locally developed and used only for the purposes of identifying the strengths and limitations of instruction that might point the way to faculty development or changes in curriculum.

It is not enough for the educated to memorize formulas, explain theories, recite facts and statistics, and perform mind-numbing feats of legal exegesis. Society needs the educated to pair these achievements with humility, empathy, and a solemn commitment to use their knowledge to advance sustainability and to protect human dignity.

Ideally, in K-12 spectrum of education, students will learn more about why public health is a serious matter, and why compliance with directives is important. They will learn about the agencies and organizations that keep people safe by monitoring health conditions, researching disease, and developing therapies and vaccines. Ideally, they will critique the values that determine priorities and agendas, and they will be able to identify special interests that may threaten society's well-being. They will evaluate of our way of life and the assumptions that perpetuate it. Ideally, instructors will develop curricula rich with real-world examples that students can use as platforms for their inquiries and analysis. Such curricula may help students to see the complexity of issues and to see them as do experts in multiple disciplines.

COVID-19 has exposed weaknesses in our current conceptualization of learning in ethics and critical thinking, whereby these matters are merely "overlays" or tangential themes rather than core content integrated across all levels of all programs. The pandemic invites us to flip the curriculum, so that the explicit centerpiece of even the most specialized and advanced academic programs is our individual and collective obligation to respect the dignity of life. Currently, many students regard the study of civility, ethics, and values, as "taxes" that faculty and students must pay in order to proceed with "real" learning. This approach reinforces the notion that sustainability, ethical business models, and social justice are nice options, but not very important values and objectives for our future corporate executives, citizens, and elected officials. Indeed, they are optional. Their importance, however, depends in part on how one reads the odds of surviving the conditions we have created.

CANNED CURRICULUM

Online instruction will no doubt be a central feature in any educational paradigm going forward. One of the critical questions in this scenario is: "Will the medium dictate the message?" Will online courses, for example, become a mandated means of public education, and if so, who will design the courses? Course design is a complex process of judgement. It involves identifying learning outcomes, setting standards for students' proficiency in knowledge and skill, selecting appropriate assessments, determining the pace of the course, selecting and developing appropriate exercises and activities, providing the means for formative feedback, and deciding the extent and direction of developmental learning that should be integrated into the course.

Will schools and universities create a stockpile of "canned courses" that "anyone could teach?" Will state departments of education perform this task? Will schools, universities and states contract with private vendors that produce the canned courses and then lease them to educational institutions? Will canned courses be produced with funding from private sources that have the right to embed commercial promotions in the courses? Will we abandon liberal arts and leave that to specialized academies, so that the business of producing people ready for business is expedited? Will the government create incentives for schools and universities to used canned courses, or punish those that do not used them? Will the state repurpose the physical campus in the wake of universal online education? Anything is possible.

Regardless of whether all education is destined for the digital platform or not, there are several ways to improve the quality of education. The following ten suggestions for changes in curricula and institutional culture will be explored in chapters 8 and 9. Interest in all of these suggestions pre-existed the COVID-19 pandemic. COVID-19 merely intensified their urgency.

1. Mandate media competency

2. Refine diversity studies

3. Increase interdisciplinarity

4. Cultivate spiritual and humanitarian competency

5. Improve reading instruction at all levels

6. Expand the school year

7. Tame tenure

8. Improve self-studies and accountability

9. Reconfigure the campus with brave new collaborations

10. Trim the fat

We have the talent and the resources to make changes. We are aware of the precariousness of human existence in the face of global warming, pandemics, over-population, and tensions between heavily armed nations and the men who rule them. We have incentives for change. What we may lack is the will to challenge every excuse we offer for not making changes.

One the arguments against the radical changes proposed in this discussion is that schools and universities will lose their autonomy as new mandates are adopted. Tyranny is unpleasant, and we reflexively rebel in its presence. Like indoctrination, however, tyranny already exists in our schools, colleges, and universities, but we do not always see it that way because it has been so deeply normed. Pressure from chancellors of state university systems to expedite students and increase persistence to degree is a form of tyranny, because it often limits the autonomy of individual campuses to administer the most exemplary education. The extent to which faculty relax their expectations for students' learning and development because they fear what deans and tenure committees might do to them if they do not, is a form of tyranny. The question therefore, is not necessarily whether radical change in education will decrease instructors' autonomy. The question may be: "What are worthwhile compromises in autonomy?"

To America's credit, its educational institutions enjoy a great deal of autonomy. Even in cases where the federal and state governments have mandated learning standards, individual institutions have had the freedom to implement them as they see fit for their local constituency. Thus far, we have had faith that "all roads lead to Rome," and that the autonomy of schools and universities ultimately get students "where they need to go." On closer inspection however, we find that all roads tend to roam. Some institutions do an excellent job with ensuring that students are proficient in their academic skills and well-prepared for advanced studies, and others not so much. Some institutions are outstanding in nurturing civic competency and ethical thinking, while others are not. Some believe that equity and excellence are the same thing; some do not. Some instructors explicitly teach that we do well to place service to humanity above the pursuit of personal profit, while others are openly cynical about that proposition.

Radical change in education may reduce the autonomy of teachers and professors, but changes need not be severe and capricious. Ideally, the reductions will result in greater consistency in what institutions ask of those who are highly educated. Ideally, local administrations and faculty will design reforms according to local needs and circumstances. Ideally, radical changes will protect the right of professors to dissent and debate curriculum reforms, and find ways for dissenting professors to remain employed while the institution undertakes reforms that may impact their teaching assignments.

COVID-19 invites educators and policy-makers across the spectrum of philosophical perspectives on education to reflect upon the gap between what schools, colleges, and universities are doing, and what the world and humanity need them to be doing. It asks us to silence the distractors and listen to creation itself. If we could still the noise about cost, time to degree, teachers' salaries, unions, endowments, alumni donations, titanic athletics, fraternities, research grants, patents, competitiveness in the market, and branding, perhaps we would hear the call to vanquish ignorance as we have never hear it before.

Chapter 8

COVID-19's Challenge to Course Content

MEDIA COMPETENCY

What we know about the world often comes to us through the filter of corporate media. In 2016, 15 billionaires owned most of America's news companies, and that number could shrink with buy-outs and consolidation.[1] The owners of news media exert considerable control over the editorial slant of their companies. This means that their newspapers, cable programs, radio shows, magazines, movie studios, and websites represent the world in the way they want it represented. The corporate boards of news media companies are frequently interlocked with other industries, such as banks, investment firms, pharmaceutical manufacturers, oil companies, and technology companies, as individuals have over-lapping and multiple board memberships.[2] This ensures that the corporate world view is well represented in news and editorials.

The effect of monopolizing the news media under tight affiliations between the media and other vital industries often compromises the way we understand the world, its people and events. News media moguls determine which stories will be covered, what information will be provided, whose perspectives on events will be featured, and whether stories will get a thorough follow-up. When we consume the news, we are also consuming a

1. Vinton, "These 15 Billionaires," 1–3
2. See FAIR, "Interlocking Directorates."

narrative about the world. Narratives are society's life's blood. In our stories we learn about good guys, bad guys, what is true, what is false, who matters, who does not matter, what we ought to value, how we should behave, and what obligations we have to the state and to our neighbors. Our narratives influence the way we vote and define our sense of what we owe each other.

There are at present no states that require students to study media in high school. At the undergraduate level, media studies may appear in the menu of general education courses required for graduation, but normally, unless students are majoring in some form of media, students are not required to take them. This leaves millions without much media literacy, and without strategies to critique information and to detect the subtle elements of propaganda.

It is possible to introduce media studies in K-12 education. The point of doing this would be to introduce students to responsible consumption of media, and to help students identify and use key criteria to evaluate information. Lessons might begin with defining "the news" and identifying the differences between "hard news," human interest, social media, and editorials, identifying sources of news and editorials, and what news and editorials do for us. They might raise the question of whether it is important to tell the truth in news and why. By the time students reach high school, they are ready to grasp the relationship between media ownership and media content. They are ready for exercises requiring them to compare and contrast how various news outlets depict the same stories and issues. In college, these lessons may continue and be fashioned to improve students' understanding of how news coverage has impacted democracy, public safety, and the way that professionals in their own fields are impacted by what the public knows and does not know.

COVID-19 laid bare the partisanship that interfered with a timely and humane response to the pandemic. It gave us lots of reasons to be concerned about whether education has done enough to mitigate the public gullibility where political rhetoric is concerned. It raised the question of whether formal education has given people the skills need to locate credible, fair, and accurate news sources.

By mandating media studies, we would also be mandating new proficiencies for instructors. They would have to know about media ownership, board memberships, conflicts of interest, editorial slants, public consumption of media, and what studies have said about the impact of media on society. They would have to acknowledge their own biases, how epistemological beliefs impact one's understanding of news and editorials, and how to foster epistemological development. Ideally, their instruction would be objective, and rich with examples of how news reports and commentary shapes democracy and our well-being. To get K-12 teachers and college instructors ready for the task, local universities might offer certificates for such curriculum development and instruction. Anything is possible.

The alternative to mandating media studies is to continue to produce a society that cannot tell the difference between veracity and venom and relevance and rubbish. There are over 3.1 million users of social media who spend an average of about 2.5 hours a day on various apps.[3] The average American spends 4.5 hours a day watching TV.[4] Nearly a third of our lives is spent consuming media that tell us who we are, what we should be, what we should value, and how we should treat others. For generations, social scientists have worked with industries and politicians to exploit public ignorance and increase the lure and appeal of certain messages.[5] For generations schools and universities have neglected to teach people how to live intelligently under these circumstances, as if sewage in the swimming pool was no big deal.

DIVERSITY STUDIES

To the credit of many instructors, school boards, and administrators, students today at all levels are learning more about social justice and diversity than what they learned fifty years ago. Instructors have enriched courses across all disciplines by integrating perspectives of minorities and vulnerable populations and by helping students understand the nature of privilege and power. They have also created stand-alone courses that study gender, sexuality, poverty, ethnic history and literature, and the experiences of vulnerable populations around the globe. Such curriculum aims to foster empathy and provide students with insights about the human condition that are necessary to build trust among diverse communities. It has added an important dimension to critical thinking and cultural competency.

Given the amazing expansion of social justice curricula and studies of diverse populations, what more could we ask? We may improve curricula by ensuring that studies of ethnic populations, people of color, sexual minorities, the poor, the disabled, the elderly, women, and religious groups rise above the temptation to become vehicles of hate and avoid the fallacies that arise in debates over who is the most victimized of all.

3. G. "How Much Time," para. 3–4.

4. Richter, "Generation Gap," chart.

5. See Jowett and O'Donnell, *Propaganda & Persuasion*, a rich and comprehensive study of media manipulation.

Scholars have observed that studies of race, gender and class represent one of the most profound challenges to higher education in the U.S., not only because it introduces students to previously ignored multicultural perspectives, but because these courses are widely *required* in post-secondary education.[6] Research indicates that diversity courses are valuable because they improve students' understanding of race and their ability to get along with others from different backgrounds.[7]

Though the value of diversity courses is generally uncontested, many students, especially heterosexual, white males are particularly critical of them.[8] White male college students typically do not willingly enroll in diversity courses, and frequently resist discussions of diversity and social justice in and outside the classroom.[9] Courses that address diversity and minorities' experiences challenge white male instructors who do not know how to engage these topics, and they are difficult for white male students who often feel that they are routinely bashed in these courses.[10]

It is not easy to remain open-minded and empathetic when classrooms become pillories for one group or the other. The responsible instructor helps students understand that everyone in the present is made to bear the sins of the past. We bear those sins differently, and to understand why this is true gives us important information about how to heal and move forward. The classroom is a crucible for truth, a place to burn the ignorance off of our world view and sense of self, but not a place to burn people at the stake because they are slow to see or even reluctant to see things from new points of view. A classroom that tolerates such metaphoric executions conveys to students the idea that social justice is just a code word for "payback," and role reversals, and that social justice is really not about bringing a new paradigm of human cooperation into reality.

Some complain that diversity courses are leftist initiatives to indoctrinate students to end white privilege and capitalism, and to distract them from essential studies. Some claim that courses on institutionalized discrimination are "specious topics."[11] These complaints raise legitimate questions about biases in the classroom. They also suggest that truly "legitimate" education does not investigate the ways in which prejudice is implicit in

6. Allsup, "What's All This," 79.

7. Lizotte, "Diversity Rationale," 634–36.

8. Vianden, "'In All Honesty,'" 465.

9. See Vaccaro, "What Lies Beneath," and Bondi, "Students and Institutions Protecting whiteness."

10. Allsup, 473.

11. Grabar, "Ugly Truth," para 4.

social institutions, and does not consider Marxist critiques when critiquing anything. Ideally in democratic societies, the college classroom is an arena wherein all ideologies are put to the test of relevance, value, and credibility, and wherein all assertions and assumptions are laid bare and debated.

Odds are that nobody goes into the classroom completely open-minded. Teachers and students all have their own memories, emotional wounds, treasured myths, and sacred cows in tow. Instructors of courses that explore racism, sexism, classism, ageism, and other institutionalized bigotry and abuse are especially challenged to know their own blind spots, prejudices, and emotional hot buttons, so that they can make wise decisions about the scope and substance of the course, and perhaps avoid spontaneous combustion when someone triggers a particularly painful memory, or says something offensive. Teachers cannot map every minute of class, but they can identify a destination and road to get there. Ideally, they are able to anticipate what students might encounter along the journey and to be ready to respond. Indeed, anticipation is a large part of teaching. The more teachers know about their students, their circumstances, and the nuances of the subject, the more teachers may anticipate and be ready to teach when students experience confusion, conflict, resistance, fear, ambivalence, resentment, withdrawal, excitement, and pain.

At the heart of good course design is a purpose that is the anchor of every exercise, discussion, assessment, and choice of teaching materials and strategies. In courses where the topics are controversial and likely to provoke strong emotional reactions, teachers are especially challenged to keep the purpose of the course front and center, and to coral students back to the center when they wander away from the agenda.

The purposes for teaching a diversity course matters. Many syllabi for these classes announce that their purpose is chiefly concerned with helping students gain cultural competence by introducing students to the histories, literature, culture, and perspectives of underrepresented and vulnerable minorities. The syllabi typically state that the course satisfies a multiculturalism requirement. The long-term objective of these courses include social transformation. People hope that as a result of overcoming ignorance about various groups, individuals will work more diligently to ameliorate suffering and promote equity in our institutions. Many syllabi, however, do not explicitly contain lessons that invite students to be introspective about the how and why they have assimilated certain believes, values, and attitudes. The danger in this curricula is that it reinforces the idea that the "enemy" of equity and justice is always external, when in fact it may at times be internal.

Like traditional curricula, diversity courses run the risk of reinforcing politically correct ideologies at the expense of objective critiques of all

ideologies. In addition, the potential for diversity courses to facilitate healing and reconciliation may be sabotaged when courses become arenas for
validating dualistic thinking, such as that the notion that all things about
Western civilization are bad, and all things about non-Western civilizations
are good. Courses in diversity are wonderful venues for fostering epistemological growth, and for immersing students in discussion about entitlement, forgiveness, moral absolutes, the source of the universal human will
to power, and the source of universal human obligations to others. As with
all pedagogy that touches the delicate aspects of our humanity, there is the
possibility that students will undertake their studies with a heightened sense
of defensiveness. It is one thing to present a rationale for overcoming one's
defensiveness, and it is another thing to help students examine what their
defenses reveal about their sense of self and how they perceive their options.

Are we teaching courses in diversity to empower people who want to
replicate oppressive and unsustainable ways of living? Are we teaching these
courses to provide a cathartic experience, or to debate who's who in the an-
nals of victimization? The best answers are the ones derived from studies of
one's own institution. The academy that investigates its own programs and
courses may assess the alignment between what is happening in diversity
courses and what was intended to happen. A key question might be: "Do
we want to teach cultural competency so that everyone agrees to distribute
the pie more equitably, or do we want to teach so that everyone walks away
questioning whether the pie should be replaced by a pineapple?" COV-
ID-19's challenge to educators is to help people understand how identity
politics and separatism have the potential recapitulate injustice and bigotry,
and why that may not be a good idea.

RELIGIOUS AND SPIRITUAL LITERACY

Religion and spirituality do not figure prominently in public education. The
absence of prayers and Bible readings is the result of litigation and community activism that has not always been peaceful. In the 1840s and 50s,
churches burned and people died as a result of clashes between Protestants
and Catholics over which Bible ought to be read in public schools.[12] In the
20th century, scores of court decisions shaped the state's role in regulating
prayer, reading from the Bible, curriculum, textbooks, and public funding for parochial education. In 1948 the Supreme Court ruled that public
schools violated the separation of church and state when they invited outside
instructors to teach religion during school hours, even when participation

12. Fessenden, "Nineteenth Century Bible Wars," 791–96.

in these special sessions were optional.[13] The case was a preview of many to come, as Americans wrestled with religious diversity in the 20th century.

The conservative position on prayer and religious instruction in public schools holds that these practices are appropriate as faith is the bedrock of civic morality. The liberal position holds that prayer and religious instruction in public schools infringes on the individual's liberty to exercise either whatever faith one chooses, or to reject religion and belief in God altogether. In the 1960s, the Supreme Court tilted toward the liberal perspective. In 1962, it ruled that prayer in public schools violated the separation of church and state.[14] In the following year, it prohibited the reading of the Bible, declaring that this also violated the separation of church and state as it smacked of the establishment of a state religion.[15] The matter of prayer in school remained contentious, in part because many Americans believe that prayer in public places affirms social unity and shared values. In 2009, a United States Court of Appeals shared those sentiments when it ruled that mandated moments of silence were permissible because they served a secular, civil purpose.[16]

As schools are regarded as parents by proxy, they naturally became battle grounds during the culture wars of the 1980s and 90s. Cultural rebellion against McCarthyism, racism, and religious orthodoxy produced greater public demand for representation and relevance in education. Americans took sides on matters of textbooks and curriculum, each side claiming that schools were obligated to teach the same values taught in the home. At one extreme, Christian fundamentalists protested books and curriculum that said it was alright for girls to do "boy things," and boys to do "girl things." They objected to studies of evolution, pollution, and science fiction. Such instruction offended their sense of world order and morality. In their view, science fiction represented witchcraft and magic, while studies of how human activity damaged the environment contradicted God's will that man should subdue the Earth.[17] The extinction of species, for example, had nothing to do with human behavior; it was God's will.

In 1987, U.S. District Judge Brevard Hand ordered Alabama public schools to remove 44 textbooks because they promoted the "religion" of "secular humanism." Christian conservatives applauded the decision as

---

13. See *People of the State ex rel. Vashti McCollum v. Board of Education of School District N. 71, Champaign County, Illinois, et al.*, 1948, 333 U.S., 203.

14. See *Engels v. Vitale*, 1962, 370 U.S. 421.

15. See *School District of Abington Township, Pennsylvania v. Schempp*, 1963, 374 U.S., 203.

16. See *Croft v. Perry*, 604 F. Supp. 2nd (N.D. Tex. 2009).

17. Del Faltore, *What Johnny Shouldn't Read*, 6–12.

they believed secular humanism had infected curricula with erroneous "doctrines" that removed God from human history, and elevated reason and science above God as the source of truth.[18] Hand essentially declared that secular humanism was a "religion," but was overturned in appeals.

It is not legal in public schools to teach religion but it is legal to teach *about* religion.[19] Americans, however, do not trust each other enough to teach about religion in public schools. People are fearful that such instruction will inevitably result in indoctrination, or at least the appearance of indoctrination. Arguably, the whole world is paying the price for this lack of trust.

There are at least two compelling reasons why studies of religion and spirituality belong in public schools and post-secondary education. First, without understanding the religious ideas that formed American culture throughout its history, it is difficult to understand the political milieu of the present. Religious literacy is a part of cultural literacy. American ideals, agendas, and values have all been flavored by piety and faith. Second, around the world, religion and spirituality continue to influence people's sense of identity. Civic leaders and clerics alike often reference faith when speaking of social progress and public morality. Some use it to justify terrorism and bigotry. It behooves us to discern when others use religious sentiment only to win votes and advance special interests, and when they are referencing it to heal, grow, and serve justice.

The need to discern these things was made clear when Trump staged a photo shoot at St. John's Episcopal Church, just after delivering a speech on how he was going to restore law and order by force in the wake of riots sparked by the murder of George Floyd in Minneapolis. He stood in front of the church with a Bible in his hand, but he led no prayers, nor delivered any words of condolence, hope, and peace-making. The absence of prayer and condolence made the event seem surreal. He posed for the cameras holding an object that seemed strange to him in an effort to link his message about law and order with the authority of the Bible. Reverend Mariann Budde, Bishop of Washington, D.C.'s Episcopal Church, was appalled by the event, stating that it was an "abuse of sacred symbols."[20] Trump denied that and said, "Most religious leaders loved it."[21]

18. See *Smith v. Board of School Commissioners of Mobile County*, 827, F. 2nd 684, 1987

19. Anti-Defamation League, "Religion in the Curriculum," para. 1.

20. Osnos, "An Abuse," para. 14.

21. Rascoe and Keith, "Trump Defends," para. 10.

Religious literacy enriches our understanding of the world. It has the potential to temper our judgements and deepen our empathy. Like all other subjects in the canon of formal education, the point of learning is not to compile facts, but to achieve greater understanding of others, ourselves, and our world. Facts alone do not vanquish ignorance. Ignorance is confronted on much deeper level when we know what facts mean to others in the context of their use, what facts imply about the human condition, and how to use those facts to improve society. Examples of how religious literacy might have altered the outcome of events are not hard to find.

Professor Stephen Prothero wrote that the tragic confrontation near Waco, Texas in 1993 between David Koresh and the federal government might have been resolved peacefully had federal agents known more about apocalyptic Christianity.[22] Led by David Koresh, the Branch Davidian sect of Seventh-day Adventist church was stockpiling arms in preparation for the apocalypse. Rumors about the weapons and Koresh's sexual abuse of children prompted the Bureau of Alcohol, Tobacco, and Firearms (ATF) to raid of the compound. Koresh was prepared for the raid and his own security team fired on ATF personnel, who then laid siege to the compound. On April 19, with the help of the FBI and local law enforcement, the ATF launched a full assault on the compound and 76 people, including over 20 children, were killed.

Apocalyptic sects are often terroristic and suicidal. Many believe that negotiating with them is not only futile, but dangerous as it encourages them to repeat their actions. Force is frequently the default strategy to "resolve" conflicts with extremists. Experts say that one cannot negotiate terrorists' belief systems or the ends they seek, but that it is possible to negotiate the *means* by which their ends are achieved. They add that, "Respect is the basic condition in any negotiation," and that making terrorists feel that they are "inferior" is unproductive.[23]

Respect is probably the last thing many people think about when they think of a terrorist. For many, respect is conditional. Respect requires not only humility, but the ability to demonstrate that one truly understands and appreciates why some people go to extremes. Respect is sometimes thought to be synonymous with acceptance and approval of whatever people do or think. The word "respect," however, refers to the act of giving something "a second look," as if to review it.[24] The point of respecting, or "reviewing" is to discover possibilities for empathy and grace. Respect confirms that

---

22. Prothero, *Religious Literacy*, 3.

23. International Institute for Applied Systems Analysis, "Negotiating," 3.

24. See Etymology Online Dictionary, "Respect," etymonline.com.

everyone has the right to personal beliefs, and that even if we do not agree them, we acknowledge that the belief is important and meaningful for those who believe it. Respect signals a willingness to see the legitimacy in other's complaints, and to feel the pain that people experience when they have been wronged.

In the case of the Branch Davidians, Professor of Religious History, Catherine Wessinger found that, for weeks prior to the April confrontation, the media aroused public fear of David Koresh, and suggested that his community was a sinister and dangerous cult. In short, people were encouraged to demonize the Davidian's faith.[25] She noted that Koresh had predicted that during Passover week of 1993 (between April 6th and 13th), his community would be attacked and killed, only to be resurrected to create God's Kingdom on Earth. When Passover week ended without the predicted attack, Koresh decided to turn himself into authorities, but not before he finished writing a commentary on the Seven Seals of the book of Revelations. On April 14th, the FBI logged that Koresh had signed a contract to retain an attorney.

On April 16th Koresh requested word processing supplies, which were delivered on April 18th. At that time, he had completed commentary on only one of the Seven Seals. At 6:00 AM the next day, the ATF assault proceeded. Negotiations broke down as the telephone line between the negotiators and Koresh was severed. Branch Davidians tried to get the FBI to restore the line, but that failed and the assault continued. Koresh had previously allowed a few of his followers to leave the compound. This, coupled with his willingness to surrender and retention of an attorney suggest that he did not want his community killed, and that there was an opportunity to save lives through negotiation.

By the time Koresh presented his terms of surrender, however, he and his community were already so stigmatized that law enforcers believed that only force would give ATF officers access of the compound to search for an illegal weapons stockpile. The negotiations might have had different results if the negotiators demonstrated greater religious competency, and found a way to express respect for Koresh's dedication to the Kingdom of God. Perhaps in telling Koresh that they respected his dedication to God, and wanted to make God part of the conversation, the carnage might have been prevented.

Most Americans can identify the sacred books, basic beliefs, key events, and central figures in Christianity, but are very limited in their knowledge

---

25. See Wessinger, "Deaths of 76."

of world religions.[26] Typically, popular knowledge about religion is confined to declarative knowledge, such as the names of holy figures or sacred books. Typically it does not concern knowledge about the role of religion in history, or the purpose of rituals, creeds, and sacraments, or what different religions have in common, or why religion has been a universal element of culture since the dawn of civilization.

With the deeper religious competency, we may have greater potential to recognize why people are attracted to secular and religious ideologies that call for isolation, vengeance, and terror. With such competency, we may be able to eliminate the reasons for joining dangerous and anti-social organizations. It is essential that we understand that membership in radical religious organizations is frequently motivated by social conditions. Reverend Jim Jones, for example, was able to draw thousands of congregants to his People's Temple in part because they were attracted to Jones' distrust—some say contempt and paranoia—of "the status quo," and to his commitment to help the poor and disadvantaged.[27] The willingness of many of his followers to kill themselves was in part due to the belief that there was no other community in the world that would understand them, recognize in them a sacred purpose, or love them as did Jim Jones.[28] In some ways, societies that create and tolerate an underclass of people who lack privilege, are trapped in poverty, and are despised because of their race, ethnicity, gender, age, or faith are are manufacturing interest in radicalism. The despised, after all, are often so desperate for love and affirmation, they turn to any well in a desert.

COVID-19 demonstrated that faith and religion were very much on people's minds during the pandemic. Some religious leaders offered prayers for healing and calls for charitable donations to the poor. Some used it as platform to justify hate. Some used it to call for change, and a renunciation of the materialistic values that lead to suffering and ruin.

Pastor Rick Wiles, an anti-Semitic evangelical Christian, declared that the coronavirus was a plague sent by God to punish those who "oppose his son, Jesus Christ."[29] Reverend Rodney Howard-Brown, Pentecostal pastor from Tampa, Florida declared that COVID-19 was a "phantom plague," and plot devised by WHO and Rockefeller Foundation to commit mass murder by way of forced vaccinations.[30] Pastor Steven Andrew of USA Christian

26. See Pew Research Center, "What Americans Know about Religion."

27. See Levi, *Violence and Religious Commitment* for an in depth analysis of what made Jonestown possible from theological, historical, and psychological perspectives.

28. See Moore, *Understanding Jonestown.* Over 900 Americans perished in the Jonestown tragedy, November 18, 1978.

29. Slisco, "Conservative Pastor Says," para. 1–3.

30. Wilson, "Rightwing Christian Preachers," para. 5–6.

Church in San Jose, California proclaimed that COVID-19 could be cured by a national commitment to obey God's laws and repent for gay rights and abortion.[31] Reverend Ralph Drollinger, of Capitol Ministries and leader of Bible studies attended by government leaders, including Secretary of Education, Betsy Vos, Vice-President, Mike Pence, and Secretary of State, Mike Pompeo, said that gays and environmentalists "are largely responsible for God's consequential wrath on our nation." He also claimed that China is to blame for the pandemic, because they were not immediately and completely transparent about the outbreak of a dangerous new virus.[32]

On the other side of the choir loft, there were Christians with a different perspective. Sixteen days before Catholics and Protestants celebrated Easter, Pope Francis delivered a sermon in which he stated that COVID-19 was not the judgment of God, but God's invitation to humanity to judge our priorities and way of life. He compared the pandemic to the storm which had overtaken the disciples when they were at sea (MK 4: 35–41), and said that everyone was in storm together, all of us afraid and disoriented. Addressing God in prayer, the pontiff called out:

> In this world that you love more than we do, we have gone ahead at breakneck speed, feeling powerful and able to do anything.
>
> Greedy for profit, we let ourselves get caught up in things and be lured away by haste. We did not stop at your reproach to us, we were not shaken awake by wars or injustice across the world, nor did we listen to the cry of the poor or of our ailing planet. . .
>
> We carried on regardless, thinking we would stay healthy in a world that was sick. . .[33]

The pope's prayer resonates with what scientists have been telling us about the role of human activity in causing pandemics. Greed has motivated encroachment into the wilderness and urbanization of previously isolated ecosystems has resulted in the transmission of zoonotic pathogens to humans. Pope Francis acknowledged that society has been sick for some time, and that the illness is not physical in nature, but spiritual. The spiritual illness made us made us believe that we could have everything we wanted on our terms and without negative consequence. Our sins congeal around our failure to be responsible co-creators with God, and our willingness to treat all people made in God's image as objects to be manhandled and exploited on our way to an entitled lifestyle.

---

31. Rosen, "God' Vengeance," para. 1.

32. See Kuruvilla, "Amid COVID-19."

33. Wooden, "COVID-10 is not God's Judgement," para. 24–26.

Society struggles with ignorance about faith for many reasons. Perhaps the worst reason of all is the refusal of academic institutions to help people understand the psychological and secular role of faith and spirituality in the world's well-being. Throughout the pandemic, we heard men and women crying in agony over the loss of loved ones. We heard them pray that the love of God would be upon the departed and those left behind. Germs or no germs, faith and spirituality help us find meaning and solace in a troubled world. Why would academicians not want people to understand that kind of human capital? The academic paralysis around exploring the role of faith, religious traditions, and sacred teachings conjures the image of the professoriate as individuals who are perhaps intimidated by or maybe contemptuous of ideas to which they do not subscribe. COVID-19's appeal to academics is to honor the metaphysical dimensions of our very physical life.

INTERDISCIPLINARITY

The idea of teaching one subject at a time has its place at all levels of education. It is great for cultivating specialized knowledge, and for introducing individuals to unique concepts, knowledge, and skills. There is also a place for interdisciplinarity, whereby instruction draws from more than one discipline and students learn about many subjects simultaneously. My first memory of interdisciplinary learning goes back to eighth grade, when the science and math teachers developed a project in which the entire class participated. We all walked over a mile to the Mississippi River to collect water, plants, rocks, and soil samples, and to "map" the area in which our teams gathered material. We made note of trash and evidence of human activity in our designated fields. We examined our samples under microscopes and described what we saw. We determined the number of plants per square foot, and we filed reports. We thought about how people affected the environment.

In college, I took a medical ethics course that was populated by students majoring in religious studies, nursing, and psychology. The course was taught by two professors, one from the Religion Department, the other from Nursing. The course required students to undertake case studies and debate the pros and cons of ethical perspectives. Students had to apply various ethical principles to situations that involved controversies over the distribution of scarce medical resources, privacy, the beginning and end of human life, the meaning of human dignity, patient consent, and heroic medicine. Lessons were rich. Just when the class thought that it had "the right answer" and buttoned up all the loopholes, one of the professors would zing the class with a detail we neglected. Students were back at square one with new concerns about some legal issue, or some overlooked stakeholder, or some aspect about social justice that escaped our attention. The professors brought their own personal experiences and training to the table, but they were singular in their mission: they wanted students to increase their understanding of how health care was a matter of human dignity, and how to factor the dignity of life into medical decision-making at all levels of decision-making.

Few educational experiences are as powerful as those wherein students behold their own instructors debating each other. In conversing with their peers, instructors immediately clarify the complexity and inter-related nature of knowledge in the disciplines, and illuminate the differences between expert perspectives and those of the student. Having two or more instructors participate in lessons gives students the opportunity to see that knowledge is not always monolithic. It also underscores the reality that expertise is not a matter of memorizing facts and procedures; it is about knowing what one does not know, the ability to use the right criteria to assess the veracity and meaning of assertions, and knowing how knowledge in one discipline relates to knowledge in other disciplines.

Interdisciplinarity is typically undertaken when courses are organized around a specific problem or project. A course might, for example raise the question of how to mitigate pandemics in the 21st century. The course might blend the disciplines of epidemiology, economics, sociology, and political science, so that students could understand the issues and potential solutions to various problems from various perspectives. This combination of disciplines might also aim to improve students' understanding of disease, how economic activity impacts human exposure to and transmission of pathogens, the role of political agendas managing pandemics, and demographic factors that impact infection, containment, and recovery. The course might also integrate a unit on statistical literacy, so that students could understand how to read graphic illustrations of data, and how to spot common errors in the representation of data.

Interdisciplinarity can be achieved in three ways. First a single instructor may facilitate learning in two or more disciplines that are germane to a single project or problem. Second, two or more instructors might co-teach the course simultaneously as a "tag-team." Third, two or more instructors might teach the course in a serial fashion, whereby one professors facilitates lessons for a period of time, then is replaced by a second professor, who takes the next leg of the course, and so on. The glue holding the course together is a strong consensus among the instructors on the matters of key course objectives, essential learning experiences and activities, and the criteria that defines various level of learning and proficiency.

As schools, colleges, and universities move students into the online environment, and as general education in post-secondary education is under scrutiny for its value, interdisciplinarity might be a pathway of sustainability for liberal arts. Institutions might create programs in which faculty contract to teach interdisciplinary courses based on the problems of a local community or the global issue. Instructors may be invited to create learning communities that create and facilitate interdisciplinary courses. The courses could be reviewed by an academic committee to see that they met the institutions requirements for rigor, accessibility, and subject mastery. Some institutions may find that by designing courses around critical issues with academic and civic competencies in mind, they could mandate the general education courses that address non-negotiable areas of knowledge, and still have room for a few electives.

LITERACY AT ALL LEVELS

As noted earlier, reading is a skill that facilitates the development of critical thinking and disciplinary mastery. Reading is developmental, and though we may leave high school with reading skills sufficient for our survival, we may leave college with far a more sophisticated level of reading and literacy. Typically, however, reading is not taught in four-year colleges, and when it is taught, it is largely episodic and aimed at remediation. COVID-19's challenge to college instructors is to be humbled by the reality that all levels of learning are developmental in nature, and that the college professor is but one instructor along the spectrum of development.

The case for integrating reading instruction across the disciplines at every level of study is compelling. In the first place, such instruction may improve the readiness of undergraduates for the workplace and advanced studies. In the second place, such instruction is appropriate as schools and universities shift instruction to online venues that require copious amounts of independent reading. Third, such instruction is probably the most accessible and logical platform for cultivating and refining critical thinking and for facilitating epistemological development. As the COVID-19 crisis reveals, Americans often found themselves wedded to assertions about disease and disease management that had no foundation in truth, and struggling to tell the difference between scientific discourse and political posturing, arguably in part because they lacked rhetorical proficiency.

In addition to reading proficiency, COVID-19 appeals to educators to integrate information literacy across all disciplines and levels of study. It takes more than a couple of lessons here and there to teach students how to locate and use information found on the internet, as the sophistication of information increases as one advances one's level of study, and as new technologies are constantly changing the face of information available.

The Association of College and Research Libraries recognizes six foundational concepts in its framework for information literacy:[34]

- Authority is constructed and contextual
- Information creation has a process
- Information has value
- Research as inquiry
- Scholarship as conversation
- Searching as strategic exploration

The framework underscores the importance of knowing about the source of knowledge, the motivations for inquiries into the subject, the objectives that were foremost in creating knowledge, the steps required to ensure the credibility of assertions, and the variables that impact the value and utility of the knowledge. In their haste to complete an assignment, many college students sprint past these considerations when they seek information required to write a paper.

Research indicates that students at higher levels of epistemological development tend to have more efficient skills when locating information and evaluating the significance of literature than do students at the lower end of the epistemological spectrum. When confronted with literature that was contradictory, students at the higher levels were able to incorporate the contradictions into compositions and speak to their significance, while students at the lower levels selected which literature would be addressed based on how many sources were in agreement with a particular assertion.[35] Studies also reveal that students often structure their research and information seeking activities around prior knowledge, convenience of access, and what they know will be sufficient to the instructor's standards.[36]

Educators should not be surprised to find that many Americans were reactionary and rumor-mongering during the pandemic. What did we

---

34. Association of College and Research Libraries Board, "Framework," 2.

35. Whitmire, "Epistemological Beliefs," 133–40.

36. Warwick et al., "Cognitive Economy and Satisficing," 2406–2011.

expect would happen as a result of mediocre efforts to teach people how to read critically and evaluate popular rhetoric? What may be surprising is our expectation that public health, economic justice, and democracy itself will be in good hands even if education proceeds along its current course. Many educators understand that lots of students find no joy in learning, and that expediency, not a deep love of learning, often drives their completion of academic work. Many educators find that they have no option but to keep courses light, uncomplicated, and user-friendly, because to do otherwise would not only disgruntle students, but might increase the amount of time they may need for lesson-planning and assessing students' work.

The integration of ethics, epistemological development, information literacy, and reading instruction is likely to frustrate faculty because, in general, they have not been trained to deliver such instruction, nor were they psychologically prepared to do work that they associate almost exclusively with K-12 education. Radical changes in curricula and instruction will challenge teachers and professors to re-conceptualize their roles. Though radical changes may require substantial pedagogical training of faculty and adjustments in their assignments, it highly unlikely and arguably undesirable that colleges and universities will purge researchers from their ranks. That said, the pandemic reminds us of the folly of trying to be all things to all people. Going forward, one of the things each college and university is challenged to consider is whether it *needs* to be a research institution in order to be an exemplary facility of teaching and learning. Going forward, institutions are also challenged to examine their own assumptions and policies regarding tenure, teaching assignments, faculty development, and developmental curricula, to determine whether they are well aligned with society's most pressing needs, and whether their assumptions and policies on these matters are actually hurting students and the communities in which they will live and work.

Chapter 9

COVID-19's Challenge to Institutional Culture

YEAR-ROUND LEARNING

Radical changes in curricula and instruction require radical changes in institutional culture. The current paradigms that define the experience of formal education in the U.S. limit our capacity to produce citizens that are well-equipped with the knowledge, skills, and moral perspectives required to radically alter the way we live. To improve the academy's ability to produce individuals ready and willing to lead humanity away from apocalyptic scenarios, schools and universities need every advantage. This means some of the academy's most treasured practices may need to change, especially with regard to: our definition of the school year; tenure; self-studies; the concept of campus; and bloated expenditure.

At present, our schools and universities are organized around an artificial calendar that gives students and teachers several weeks off throughout the year. The numbers of days required by states for the public school year is roughly 180, and colleges typically run about 16 weeks per semester. A century ago, this suited the agrarian needs of American families. Currently, we justify this practice with assertions that instructors and students need a break, because teaching and learning are especially exhausting, and because teachers need time for conferences, research, and course development.

The idea that classes at all levels should be year-round arouses intense controversy. Some parents dislike the idea because it interferes with family vacations and athletic camps that groom kids for college scholarships. Others like the idea because it means they do not have to find day care, and can be assured that their children will receive nutritious meals that they may not get at home.[1] Most instructors with whom I have worked relish the idea of having more time for courses on one hand, because they would like to have more time to "cover the material" and dig deep into content, analysis, problem-solving, and creative work. They do not, however, like the idea of adding more time to courses if they are not relived of other duties, such as student advising, committee work, research, grant-writing, program coordination, and clinical supervisions. In any event, students' demand for summer college courses tend to keep campuses open year-round. Earning credits over the summer is a "fast track" to graduation.

The pedagogical arguments for year round K-12 education include the fact that during vacation, many students forget what they learned the previous spring and thus, significant time in fall classes is spent reviewing and re-teaching. Opponents make the case for family time around the holidays and reasonable breaks for children. Year-round schooling proponents note that there are several ways to structure the school year that would allow for family time. Three of the most common schedules for year round school are: 1) 45–15 calendar calling for nine weeks of instruction followed by three weeks of vacation; 2) 60–12 calendar calling for 12 weeks of instruction followed by four weeks of vacation; and, 3) 45–10 calling for nine weeks of instruction followed by ten says of vacation. Between 2007 and 2014, the number of year-round schools in the U.S. increased by 26 percent.[2] By 2014, roughly 4 percent of K-12 schools were year round, and 57 percent of those schools were elementary.[3]

Arguments against year-round schooling include the reality that it is expensive. Teachers and staff must be paid for the added weeks of service, and businesses that depend on summer family vacations and tourism stand to lose some of their bread and butter. The cost certainly does increase, yet, many communities find the investment in their children yields valuable dividends. Research finds that the year-round school is beneficial as children retain more knowledge, sustain physical fitness, and have a better chance to

1. In 2018, about 20 million children qualified for free meal programs in school, and another 2 million qualified for reduced-price meal plans. See Domina, "Coronavirus School Closings," interactive graph.

2. Towler, "Districts Weigh Pros and Cons," para. 5.

3. Skinner, *Year-Round Schools: In Brief*, 2

overcome achievement gaps.[4] It is also especially helpful to students from disadvantaged families, as it provides structured learning events and resources not always found at home.[5] Even in schools where the achievement gap is very small, students may benefit from year-round learning. Another six or seven weeks in the school year might provide more time for field trips, community service, and refinement of skills. The point of year-round schooling is not to speed up the processes of graduation, but to have more time to explore knowledge, develop problem-solving skills, remediate, critique our values and expectations, and cultivate critical and ethical thinking.

The year-round school presents us with many obstacles, and every obstacle is a manifestation of our values. We sincerely value education in the U.S., but cannot seem to find enough money from private and public sources to pay teachers well—let alone pay for year-round schooling. We sincerely appreciate good teachers, but not enough to stop unions from putting incompetent teachers in charge of classrooms. We put these obstacles in our way. That means we can remove them. So far, we do not seem to value education enough to change things.

Public revenue for teacher salaries at all levels could be generated through imposing taxes on the wealthiest two percent of Americans, and could be found by closing tax loopholes for corporations. Incentives might be created for private businesses to "adopt a school" and commit funding for educational materials and special services. Different institutions may find some strategies for cost-reduction more appropriate than others, but in general these strategies include: reducing the number of administrators, reducing the salaries of administrators, reducing the number of athletic teams, eliminating redundancy in the staff, contracting with vendors that offer discounts to schools, and using energy-efficient heating and lighting systems.

Increases in teachers' salaries would, in theory, draw more individuals who are talented and committed to teaching into the profession. To ensure that increases in teachers' salaries actually pay for excellent instruction, administrators require greater support for dismissing mediocre teachers, and districts my need to set higher bars for pedagogical proficiency. Unions may need to adjust their criteria for protecting jobs. All of the strategies mentioned so far are relatively puny when compared to the one thing that is more potent than a thousand blue-ribbon school boards and teachers, and that is the family.

No variable in education reform at the K-12 level is as profound as that of the parents. The power of parents to teach children how to delay

4. Lynch, "Top 3 Reasons," 3–11.

5. Lynch, "Year-Round Schools," para. 6–7.

gratification, read, and to take pleasure in learning, plays a far more power-ful role in academic achievement than do teachers' salaries, computers, and the numbers of administrators in a school district combined.[6]

In 1966 James Coleman and his colleagues published a ground-breaking report, *Equality of Educational Opportunity*, which contained data from 3,000 schools, nearly 600,000 students, and thousands of teachers. It examined class size, per pupil expenditure, textbooks, teacher credentials, and other institutional variables that might have had an impact on academic achievement, but nothing compared to the impact of the family.[7] Coleman's study was released a year following President Lyndon Johnson's (D-TX) approval of the *Elementary and Secondary Education Act*, that gave K-12 educators $14.4 billion (over $115 billion in 2020 dollars) to improve educa-tion and the academic achievement of minority students.

Coleman's report was released in a political atmosphere ripe with lib-eral convictions that if the government simply pumped enough money into K-12 education, inequality in educational opportunities would disappear, and equality in the academic achievement of Caucasians and people of color would be secured. Many people believed that low academic achievement of African American, Hispanic and other minorities were due only to dilapi-dated schools, lack of educational resources, poor quality of teachers, and lack of special academic support services.

Coleman's report found that schools attended largely by minorities had less science and language labs, poorer libraries, and insufficient numbers of textbooks when compared to schools attended by whites. It also found that the type of school students attend had a greater impact on African Ameri-can academic achievement than it had on Caucasian academic achieve-ment. Why the difference? Coleman contradicted liberal assumptions about the causes of low minority academic achievement with evidence that the type of school students attended and curriculum played a smaller role in students' achievement than did the backgrounds of one's classmates, the family's economic status, parents' interests, parents' education, and parents' reading matter.[8]

Fifty years after Coleman's report, researchers validated his original findings. Most studies confirm that parents' education level is among the top predictors of children's academic success, and that school suspensions

6. Garcia and Weiss, *Reducing and Averting Achievement Gaps*, 5.

7. Coleman et al., *Equality of Educational Opportunity* was the result research com-missioned by President Johnson as part of a request embedded in the Civil rights Act, 1964. Few studies of education are as comprehensive and as far reading in data collec-tion as this seminal work.

8. Coleman, "Nearly 6 in 10," 9–11; 22; 302.

of students and the need to repeat grades for children in single-parent or guardian families are twice that of children in families with two parents.[9] Parents are year-round teachers. *Their* examples, *their* expectations, *their* cultivation of children's interests and skills, and *their* willingness to support high standards of learning and academic discipline—even if they are tough on their own children—are essential to meaningful educational reforms. Decades after Coleman's report, many teachers and educational reformers are afraid to contradict the liberal narrative that families are not to blame for poor student achievement. Many do not want to be accused of being racist, and many struggle to assign at least some measure of responsibility to anybody who is a victim of institutional neglect.

"The apocalypse" will not wait until we figure out who is to blame. Parents, educators, and policy-makers will either reach a consensus on their obligations to educate society, or arguments will continue while exemplary education for all eludes us. The year-round school has the potential to bring parents and schools closer together in an alliance for education that is built on a strong consensus of what should happen in school, what should happen at home, and how teachers and parents may support their mutual goals.

TENURE

Higher Education

As the mantra in higher education goes, "When I get tenured, then I will voice my concerns about broken policies, grade inflation, and bullying in my department." As the reality goes, many who utter those words never articulate their case for institutional reforms once they achieve tenure. The fact that tenure plays a role in whether people feel safe enough to raise concerns is itself an indicator that the system is broken. In an institution, ostensibly populated by some of the brightest people in the community, one would think that people would be enlightened enough to handle conflict, dissent, and complaint in healthy ways that do not threaten people's employment. The unspoken rule against being critical of policies and practices, and the unspoken threat that those who break the rule will compromise their tenure is a form of extortion in the service of institutional stagnation.

Officially, in higher education, tenure is an objective, non-political process, but it is not always that way in practice. Generally, tenure is based on the quality of instruction, research, and community service, but data on those factors are filtered through human beings who often have political

9. Egalite, "How Family Background Influences," 72; 74.

agendas or personal biases. Politics are introduced to the process whenever the people involved have opposing perspectives on policies, or compete for the same pool of scarce resources. Politics are implicit in the process when those involved have different visions for program development, or different beliefs about who should be hired, and who should be assigned which classes. Tenure is more than job security. It is prestige and it is a salary increase.

Student evaluations of teachers (SETs) play a significant role in the tenure process, and they too are sometimes political. They have been a source of controversy for decades, as scholars have contested the value of feedback from students who may not have reasonable expectations for exemplary teaching. Most studies of SETs conclude that SET scores moderately correlate to student achievement and pedagogical practice, and that SETs generate reliable and consistent results.[10] Despite these findings, researchers have also detected gender and race bias in SETs. The literature on the subject goes back more than 100 years, and scores of studies document the existence of student prejudices in SETs.[11] While SETs may provide valuable information about how to improve instruction, their role in the tenure process may be larger than what is prudent.

More than being problematic because of SETs, tenure is problematic for the adverse impact it has had on instruction. Many instructors have confided over the years that they are not interested in pedagogical development and the nuances of course design, epistemological growth, and integrating literacy development into lessons and assessments, because they have no time for such things. They say are overwhelmed with research, publications, grant-writing, student advising, and committee work, because these things matter more to tenure committees than does teaching. Many instructors live in perpetual paradox. On one hand, they are passionate about teaching, and on the other hand, they resent the amount of time it takes to design lessons, grade papers, and help struggling students because these things take time away from other things vital to their tenure and promotion. Many confide that if they did not have to chase tenure, they would be more enthusiastic about pedagogical development and course improvement.

For the sake of improving the quality of curriculum and instruction, colleges and universities are challenged to justify their own tenure protocols and policies, and to determine whether their own approach is helping or hurting the quality of education at their institution. This discernment may

10. Flaherty, "Even 'Valid' Student Evaluations," para. 3.

11. See Holman et al., "Evidence of Bias," a running file of research on SETs and student biases.

be informed by the caliber and relevance of the research its professors produce, and whether its investment in research ought to be refined.

A one-size-fits-all approach to tenure policies and protocols is not
necessarily in the best interest of every institution. Institutions that have
achieved the status of a national leader in research, for example, may find
it prudent to sustain strident research requirements for tenure. Their decisions may be influenced by their selectivity and a relatively low level of demand for pedagogy tailored for under-prepared or under-skilled students.
Institutions that have dedicated themselves to serving under-prepared and
under-skilled students may find that the prudent choice is to eliminate tenure or create alternative ways to assess whether instructors merit contract
renewal or promotion.

K-12

Tenure is also problematic at the K-12 level, and has been so for generations.
In the U.S. it is very difficult to fire bad teachers. The Department of Education estimates that schools districts dismiss an average of about 2 percent
of instructors for bad performance.[12] It, as well as other scholars, estimate
that between 5 and 15 percent of teachers are incompetent, and find that it is
difficult to obtain exact figures on the distribution of incompetence because
administrators do not universally define it in the same way.[13] The federal
government does not have the authority to fire teachers, but it does have the
power to influence dismissals. As he announced funding for "Race to the
Top" in 2010, President Barak Obama encouraged schools to find their own
way to ensure that their teachers were worthy of the jobs and stated:

> If a teacher is given a chance or two chances or three chances
> but still does not improve, there's no excuse for that person to
> continue teaching. I reject a system that rewards and protects
> persons from its consequences. The stakes are too high. We can
> afford nothing but the best for our children's teachers and the
> school where they teach.[14]

Obama's remarks confirm that even when troublesome teachers fail to be
remediated, many manage somehow to keep their jobs. This phenomenon
occurs for at least three reasons: flawed assumptions about teaching; unions'

12. U.S. Department of Education, "Schools and Staffing," Table 8.

13. See U.S. Department of Education, "America's Teachers," and Yariv, "'Challenging' Teachers."

14. Obama, "Remarks to the United States," para. 28.

resolve to protect the job and not the profession; and, lack of district support for school administrators who want to dismiss teachers.

In 2009, The New Teacher Project published a report based on surveys of approximately 15,000 teachers and 1,300 administrators who were asked to describe the problems they faced in hiring good teachers and firing bad teachers. The researchers discovered that education suffers from the "Widget Effect," whereby people assume that teachers are like machine parts that can be interchanged without seriously damaging the quality of "the product."[15] They found that many educators themselves had difficulty defining the difference between excellent and poor teachers, and that teacher performances are not evenly or consistently applied to decisions about teachers and teaching. In particular, they noted that, while teacher performance is universally considered in teacher remediation and dismissal, it is far from universal in decisions regarding hiring, faculty development, layoffs, recruitment, and retention.[16]

Having worked in education for over 35 years as a teacher, administrator, and faculty consultant, I know that decisions about teacher recruitment, hiring, retention, tenure, and dismissal are frequently based on matters other than teacher performance. Other variables may include: the popularity of instructors, the instructor's age, race, or gender, whether the instructor is a winning athletic coach, whether the instructor is likely to file a law suit, and whether administrators are good friends with the instructor or "the folks downtown." Administrators are also sensitive to the impact a dismissal might have on the rest of the faculty. As one teacher opined, terminating a teacher can diminish morale in schools were "staff morale already sucks."[17]

Unions also complicate decisions related to hiring, remediation, tenure, and dismissal, and they often keep the authority of principals and districts supervisors in check. A recent study of teachers across the U.S. found that 62 percent of teachers in unions, and 64 percent of teachers not in unions agree that unions make it difficult for administrators to fire bad teachers.[18]

Some argue that, while unions are warranted in the private sector, they are detrimental in the public sector because they negotiate with public officials that they themselves elect.[19] It is argued that, when unions support candidates for office, they expect those they helped elect to do their bidding.

15. See Weisberg et al., *Widget Effect*, a 48-page report that explores key findings.
16. Weisberg et al., *Widget Effect*, 4.
17. Murphy, "Why Districts are Reluctant," para. 12.
18. Wigfall, "Teachers Agree," para. 5.
19. Ring, "Why Teachers' Unions are the Worst," para. 3.

Some teachers complain that union-supported regulations, such as those concerning required hours of instruction during shelter-in-place, interfere with best pedagogical practice. Others hold that teachers' unions are necessary, because without them, decisions about teaching duties, salaries, and teaching conditions would be made capriciously and without regard for civil rights.[20] Teachers' unions are populated by teachers, and so, whatever obligations the unions have to protect the caliber of instruction by way of dismissing those who are unfit to serve presents a glaring conflict of interest with the union's promise to protect teachers' jobs.

Some principals find it very difficult to fire incompetent teachers because their district supervisors will not support their decisions.[21] Although most schools districts proceed with dismissal in cases of gross violations such as sexual misconduct or assault, they are sometimes forced to pay monetary compensations for violators, and are sometimes not supported by local police or the law itself. Many want to avoid the cost and public scandal that dismissals can bring, and so find alternatives ways to address concerns.[22]

In some instances, the state has interfered with the authority of local administrators to use performance data when determining tenure. Joel Kline, former Chancellor of New York City Department of Education, recalled that when he wanted to use data collected from federally mandated math and English tests of students in third through eighth grade to assess the teachers' performance, and use that data as one of many factors in tenure decisions, the unions objected. Kline proposed that the data should be applied only for the top 20 percent and bottom 20 percent of teachers, as to significantly impact rewards for the best teachers, and to target the worst teachers for remediation or termination. The New York State Assembly rejected Kline's ideas anyway, and banned the use of performance data in tenure decisions. Those in the New York State Assembly who had initially championed Kline, acquiesced to union demands under the threat of retaliation in future elections.[23] The collateral damage of the union's desire to protect jobs, and the Assembly representatives' desire to get re-elected was the quality of instruction. The administration's ability to fire incompetent teachers is a big deal because, next to parental influence, the quality of instruction is one of the most vital factors in student achievement.[24]

20. See Ravitch, "Why Teacher Unions are Good."
21. Range et al., "School Leaders' Perceptions," 315.
22. See Friedersdorf, "Firing Bad Teachers."
23. Kline, "Failure of American Schools," para. 7–8.
24. See Owings et al., "Teacher Quality and Troop Teachers."

Dismissals present problems that go beyond the quality of instruction and student learning, as they are expensive. Each dismissal triggers the need for the district to find and train a replacement, and that translates to an investment of time and money that district supervisors may not want to spend. Litigating a contested termination can cost districts hundreds of thousands of dollars and take months to resolve.[25] There is also an intangible price to pay for appearing to be "quick to dismiss," and that is the trust between teachers and administrators, administrators and district officials, and between the district and the families they serve.

COVID-19's challenge to educational leaders, unions, and public policy-makers is to restore the integrity of the teaching profession by placing learning outcomes and students' academic progress front and center of decisions about hiring, retaining, promoting, developing, and dismissing teachers. The challenge is to confront the overarching malady, which is the subordination of the well-being and improvement of our society as a whole to the personal interests of individuals, whose voices are amplified a thousand times over the voice of the people in political processes wherein educational matters are resolved.

SELF-STUDIES

Self-studies of schools and colleges are widely undertaken for the purpose of accreditation by an external agency. In addition, some schools and departments within universities are required to conduct self-studies in order to sustain accreditation for their programs. Schools of nursing, for example, might be accredited by the American Association of Colleges of Nursing or the Commission on Collegiate Nursing Education. Schools of nursing may also be affiliated with the state's Board of Registered Nurses and the American Nurses Association. They may closely follow recommendations and standards generated by external institutes, such as those issued by the QSEN Institute (Quality and Safety Education for Nurses, Case Western Reserve University), or the Institute of Medicine. The purpose of holding any program up to the scrutiny of professional agencies and state boards is to protect and advance the quality of programs.

The advantage to welcoming external agencies and consultants into the process of institutional evaluation is twofold. First, it relieves the institution of having to re-invent the wheel of self-study instruments and criteria that are vital to the quality of program evaluation. Second, it generates

---

25. Chait, "Removing Chronically Ineffective Teachers," 10.

feedback from individuals who are not associated with the program, who may therefore be more objective than in-house faculty in their observations.

In my experience with institutional self-studies, I have found that there is often some resistance to self-studies, either because faculty and staff do not want to take on additional tasks related to self-studies, or, in rare cases, because people think that their programs are so good that it is pointless to evaluate them. In addition, the quality of self-studies is impacted by what evidence may be used to evaluate programs. Not all programs in the same institution use the same pool of evidence to support their claims. In the case of nursing, for instance, students' scores from the National Council of State Boards of Nursing's NCLEX test (National Council Licensure Exam) represent data that many programs do not generate. With the exception of K-12 teachers, majors in philosophy, art, physics, and other subjects are not generally required to take licensure exams before they may "practice their trade."

Self-studies are only as credible and as valuable as institutions make them. The Western Association of Schools and Colleges (WASC) provides accreditation for public and private schools and colleges in the western region and Pacific territories of the U.S. WASC represents a "peer accreditation" rather than a state accreditation. Its protocols require local schools and colleges to establish committees that will conduct a self-study and present a report to a visiting WASC team that consists of educators from other institutions. The visitors are volunteers who observe operations on campus and meet with various members of the campus community to determine whether the school or college merits accreditation. My service on WASC committees and WASC visiting teams taught me that it is possible for institutions to over-rate certain aspects of their institutions while under-rating or ignoring others.

The keys to meaningful self-studies are humility and courage. All other variables that impact the quality of self-studies will be influenced by these things, including thoroughness, honesty, fairness, and the credibility and quantity of evidence. Humility enables administrators, teachers, staff, students, parents, and board members—all of whom play a role in the WASC process—to keep in mind that they are not participating in the study to prove that they are superior to others, but to determine how well every operation in every domain of the institution is aligned with the values, ideals, and vision that the institution espouses. Courage enables participants to remain open-minded, fair, honest, and persistent, especially when other members of the team exert pressure to ignore and misrepresent matters, or to rush one's judgement.

In theory, the cornerstone of exemplary and useful self-studies is the mission, or what some may call the vision and purpose of the institution.

It is not easy to remain moored to the mission when evaluating operations, policies, and practices, because missions can be slippery and shape shifting. Those who control the dictionary control the narrative, and those who control the narrative have power that others do not have.[26]

I recall a committee meeting in which my colleagues and I were tasked to respond to the question of how the institution articulated its commitment to social justice. A committee member raised the question of how we were to define or conceptualize "social justice." It was a legitimate question. The answer would determine the perimeters of our investigations and what sources of information to tap. The chair of the committee slammed his hand on the table and thundered, "We are not defining social justice! That is the job of the administration! Our job is to look at what they tell us to look at!" The committee could have examined all sorts of things, like hiring practices, distribution of resources, patterns in litigation, salaries, representation in key campus committees, special contractual arrangements, data from our community service programs, and what organizations that partner with the institution had to say about our commitment to social justice. In the end, we were directed to count the number of courses that had the words "social justice" or words connoting social justice either in their titles or course descriptions, and then report our findings.

While sticking to the mission as the touchstone for all domains of operation is vital, it might not get institutions to where they want to be. Mission statements and visions that do not explicitly state the institution's commitment to advance students' literacy in specific ways, and that do not explicitly state that all students will demonstrate proficiency with specific literacies, rhetorical critiques, ethical thinking, and discrete knowledge about the world, may produce blind spots in program evaluation.

The beauty and strength of self-studies is that it allows institutions to create research questions that speak to its most vital concerns. Those that control the questions control the scope and depth of the investigation. It is important, therefore, that those who create the research questions represent the broadest scope of stakeholders not only according to role and status, but according to perspective. "Cheerleaders," bureaucrats, and dissenters all have legitimate concerns.

COVID-19's challenge to administrators is to perennially take an inventory of the institution's integrity. It is to embrace the idea that an authentic study that is highly critical is more valuable than a fake study that is

26. Senator Patrick Moynihan (D-NY) once noted that, "Those who control the dictionary control the debate" (see Daniels, *Keeping the Republic*, 71). Professor of English, Gretchen Busl posits that whoever controls the narrative has the power to control what is real and rational (see Busl, "Narrative Rationality").

self-congratulatory and indifferent to serious problems. The authentic study attends the institution's needs for growth and self-improvement, and gives people a map to the finish line. The fake study attends the psychological need for homeostasis and security, and keeps everyone on the merry-go-round. The pandemic teaches us that sometimes, as we attend to our psychological needs, we miss the big picture, and often miss opportunities to be better than we thought we could be.

REAL ESTATE

No university president announces at the ribbon-cutting ceremony that, thanks to the generosity of its alumni and patrons, it proudly opens a 100 million dollar recreational facility that is "a testimony to its lack of imagination, and enslavement to the corporate paradigm that is raw in its treatment of students as customers." COVID-19 invited us to think about whether these words might be more honest than the one's we hear when capital campaigns come to fruition.

Not all capital campaigns and institutional initiatives are equal. Capital campaigns exist to raise money for a special projects, such as building new facilities, refurbishing libraries and labs, and even general operations. Some campaigns are very narrow in their vision, and are essentially investments in marketing and sustaining high enrollment by way of building things that attract young adults, such as luxury housing, fitness centers, and game rooms. A broader vision of higher education might look beyond students' preferences, or at least challenge the necessity of the institution to cater to every preference. It might look toward community needs, and the ways that the institution might partner with external organizations and government agencies to create something that serves the interests of students, the community, and the institution in new and meaningful ways. A broader vision might repurpose campus real estate.

Many colleges and universities have institutes or offices for civic engagement or community service. Community service requirements are nearly universal fixtures in secondary and higher education. Students earn academic credit for volunteering to serve meals to the poor, clean up local parks, and provide other services. What if the paradigm were flipped?

What if, instead of designing campuses to be centers of student life, learning, and research that sent its students out into the world to provide community service, the campus brought the world's needs to itself. Instead of cutting a ribbon for a recreation center, the president might cut a ribbon for an assisted living home for the elderly, a hospice for the dying, or a bakery that distributes food to homeless shelters. These facilities might be run with funding from a variety of sources and operated in concert with local public agencies. These capital campaigns might attract financial support that the institution previously did not attract. The facility itself might be funded and staffed in a way that sharply reduces the cost of using the services. In the case of an assisted living center for poor elders, students majoring in nursing, physical therapy, dietetics, social work, accounting, management, and counseling might complete internships in the facility. Engineering and public policy majors might participate in the project's planning. Low-income elders might have access to outstanding care. The university might become a national role model for 21st century professional formation in health care. These things are possible.

COVID-19 challenges colleges and universities to examine their priorities and whether they are aligned with the pressing needs to heal the planet and care for those who are in desperate need of human services. Some institutions might find that after studying land use on campus that far too many acres are devoted to sports and recreation. They might decide that it is better for them to open a construction shop that builds pre-fabricated walls for public housing or a day care center for low-income parents, than it is to have a competitive sports program.

The current paradigm for higher education does not always thrust students into adulthood, and in some cases it allows them to wallow in adolescence. A 2014 study revealed that nearly 43 percent of students believe that the college's reputation for social activities was more important its graduation rate.[27] Students often expect colleges to pamper them, make learning easy, and entertain them. For many students, the college experience is a "rite of passage" from adolescence to adulthood that is frequently characterized by excessive drinking, sexual experimentation, parties, and bragging about writing term papers five hours before they were due. What if the "rite of passage" were something else—something less self-indulgent?

With greater numbers of courses going online, the demand for classroom space might decline significantly, and buildings may be repurposed. Buildings that once housed offices and classrooms might be converted into clinics, bakeries, or shops. They could become inexpensive housing units for students and faculty that have meeting spaces for tutoring, book clubs, guest speakers, and free courses for high school students thinking about being parents. Anything is possible. The ultimate goal of flipping the campus and bringing the community to the campus is to increase students contact with communities. It is to reinforce the notion that college life need not orbit

27. Struamsheim, "Connected," para. 8.

around stereotypical rituals. It is to widen possibilities for service learning, and multiply the connections between the university, vulnerable populations, and others in the community who serve and care for them.

TRIM THE FAT

Since the 1980s, the number of administrators in higher education has swollen for a variety of reasons. When student course evaluations began to play a major role in tenure and promotion processes, somebody had to oversee data collection and analysis. When institutions wanted to create a curricula for social justice and equity and services for under-represented minorities and students at risk, somebody had to oversee their development and progress. When colleges and universities wanted to enroll students with marginal reading and writing proficiency, somebody had develop and supervise bridge programs and remediation. When federal laws regarding accessibility and protection against harassment and discrimination went into place, somebody had to ensure that campuses were compliant. When federal and state funding went into decline, somebody had to coordinate greater outreach to donors, alumni, and foundations.[28] Despite the legitimacy of these demands, the way colleges and universities have responded to them leaves room to question the prudence of their spending.

The cost of adding scores of administrators to the institution's payroll includes not only salaries and benefits for directors, vice-presidents, deans, and their support staff, but in many instances, it means creating and furnishing offices, purchasing computers and supplies, and the cost of recruiting new personnel. These costs often lead to tuition hikes, and administrative costs will naturally compete with instructional costs.

Administrations have grown all over the country in both private and public institutions. One study found that between 1993 and 2007, the number of full-time administrators grew overall by 39 percent.[29] Another found that during the 1980–81 academic year, public and private colleges and universities spent $20.7 billion on instruction and $13 billion on administration, and by 2014–15, they spent $148 billion on instruction and $122.3 billion on administration. Over these 35 years, the cost of instruction increased by about 7 percent while the cost of administration and student support increased by about 9 percent.[30] In some cases, administrative posi-

28. See Staddon, "Administrative Bloat;" Ginsberg, *Fall of the Faculty*; and Simon, "Bureaucrats and Buildings."

29. Throne, "5 Consequences," para. 2.

30. Simon, "Bureaucrats and Buildings," para. 5.

tions grew while faculty positions decreased. Between 2014 and 2017, in the University of Wisconsin System, for example, administrative positions grew by 3.5 percent while the positions for faculty *declined* by 7.7 percent.[31]

In the California State University (CSU), administrative bloat has been tracked by audits, but they do not always capture the puffy proclivities of the institution. In 2017, an audit acknowledged that, from 2007 to 2014, the CSU added administrators at twice the rate of faculty, and that compensation for administration increased by 24 percent while faculty compensation rose by 10 percent.[32] Peter Herman, Professor of English Literature at San Diego State University, provided insight to what was missing in the audit:

> According the Sacramento Bee State Worker Salary Database, in 2011, the total compensation cost for the Chancellor's Office... was $49.9 million for 634 employees; by 2016, that number rose to $59.7 million for 732 employees. That's *ten million dollars more* for about one hundred more administrators...
>
> The CSU responds that it needs more administrators because of increased demands and obligations. No doubt some of that it true. But the report also reveals that when the auditors asked individual campuses to justify the numbers of administrators hired, they couldn't do it. Cal State Los Angeles increased its student services administrators by 10 (a "55 percent" increase), but when asked for some concrete evidence for why they need 10, as opposed to, say five more people, the auditors discovered that CSULA, and other campuses, do not require "a documented staffing analysis to support the hiring of new management personnel." Consequently, the report continues, "CSU cannot adequately justify the significant increase in management personnel it has hired in the last nine years."
>
> But it gets even worse, and of course, it has to do with athletics. The collective bargaining agreement classifies all coaches as faculty unless they supervise two or more full-time employees. This means that football coaches cannot command stratospheric salaries. So, Chuck Lang, the "associate director of business administration" at San Diego State University, decided on a simple, easy solution: in order for these coaches to "receive starting annual salaries of $150,000 each," all the assistant football coaches would "be reclassified as management personnel and receive the same higher salary." . . .When the auditor asked the "assistant director of employment services" for further explanation," she claimed that the assistant coaches are "program

31. Kremer, "Administration Within," para. 2.

32. Herman, "Opinion: There's No End," para. 2.

managers." After examining the position descriptions, the au-
ditors "did not find adequate support" for this claim. A fairy
tale. . . to justify "inappropriately [granting] the three existing
assistant coaches raises averaging 33 percent at a total annual
cost of more than $111,000. . ."

However, the most disturbing part of this report is the
CSU's evident refusal to accept any responsibility, or accountability, for administrative bloat.[33]

Bloated budgets are also the result of what the American Council
of Trustees and Alumni calls "chaos in the curriculum," which is general
education characterized by elective course options that fail to target core
competencies. It suggests that the chaos and budgetary nightmares general
education create can be overcome by eliminating narrow niche courses, requiring minors, prescribing courses, and consolidating departments.[34]

In public K-12 schools, revenues are not impacted by tuition, and so
every school receives whatever funding the local district and state can bear.
The wealthiest districts in the U.S. regularly spend ten times the amount
on their public schools as do the poorest districts.[35] Rich districts support schools that have modern libraries, laboratories, textbooks current in
their discipline with enough for each student, buildings in good repair, and
handsomely paid teachers, counselors, and support staff; poor schools do
not. To complicate matters, when schools abolished tracking and honors
or advanced courses, (largely to remove the stigma being tracked), they
increased the demand for teacher's assistants who could work with special
needs students where students of all levels in their grades were blended in
a single class.[36]

Administrative and instructional costs in K-12 are driven by some
of the same variables that drive administrative costs in higher education,
and vary from state to state and district to district. The federal budget for
K-12 education for the 2017–2018 academic year was $705.6 billion, an
increase of $123.4 billion since 2000.[37] The federal government has covered
the cost of public K-12 education at a relatively consistent rate from 1965
to 2015, ranging from 6.7 to 9.1 percent. Fluctuations in local support for
K-12 schools from 1965 to 2015 were greater, as they ranged from 53 to 43.9

33. Herman, "Opinion: There's No End," para. 3–7.

34. Phillips and Poliakoff, "Cost of Chaos," 1–2.

35. Raikes and Darling-Hammond, "Why Our Education Funding," para. 3. Also
see Semuels, "Good School, Rich School."

36. See Buck, "I'm a Teacher and a Waste of Money."

37. *Education Week*, "Data: Breaking Down the Where and Why of K-12 Spending,"
first graph.

percent. This was largely due to popular tax revolts that led to decreases in local property taxes that were used to fund public schools.

Enrollment plays a role in the size of administration, though reductions in administrative cost do not necessarily follow decreases in enrollment. Despite decreases in student enrollment between 2007 and 2017, administrative costs in the state of Mississippi increased by nearly 18 percent, while the cost of instruction increased by about 11 percent.[38] A similar pattern emerged in Illinois, where between 2014 and 2018, student enrollment dipped by 2 percent, while administration grew by 1.5 percent.[39] Demographic changes over the last 50 years have perhaps impacted spending more than enrollment itself. As the government increased its commitment to see that minorities and students with special needs were successful in schools, the cost of providing for special needs and equity initiatives has increased. Between 1975 and 2015, there was an 83 percent increase in the number of students with disabilities and special learning needs in K-12, and from 2000 to 2015, there was a 29 percent increase in the number of students who were English language learners. In addition, between 2000 and 2015, the number of students who qualified for free and reduced-price meals spiked by 45 percent.[40]

A significant portion of all administrative costs are related to diversity programs. Schools and universities have responded to the need for equitable education and social respect for diversity by creating task forces, hiring directors to develop and oversee a new programs, and mandating employee training that addressed cultural competency and the legal ramifications of discrimination. Research suggests that diversity in the student population helps to improve students' empathy, understanding of diverse cultures, and how to work with diversity in the democratic process.[41] Diversity programs, however, have not always closed achievement gaps between Caucasians and non-Caucasian minorities, so they deserve a second look.

Diversity

Roughly two thirds of colleges and universities employ diversity officers, who are typically low-level administrators.[42] These officers oversee the

---

38. Wilson, "School Administrative costs," para. 1–3.

39. Schuster, "Illinois K-12," para. 2–3.

40. Schuster, "Illinois K-12," para. 2–3, "Demographics." Improvements in diagnostics accounts for some of the increases in the number of students with special needs.

41. Shaw, "Researching the Educational Benefits," 6.

42. Leef, "What Do College Chief Diversity Officers Accomplish," para. 12.

institution's initiatives and programs to promote and support equity and diversity on campus. Diversity officers are expensive. In 2017, the average salary for a diversity officer at top universities was $175,088, while the average professor made $79,424, and the American worker earned $44,980.[43] A study at the University of Michigan revealed that it employed 25 such administrators who earned over $100,000 annually plus benefits, a cost of roughly $14 million a year.[44]

Many believe that diversity-related expenses are justified as long as they lead to academic success for under-represented minorities.[45] A study by the National Bureau of Economic Research found that diversity programs are a way of articulating compliance with federal equal employment laws and other government initiatives aimed at achieving equity in education. The study asserts that the logic of hiring ethnic minorities and people who represent cultural diversity is grounded in the assumption that, "positive educational outcomes will result from congruency of student and professor race/ethnicity, thereby reducing achievement gaps for minority students."[46] Studies suggest that the integration of multiculturalism and diversity into college curriculum is linked to increases in student retention and high grades.[47] Research also asserts that graduation rates for underrepresented minorities are positively impacted by faculty diversity.[48] However, these findings are contradicted by persistent achievement gaps in higher education, as evidenced by gaps between the graduation rates of Caucasians and African Americans and Hispanics.[49] In 2017, for example, 58.8 percent of college students obtained a degree in six years, while graduation rates fluctuated by race. The Asian rate was 63.2 percent, the Caucasian rate was 62 percent, the Hispanic rate was 45.8 percent, and the African American rate was 38 percent.[50]

At the K-12 level, the achievement gap between Caucasians and non-Caucasians has persisted since the 1950s.[51] Between 1992 and 2011, reading tests' scores for 4th grade students reveal an average gap between Caucasians students and African American students of about 30 points, and

43. Vacchiano, "College Pay Diversity," para. 1–3.

44. Vedder, "Diversities and Other Monstrosities," para. 1.

45. Kaplan, "Breaking Down," para. 7–24.

46. Bradley et al., "Impact of Hiring Chief Diversity," 4.

47. See Association of American Colleges and Universities, *Diversity Blueprint*.

48. See Stout et al., "Relationship between Faculty Diversity."

49. Ross et al., *Higher Education*, xi–xii.

50. Tate, "Graduation Rates," para. 3–4.

51. Hanushek et al., "Achievement Gap," para. 5.

an average gap between Caucasian and Hispanic students was roughly 29 points. Scores for 10th grade reading scores showed the gap had narrowed between Caucasian and African American scores to an average of about 25, and between Caucasian and Hispanic scores to an average of about 23.[52]

The gap takes form long before children enter kindergarten, as family poverty, lack of neighborhood resources, and parental educational levels lay foundations for how children approach learning, and determine the knowledge and skills that they bring to their first formal educational experiences. In the U.S., poverty, lack of neighborhood resources, and low levels of education are correlated with race. Scholars recognize that race and ethnicity do not determine academic success, but the environmental conditions in which many minorities raise their children have a profound impact on academic success.[53] Diversity programs aim to close the achievement gap, but often do not begin until children have entered kindergarten, and are thus intervening relatively late in children's development, after the effects of the family's conditions have taken root.[54] Diversity programs, for instance, did not control the reality that between 1998 and 2010, the number of children from poor families increased by 14 percent.[55]

Studies reveal that when African American students take academic tests with the understanding that their performance will be compared to those of Caucasians and Asians, their scores go down, but when African American students are given the test and told that it is merely a research tool, their scores increase.[56] This suggests that African American students bring the trauma of racism to the classroom in the form of self-defeat. Educational equity initiatives do not change the culture that produces race-based trauma. They do not lift families out of poverty, nor expunge racism from the community, nor radically alter family dynamics. Some believe that diversity programs are ineffective because they do not, or cannot produce substantial social transformation.[57]

The achievement gap is not something that can be overcome only by diversifying the school. It requires curriculum and instruction that specifically targets students' developmental needs, and parental support for placing students in courses that focus on these targets. There are essentially two ways initiatives for closing the gap can go. The first is to channel resources

---

52. National Center for Educational Statistics, *Reading, 2011*, 11, 40.

53. Bainbridge and Lasley, II, "Demographics, Diversity and K-12," 425–28.

54. Garcia and Weiss, *Reducing and Averting Achievement Gaps*, 4, 7, 10.

55. Ibid, 8.

56. Bainbridge and Lasley, II, 424.

57. Kezar, "Curing Programitis," para. 1.

exclusively to special instruction and tutoring for the lowest achievers with the intention of *leveling everyone's achievement*. The second is to channel resources to instruction and support that is likely to *raise everyone's level of achievement*. The difference is important. When the first option is exercised, it is possible that schools neglect the needs of students who are ready for advanced learning, and when the second option is exercised, there may still be significant gaps in scores between various demographic groups, even though the general trend is upward for all.

Investing in the diversification of campus demographics is different from investing in instruction that is likely to improve student achievement. This compels colleges and universities to critique their own expenditures, and to determine whether their investments and practices relative to diversification and equity can be justified. The institution may take pride in graduating a "rainbow" of students, but questions remain. Would the "rainbow" be just as ignorant as the average American on topics of world geography, the Constitution, world religions, and science? Do "rainbows" guarantee that graduates' intellectual habits and skills are significantly different from those who did not complete college? These are very difficult questions for educators, but we are the ones who said that we were going to prepare students to meet the challenges of the 21st century, and so we need to provide answers.

Scrutiny of the Bounty

The price tag for administrators varies by institution and correlates with the wealth and status of institutions. In 2018, the administrative cost per student at Stanford University was $35,513.00, the cost per student at California State University, Sacramento was $1,759.00, and at the University of California at Berkeley it was $7, 322.00.[58] Between 2000 and 2012, the average number of administrative and executive employees per 1,000 students increased from 67 to 73 in research universities, and decreased from 10 to 9 in bachelors and masters universities.[59] Faculty salaries vary not only by institution, but by discipline, with professors in the STEM subjects often earning more than professors who teach subjects in the arts and humanities. Over the last few decades, faculty salaries have stagnated. Since the Recession of 2008–2009, they have averaged increases of half a percent above the increases in the consumer price index.[60]

58. See "How Colleges Spend Money."
59. Hiltonsmith, "Pulling Up," 5.
60. Colby and Fowler, *Annual Report of the Economic Status*, 4.

Whopping salaries for high level administrators have often been justified on the claim that these men and women are responsible for the financial well-being and fund-raising, and so deserve to be well-compensated. As the narrative goes, "The president who will bring big bucks to the academy must be lured by big bucks to the academy." It is not uncommon for presidents of colleges and universities, public and private alike, to receive over a half a million annually in salary, amenities, and benefits. Some get housing stipends and travel allowances, others get signing and completion of contract bonuses.[61] There is, however, no guarantee that luxurious presidential salaries translates into exemplary learning and persistence to degree.

As noted, the administrative cost per student at California State University, Sacramento was $1,759 in 2018, and at Stanford University was $35,315. The percent of undergraduates completing their degree in four years at these institutions varied with Sacramento State at 9 percent and Stanford at 75 percent. At first glance, it appears that money spent on administration immediately translates to graduation rates. In reality graduation, rates are affected by institutional selectivity, whereby admissions criteria for elite institutions tend to favor students that acquired self-motivation and academic discipline early in life, and who attended excellent schools and had access to abundant district resources in their K-12 education. The relationship between administrative cost and graduation rates are all over the map. Here are some examples:[62]

- St. John's College in Santé Fe, New Mexico, administrative cost per student $10,195, with a four-year graduation rate of 55 percent

- Gustavus Adolphus College in St. Peter, Minnesota, administrative cost $5,326 with four-year graduation rate of 76 percent

- Alabama State University, administrative cost per student $9,219 with a four-year graduation rate of 10 percent

- Yale University, administrative cost per student $20,352, with a four-year graduation rate of 88 percent

- University of Georgia, Athens, Georgia, administrative cost per student $2,926, with a four-year graduation rate of 65 percent

- Kansas State University, administrative cost per student $1,504, with four-year graduation rate of 31 percent

- University of Wisconsin, Eau Claire, administrative cost per student $1,706, with a four-year graduation rate of 37 percent

61. Finkelstein and Wilde, "Bonuses and Benefits," para. 6–7.

62. Data located at How Colleges Spend Money: howcolegesspendmoney.com.

- Mississippi State, administrative cost per student $3,538, with four-year graduation rate of 31 percent

- Oklahoma State University, main campus, administrative cost per student $676 (yes, less than a thousand), with a four-year graduation rate of 39 percent.

So, what does COVID-19 have to do with bulging budgets? Simply put, the crisis raised the question of whether the astonishing amount of money we spend on education is actually invested in activities that significantly reduces ignorance, and that significantly increases civility and compassion in society. Given the scope and stature of problems headed our way, it seems that expenditures for competitive sports programs, luxury dorms, and multiple layers of middle management might not be as prudent as expenditure for reforming curriculum and instruction.

Many teachers have acknowledged that, in the ideal world, education would bring about a better world, but "people don't want that." Some instructors believe that they must give people what they want, because that is what they are paid to do. Some sigh, "Let's be honest; parents send their kids to school so they can do better than they did, and not because of some highfalutin philosophical thing." Others plead, "Look around—this country produces some of the greatest innovators who really care about sustainability and social justice—look at all the people who risked their lives and political careers fighting COVID-19 and speaking truth to power."

I get it. I admire and respect those in "the good fight," which is to oppose ignorance, bigotry, selfishness, sloppy reasoning, short-sightedness, and injustice. I also get that part of the good fight is to increase the number of people who are committed to it, and embrace the notion that educators are obligated to help people see the difference between the good fight and the not-so-good fight. I grew up assuming that all teachers, principals, professors, and educational administrators automatically subscribed to the good fight. It is safe to say that—at least rhetorically—most of these people do subscribe to the good fight. Our own conditions, however, accuse us of failing to consistently and sincerely fight the good fight.

Chapter 10

Conclusion

WHAT DID WE EXPECT?

As Americans turned out the lights and went to bed on Memorial Day, 2020, they would learn two days later that the United States reached the milestone of 100,000 deaths due to COVID-19. For many people, Memorial Day had been one of celebration and defiance. People gathered at beaches on both coasts to play and sunbathe, while others in between mingled at pool parties and bar-b-ques. The weekend's festivities included car races in Altamahaw, North Carolina and Daytona Beach, Florida, where folks made their way, "elbow to elbow" through the gates as police concluded the swarm was just too big to enforce social distancing.[1] Tired of social distancing, many decided that the threat of illness was so remote, that caution was unnecessary.

As they tucked themselves into bed on that Memorial Day, Americans did not anticipate the rupture of civic peace caused by Officer Derek Chauvin's brutal murder of Mr. George Floyd in Minneapolis, Minnesota. The homicide and demonstrations that followed magnified the nation's failure to eradicate racism and police brutality. It seemed that the marches, looting, and arson following Floyd's death did more to get the attention of policy-makers and average Americans than did the disparities in COVID-19's morbidity and mortality rates between Caucasians and racial minorities. Both racism and indifference to health hazards tell us that we are

1. Maxouris, "Some Americans Take a Holiday," para. 1–7.

not always governed by reason and compassion, and the world is waiting for our hearts and minds to mature, so that we can get on with life without the "soft" genocide of hate and poverty.

As an educator, I am profoundly disappointed that when people in my profession were given opportunities to help students confront and remove ignorance, bigotry, and entitlement from their hearts and minds, we often made excuses for not doing so. We complained that we lacked the time and training. We said that ethics was "someone else's department." We said that it was not our job to address values, morality, and human dignity because "that stuff" was "all mushy and personal," and that it took away precious time away from "real education"—and besides that, students disliked instruction that "picked at" their personal values. In our colleges and universities, we declared that developmental education focused on literacy and epistemological beliefs was beneath us. We rationalized that with upward mobility would come civic decency and justice. So firmly has the rational for education been chained to economic ends and material objectives, that people in my profession have imagined that by requiring a couple of courses related to critical thinking and cultural competency in a program of 32 courses, they have done their duty to promote equity and cultivate empathy.

We have not yet learned that equity is greater than the sum of families who gain entrance into the middle class, as it concerns the knowledge and discernment required to participate effectively in the democratic process, and the need to view equity through the lens of ecology and environmental justice. Many colleges and universities are content to declare victory for equity when more have been removed from the ranks who are paid hourly and added to the ranks of those who earn salaries, benefits, and bonuses, even when those salaries, benefits, and bonuses are earned in conditions that are far from equitable for all. Our educational system is not *designed* to, nor does it *aspire* to, nor is it legally *obligated* to provide the kind of education that would bring the masses into the peerage of those who own the country.[2] In many ways, higher education is about producing middle managers and service providers while leaving the larger economic and political systems intact. That might not be so bad if our current systems were fair and dominated by people who want environmental sustainability, but they are not.

We should not be surprised when 25 year-old college graduates feel entitled to executive offices and six-figure salaries, or when our neighbors refused to wear masks and comply with social distancing rules, or when our fellow citizens voted for bigots. Human nature urges us to put ourselves first

---

2. For an introduction to America's aristocracy, see *American Ruling Class*, directed by John Kirby (Bullfrog Films).

and to place ourselves above all others. Human nature had a little help, however, as we—the aggregate of teachers, administrators, parents, commercial media, and elected officials—taught folks that such behavior is OK. We did this by convincing ourselves that we had no legitimate business putting the content of character front and center of our curriculum and instruction. We taught each other that self-interest is a good thing, and that only fools and liberals care equally about others as they care about themselves. We taught each other that short-term profits matter more than long-term sustainability, and that economies must expand or we will wither and die. We taught each other to fear truth, and to believe that adapting to what we know is wrong is better than dissenting, because adapting means we get to keep our toys and privileges. We held that as long as we "cared about" the poor by way of serving a turkey dinner once a year, or giving cast-off clothing to a local charity, we need not feel uncomfortable about inequities built into our economy—so what did we expect?

Memorial Day, 2020 is a metaphor for American entitlement; it is a symbolic middle finger trust into the faces of law-makers, scientists, and health care workers who told everybody to stay home for the sake of containing a deadly disease. It is also a metaphor for our willingness to absorb a staggering number of deaths as the collateral damage we pay for our "right" to "our lifestyle." The haste to reopen businesses and relax social distancing did exactly what scientists told us it would do: it resulted in a surge of infection. In the spring of 2020, it took about two months to reach 50,000 cases of COVID-19 in the U.S., and by the first of July, the U.S. was recording that many new cases in a single day.[3]

The day was a logical culmination of four critical factors that made defiance of health and safety measures inevitable. First, when COVID-19 appeared in the U.S., the federal government was slow to mandate radical precautions. The president left matters in the hands of governors, who responded to the crisis at their own pace and with variation in policies.[4] Second, Americans were barraged by conflicting information and misinformation about coronavirus that often confused them. Third, by May, the president's task force on the pandemic and the CDC were marginalized in public discourse. This left people wondering about whether their absence from presidential press conferences meant that the crisis was over. Fourth, April's unemployment rate tipped 14 percent. For many people, shelter in place meant zero income.

3. Mossburg et al., "US Sees a Record," para. 1–8.
4. See Andrew and Froio, "These are the States."

The COVID-19 crisis was more than a biological event. It was a test of character. The crisis began long before the novel coronavirus surfaced in China. It began with choosing a way of life that is woefully indifferent to how unchecked materialism and egos can lead to pandemics and serious errors in managing them. It continued with school and college curricula that reinforced the idea that knowledge is best used to acquire the lifestyle to which we feel entitled. It continued every time educators and policy-makers made excuses for why schools that serve ethnic minorities and the poor must tolerate bad teaching, lack of resources, and crumbling facilities. It continued every time professors protested the need for universal curricula aimed to remove ignorance about the world, nature and the scientific methods, the U.S. Constitution, and the philosophical and religious ideologies that have shaped and continue to shape civilization. It continued each time an instructor designed lessons that were void of the need to think critically, explore the meaning and significance of ideas, and to relate knowledge to our problems and conditions. It continued each time schools and universities expedited students like they were sausages rolling off an assembly line.

WHAT THE CONSULTANT LEARNED

As instructors and students made the incredible shift en masse to remote instruction, they told us about their experiences, anxieties, frustrations, and successes. Many instructors and students completed courses with ease, and, no doubt, many students had satisfying and substantial instruction. As expected, however, many were troubled by remote instruction not only because they were challenged to learn new software, but because they struggled to re-conceptualize their own courses. Some instructors were confronted with a pedagogical lexicon that was alien to them. Some did not know what was meant by backwards design, scaffolding, universal design, formative assessment, epistemological development, and metacognition.

There were many instructors who were expected to convert their courses into the online environment who had never studied curriculum design from the perspective of pedagogical experts and cognitive developers. For some, "course design" was simply a matter of learning how to use software to facilitate teaching and assessing. This reality is the logical conclusion of excusing professors from having to learn about teaching and learning before they undertake their teaching assignments. Traditionally, we assume that people with doctorates in their field automatically know how to teach, so what did we expect?

As instructors prepared for summer and fall courses in the online environment, the literature they read on the topic of course design routinely reinforced the notion that exemplary instruction was primarily about effective use of technology. An avalanche of articles and books spoke to the importance of equitable and inclusive instruction, student engagement, connecting with students, transparency of instruction, and helping students cope with trauma. These are important topics, but they have occupied center-stage of pedagogical conversations to the near exclusion of topics such as academic reading proficiency, critical thinking, interdisciplinary understanding, information literacy, civic and scientific literacy, and writing proficiency. One may argue that these topics are not appropriate for conversations about the big learning picture, and that it is up to instructors in certain departments to address these things. Yet, these things concern teachers at all points on the educational spectrum.

During the pandemic, many instructors learned how to use digital tools to engage students, assess students' work, and deliver content. Technology, however, will not cure what ails America and its educators. Learning how to click buttons on an LMS does not mean that instructors will be more willing to explicitly teach critical reading skills, or require students to improve their civic, scientific, and information literacy, or actively develop students' epistemological beliefs, or to develop their moral judgement, or to improve their capacity to detect and analyze propaganda. Technology enables one to transform face-to-face instruction into a digital venue; it does not organically alter the depth, sophistication, or quality of curricula.

A TEST OF CHARACTER

The COVID-19 crisis presented us with choices. Would we take responsibility for the pandemic, or blame others? Would we set aside partisan feuds and work together to fight the disease, or would we throw sand in each other's faces? Would we examine the impact that poverty had the wellness of our brothers and sisters, or would we ignore that reality? Would we increase our respect for nature's vulnerability, or continue destroy ecosystems that makes our lives possible?

Is education to blame, for the COIVD-19 crisis? Yes, to some degree, education is at least *partially to blame* for the crisis. The pandemic revealed an embarrassing amount of ignorance in America's citizenry and in America's leadership. Educators at all levels could do more to help people understand nature, the scientific method, and what happens when human activity disrupts ecosystems. We can do more to help people understand how government is supposed to work, and to cultivate intellectual skills necessary to resist propaganda about what is best for us and what we ought to treasure.

The purpose of our schools and universities is to lead us away from ignorance, bigotry, irrationality, and intellectual sloth. However, since our schools and universities are creatures of culture, they frequently embody, in their own ways, ignorance, irrationality, bigotry, and intellectual sloth. The academy is a porous institution, and the biases and assumptions that rain on society leak into their offices and classrooms. As with society as a whole, schools and universities can rationalize anything, even when to do so contradicts their fundamental purpose. We can rationalize converting a child's education to a wholly digital learning environment. We can rationalize giving the unions the power to determine whether teachers should get extra pay for preparing their own lessons. We can rationalize paying professional football players an average of $2.7 million a year, and paying teachers less than $2 million over a thirty year career.[5]

Many believe that as we rationalize, we are too smart to shoot ourselves in the foot. COIVD-19 was just nature's way of pointing to the smoking holes in our shoes. The pandemic suggested that we are running low on common sense, and may need robust educational intervention to get us firing on all intellectual cylinders. The virus said to us: When you teach people that it is OK to disrupt ecological habitats for the sake of economic growth, put wealth before people, ignore science, and bring ignorance to the voting booth, odds are that unpleasant consequences will follow—what else would one expect?

During the pandemic, we beheld the possibility that we might not be a democracy for long. We saw with our eyes and heard with our ears, that even people who are highly educated are willing to be sycophants and lapdogs to powerful people, either out of fear of being fired or as a gamble that blind loyalty would bring favors in the future. We saw and heard that even people with college degrees who were surrounded by experts, were willing to dismiss experts because those experts' assertions were not aligned with a particular political narrative. What can we take away from these things? To put it bluntly, we may not be smart enough, or courageous enough to elect the kind of leaders we need to sustain democracy.

---

5. The average teacher's salary in 2019 was about $60,000, the average starting salary was $40,000, with some districts starting teachers at $30,000 a year. See Weir, "10 Alarming Facts." Also see Renzulli and Connley, "Here's What the Average NFL Player Makes," para. 8.

Could *all* of the chaos, carelessness, suffering, mismanagement, and death wrought by COVID-19 have been eliminated if schools, colleges, and universities been doing a better job?

No way.

Even the best institutions and teachers cannot guarantee that their students will want knowledge, or want to improve their intellectual habits and moral character. One of the elephants in the academy packed with pachyderms is that education will not be the "salvation" of humanity because too many humans do not want to be "saved." This is just another way of saying that many will never be humbled by their own ignorance. Leading human beings to knowledge, reason, and the "better angels of our nature" often feels like a Sisyphean task."[6] One might ask, "If education is so impotent and futile, then why bother with it at all?"

MONKEY SUITS

We send our children to schools and universities for many reasons. Some expect education to ensure that the nation dominates others in the global economy. Some expect the academy to make us self-sufficient and effective in our civil relations. Some see schools as day care centers and a way to feed their children. Some see universities as a home for researchers with government contracts, or a farm for professional athletes.

Arguably, the most hopeful and important reason why we bother with education is because it is not in our best interest to be at the mercy of ignorance.

We live with constant propaganda urging us to surrender our dignity, conscience, and well-being to charlatans and wolves. This justifies reforms that may be summarized as follows:

- Mandate media studies that improve students' proficiency with critical consumption of media and the ability to participate in social media responsibility

- Direct diversity and equity resources to the improvement of instruction and academic achievement, rather than administration and marketing

6. President Abraham Lincoln referred to the "better angels of our nature" in his First inaugural Address. In Greek mythology, Sisyphus was a deceitful and selfish king of Ephyra (Corinth), who so angered the gods that they condemned him to roll a huge boulder up a hill, only to have it roll down when it neared the summit, thus requiring an eternity of rock-rolling for the unfortunate monarch.

- Broaden the scope of cultural competency to include the role of religion and spirituality in the world, moral development, and social well-being

- Increase interdisciplinarity so students' may grasp the relationship between knowledge in disparate fields and appreciate the complexity of problem-solving

- Explicitly and systemically teach critical reading across all levels of education

- Expand the school year to enrich learning and overcome achievement gaps

- Reform or eliminate tenure, and enforce high standards of teacher competency

- Improve institutional self-studies that place evidence for student proficiencies front and center

- Repurpose university real estate and capital projects to enhance instruction and fortify the university's commitment to community service

- Eliminate wasteful spending, and curb administrative bloating

The question addressed in this essay is not about whether remote instruction is the way of the future. That ship has sailed; we will, no doubt, increase its reach. This essay is not about whether higher education in the future will be public or private, or accessible, or affordable. At the end of the day, these things might not matter, especially if whatever education we get does not improve our understanding of the world and our commitment to be its good shepherd. The key questions here are to what extent are we listening to what the Earth and its people are telling us about the need to change our way of life, and to what extend we will honor what they tell us.

Our way of life has normed greed, entitlement, and all forms of bigotry. As we make excuses for why things are the way they are, we often rely on assumptions, rumors, and popular opinions about the world and its people, as if these things were well-established facts. We do not have to do this. We have a choice. We may get the monkey off our back, or we may simply put a new suit on the monkey and sent it back into the circus.

Meaningful educational reform does not begin with ambition, because ambition can be blinding. Meaningful reform beings with humility. It starts with embracing the reality that we are not all-knowing and infallible, and that sometimes schools and universities are education's worst enemy. It begins with accepting that all learning exists on a continuum, which makes the pre-school teacher and the professor kindred spirits in the endeavor of human development. The humble instructor understands that she or he has gained access to sacred space, which is where students' construct their sense of self, purpose, and orientation to the world and everyone in it. The humble teacher respects the terrible power of ignorance as it may not only corrupt one's grasp of the facts, but one's knowledge of self and the narratives from which one derives life's meaning. The humble teacher serves an elusive master, which is truth, and which engages the servant in a life-long quest.

Meaningful and authentic reform is an act of courage because it brings us face to face with the indignities and suffering that are implicit in the status quo, and asks us to examine our role in maintaining that status quo. It takes courage to admit that some of the privileges we enjoy and "our way of life" perpetuate injustice and threaten our planet. Education is essentially about our way of life. More than a means of acquiring job skills, it regards the individual's assimilation of prevailing attitudes, norms, and values. Education is also dynamic and responsive to changes in our conditions and perspectives. It is concerned with emerging visions for the future and how we manifest our ideals. If all we ask of education is to secure our children's place in the middle class, and to produce the cadres of professionals needed to sustain the nation's military prowess and dominance in global markets, we might say that we have asked too little. The better summation, as our condition suggests, is that we have unwisely asked for the wrong things.

Bibliography

Aberth, John. *Plagues in World History*. Lanham, MD: Rowman & Littlefield, 2011.

Alexander, Patricia A. "The Path to Competence: A Lifespan Developmental Perspective on Reading." *Journal of Literacy Research* 37.4 (2005) 413–36.

Aljazeera. "Iran Leader Refuses U.S. Help; Cites Coronavirus Conspiracy Theory." *Aljazeera*, March 23, 2020. https://www.aljazeera.com/news/2020/03/iran-leader-refuses-cites-coronavirus-conspiracy-theory-200322145122752.html.

Allen, I. E., and J. Seaman. *Changing course: Ten years of tracking online education in the United States*. Babson Survey Research Group and Quahog Research Group, LLC, 2013. http://files.eric.ed.gov/fulltext/ED541571.pdf.

Allsup, Car. "What's All This White Male Bashing?" In Renee J. Martin (Ed.), *Practicing What We Teach: Confronting Diversity in Teacher Education*, pp. 79–94. Albany, NY: State University of New York Press, 1995.

Alltucker, Ken. "Labs are Testing 100,000 People Each Day for Coronavirus. That is Still Not Enough." *USA Today*, April 2, 2020. https://www.usatoday.com/story/news/health/2020/04/02/coronavirus-testing-number-labs-covid/5099458002/.

Allyn, Bobby, and V. Romo. "Trump Suspends All Travel from Europe for 30 Days to Combat COVID-19." NPR. KQED, March 11, 2020. https://www.npr.org/2020/03/11/814597993/trump-set-to-deliver-address-as-coronavirus-deemed-a-pandemic.

American Council of Trustees and Alumni. *A Crisis in Civics Education*. American Council of Trustees and Alumni, Washington, DC, 2016. https://www.nationalreview.com/2017/03/americans-history-civics-knowledge-education-federal-government/.

American Council of Trustees and Alumni. "No U.S. History?" American Council of Trustees and Alumni, July 2016. https://www.goacta.org/wp-content/uploads/2016/07/no-us-history.pdf.

———. "What Will They Learn? 2019–2020." American Council of trustees and Alumni, September 9, 2019. https://www.goacta.org/wp-content/uploads/ee/download/what-will-they-learn-2018-19.pdf.

American Revolution Center. "The American Revolution Center: Who Cares?" Press release, October 12, 2011. Philadelphia, PA. https://www.amrevmuseum.org/sites/default/files/media-uploads/Updated%20Website%20Press%20Release%2010–12–11.pdf.

American Ruling Class. Directed by John Kirby. London. Alive Mind Media. DVD 2005.

Anderson, Lorin W., and D. R. Krathwohl. *A Taxonomy for Learning, Teaching and Assessing*. New York: Pearson, 2000.

Andrew, Scottie, and J. Frorio. "These are the States that Require You to Wear a Face Mask in Public." CNN, April 20, 2020. https://www.cnn.com/2020/04/20/us/states-that-require-masks-trnd/index.html.

Anti-Defamation League. "Religion in the Curriculum." Religion in the Public School. New York: Anti-Defamation League, 2012. https://www.adl.org/education/resources/tools-and-strategies/religion-in-public-schools/curriculum.

Arendale, David R. "Then and Now: The Early Years of Developmental Education." *Research and Teaching in Developmental Education* 18.2 (2002) 5–23.

Arum, Richard, and J. Roska. *Academically Adrift. Limited Learning on College Campuses.* Chicago: University of Chicago Press, 2011.

Association of Colleges and Research Libraries Board. "Framework for Information Literacy in Higher Education." Association of Colleges and research Libraries, February 2, 2015. http://www.ala.org/acrl/sites/ala.org.acrl/files/content/issues/infolit/Framework_ILHE.pdf.

Association of American Colleges and Universities. *Diversity Blueprint: A Planning Manual for Colleges and Universities.* Washington, DC: Association of American Colleges and Universities, 1998.

———. "Joint Statement on the Value of Liberal Arts Education." May 31, 2018. https://www.aacu.org/about/statements/2018/joint-statement-value-liberal-education-aacu-and-aaup.

Avert. "HIV and AIDS in the United States of America (USA)." October, 2019. https://www.avert.org/professionals/hiv-around-world/western-central-europe-north-america/usa.

Bagdikian, Ben. *The New Media Monopoly*, 20th ed. Boston: Beacon, 2004.

Baier, K., C. Hendricks, K. W. Gorden, J. E. Hendricks, and L. Cochran. "College Students' Textbook Reading, or Not! *American Reading Forum Annual Yearbook*, 31 (2011). http://americanreadingforum.org/yearbook/11_yearbook/documents/BAIER%20ET%20AL%20PAPER.pdf.

Bainbridge, William L., and T. J. Lasley. "Demographics, Diversity, and K-12 Accountability: The Challenge of Closing the Achievement Gap." *Education and Urban Society* 34.4 (2002) 422–37.

Baldwin, Chuck. "A Contagion of Fear." [Video]. Liberty Fellowship, March 13, 2020. https://libertyfellowshipmt.com/News/tabid/56/ID/3990/A-Contagion-Of-Fear.aspx.

Barzun, Jacques. *House of Intellect*. New York: Harpers, 1959.

Bauder, David. "Trump Uses Coronavirus Briefing to Attack Reporter." ABC News, March 20, 2020. https://abcnews.go.com/Entertainment/wireStory/trump-daily-coronavirus-briefing-attack-reporter-69717997.

Baumgartner, Emily, and J. Rainey. "Trump Administration Ended Early Warning Program to Detect Coronaviruses." *Los Angeles Times*, April 2, 2020. https://www.latimes.com/science/story/2020–04-02/coronavirus-trump-pandemic-program-viruses-detection.

BBC News. "Li Wenliang: Coronavirus Kills Chinese Whistleblower Doctor." BBC News, February 7, 2020. https://www.bbc.com/news/world-asia-china-51403795.

Bluestein, Greg. "Kemp Rejects Statewide Shutdown to Contain Coronavirus." *AJC*, march 19, 2020. https://www.ajc.com/news/state—regional-govt—politics/kemp-rejects-statewide-shutdown-brace-for-coronavirus-scrambles-for-health-supplies/opYYAFVOkyV4VIhLkEJajK/.

Bok, Derek. *Our Underachieving Universities*. Princeton, NJ: Princeton University Press, 2006.

————. *Universities and the Marketplace. The Commercialization of Higher Education*. Princeton, NJ: Princeton University Press, 2003.

Bondi, S. "Students and Institutions Protecting Whiteness as Property: A Critical Race Analysis of Student Affairs Preparation." *Journal of Student Affairs Research and Practice* 49.4 (2012) 397–414.

Booker, Brakkton. "Fauci Says Its 'Doable' to have Millions of Doses of COVID-19 Vaccine by January." NPR, April 30, 2020. https://www.npr.org/sections/coronavirus-live-updates/2020/04/30/848478507/fauci-says-its-doable-to-have-millions-of-doses-of-covid-19-vaccine-by-january.

Borges, Thais and S. Branford. "Rapid Deforestation of Brazilian Amazon Could bring Next Pandemic: Experts. *Mongabay*, April 19, 2020. https://news.mongabay.com/2020/04/rapid-deforestation-of-brazilian-amazon-could-bring-next-pandemic-experts/.

Bosley, Lisa. ""I Don't Teach Reading": Critical Reading Instruction in Composition Courses." *Literacy Research and Instruction* 47.4 (2008) 285–308.

Bowden, John. "Demonstrators at Michigan State Capitol Protest Stay-at-Home Order." *The Hill*, April 15, 2020. https://thehill.com/homenews/state-watch/492941-demonstrators-at-michigan-state-capitol-protest-stay-at-home-order.

Bradley, Steven W., J. R. Graven, W. W. Law, and J. E. West. "The Impact of Hiring Chief Diversity Officers on Diver Faculty Hiring." Cambridge, MA: National bureau of Economic Research, 2018.

Breuniger, Kevin. "Trump Wants Packed Churches and Economy Open again on Easter Despite the Threat of Deadly Coronavirus." CNBC, March 24, 2020. https://www.cnbc.com/2020/03/24/coronavirus-response-trump-wants-to-reopen-us-economy-by-easter.html.

Bright, Rick. *Complaint of Prohibited Personal Practice or Other Prohibited Activity, OSC From-14*. Katz, Marshall, and Banks, LLC. https://www.kmblegal.com/sites/default/files/NEW%20R.%20Bright%20OSC%20Complaint_Redacted.pdf.

Brost, Brian D., and K. A. Bradley. "Student Compliance with Assigned Reading: A Case Study." *Journal of Scholarship of Teaching and Learning* 6.2 (2006) 101–11.

Brown, Anna. "Most Americans Say Higher Ed is Heading in Wrong Direction, but Partisans Disagree on Why." Pew Research Center, July 26, 2018. https://www.pewresearch.org/fact-tank/2018/07/26/most-americans-say-higher-ed-is-heading-in-wrong-direction-but-partisans-disagree-on-why/.

Brozo, William G.,G. Moorman, C. Meyer, and T. Stewart. "Content Area Reading and Disciplinary Literacy: A Case for the Radical Center." *Journal of Adolescent & Adult Literacy* 56.5 (2013) 353–57.

Buck, Daniel. "I'm a Teacher and a Waste of Money," Arc Digital. November 7, 2019. https://arcdigital.media/im-a-teacher-and-a-waste-of-money-acd4a6a8392d.

Bunge, Nancy. "Students Evaluating Teachers Doesn't Just Hurt Teachers. It Hurts Students. *The Chronicle of Higher Education*, November 27, 2018. https://www.chronicle.com/article/Students-Evaluating-Teachers/245169.

Burns, Kristin. PREDICT Receive Extension for COVID-19 Emergency Response." U.C. Davis, March 31, 2020. https://www.ucdavis.edu/coronavirus/news/predict-receives-extension-covid-19-pandemic-emergency-response/.

Busl, Gretchen. "Narrative Rationality." Ted Talk, June 6, 2016. https://www.youtube.com/watch?v=rNuzkAosEDw.

Bustamante, Jaleesa. "College Enrollment & Student Demographic Statistics." Educationdata.org, 2019. https://educationdata.org/college-enrollment-statistics/.

Cabrera, Christina. "McConnell Blames Impeachment for Trump Administration's Slow Response for Coronavirus." *Talking Point Memo*, March 31, 2020. https://talkingpointsmemo.com/news/mcconnell-blame-impeachment-trump-administration-slow-response-coronavirus.

Cachero, Paulina. "Carnival's CEO Says Coronavirus Can Be Contained on Cruises because 'the Ship is So Large.'" *Business Insider*, March 23, 2020. https://www.businessinsider.com/carnival-ceo-defends-lagging-response-coronavirus-infection-onboard-social-distancing-2020-3.

Camera, Lauren. "High School Seniors Are Not College-Ready." *U.S. News and World Report*, April 27, 2016. https://www.usnews.com/news/articles/2016–04-27/high-school-seniors-arent-college-ready-naep-data-show.

Carnegie Classification of Institutions in Higher Education. *2018 Update Facts and Figures*. Bloomington, IN: Indiana University, 2019. https://carnegieclassifications.iu.edu/downloads/CCIHE2018-FactsFigures.pdf.

Carnegie Foundation for the Advancement of Teaching. *Missions of the College Curriculum: A Contemporary Review with Suggestions*. The Carnegie Council Series. San Francisco, CA: Jossey Bass, 1977.

Carnevale, Anthony P., B. Cheah, and H. R. Hanson. *The Economic Value of College Majors*. Center for Education and the Workforce. Georgetown University, 2015. https://cew.georgetown.edu/wp-content/uploads/Exec-Summary-web-B.pdf.

Carr, Austin, and C. Palmeri. "Socially Distance This. Carnival Executives Knew They had a Virus Problem, but Kept the Party Going." *Business Insider*, April 16, 2020. https://www.bloomberg.com/features/2020-carnival-cruise-coronavirus/.

Center for Sustainable Systems. "U.S. Environmental Footprint Factsheet." University of Michigan, 2019. Pub. No. CSS08–08. http://css.umich.edu/factsheets/us-environmental-footprint-factsheet.

Centers for Disease Control and Prevention. "1918 Pandemic." Influenza. U.S. Department of Health and Human Services, 2020. https://www.cdc.gov/flu/pandemic-resources/1918-pandemic-h1n1.html.

———. "2009 H1N1 Pandemic (N1H1pdm09 Virus)." Centers for Disease Control, Atlanta, GA, 2019. https://web.archive.org/web/20200318191813/https://www.cdc.gov/flu/pandemic-resources/2009-h1n1-pandemic.html

———. "2009 N1H1 Timelines." Influenza (Flu). U.S. Department of Health and Human Services, 2019. https://www.cdc.gov/flu/pandemic-resources/2009-pandemic-timeline.html.

———. "COVID-19 in Racial and Ethnic Minority Groups." Centers for Disease Control and Prevention, June, 2020. https://www.cdc.gov/coronavirus/2019-ncov/need-extra-precautions/racial-ethnic-minorities.html.

Chait, Robin. *Removing Chronically Ineffective Teachers*. Washington, DC: Center for American Progress, 2010. https://cdn.americanprogress.org/wp-content/uploads/issues/2010/03/pdf/teacher_dismissal.pdf.

Chertoff, Meryl Justin. "The Calvary Isn't Coming: Governors and Mayors Take Lead on Coronavirus Pandemic." *Georgetown Law*, March 22, 2020. https://www.law.

georgetown.edu/salpal/the-cavalry-isnt-coming-governors-and-mayors-take-lead-on-coronavirus-pandemic/.

Chickering, Arthur W., and G. D. Kuh. "Promoting Student Success: Creating Conditions so Every Student Can Learn." Occasional Paper No. 3. Bloomington, IN: National Survey of Student Engagement. (2005).

Christenbury-Emory, Janet. "Study in ICU Finds 30.9% Mortality Rate to COVID-19." *Futurity*, June 1, 2020. https://www.futurity.org/covid-19-mortality-rate-237 7362-2/.

Clark, Doug Bock. "Inside the Nightmare Voyage of the Diamond Princess." *GQ*, April 30, 2020. https://www.gq.com/story/inside-diamond-princess-cruise-ship-nightmare-voyage?utm_source=pocket-newtab.

Clump, M.A., Bauer, H., & Bradley, C. "The Extent to Which Psychology Students Read Textbooks: A Multiple Class Analysis of Reading across the Psychology Curriculum." *Journal of Instructional Psychology* 31.3 (2004).

CNN Politics. "Trump Berates Reporters When Asked about Report by His Own Administration." CNN, April 6, 2020. https://www.cnn.com/videos/politics/2020/04/06/trump-inspector-general-report-christi-grimm-vpx.cnn.

Coates, Daniel R. *Worldwide Threat Assessment of the U.S. Intelligence Community*. United States Office of Intelligence Community, 2018. https://www.dni.gov/files/documents/Newsroom/Testimonies/2018-ATA—-Unclassified-SSCI.pdf.

Cochrane, Emily, and S. G. Stolberg. "$2 Trillion Coronavirus Stimulus Bill is Signed into Law." *New York Times*, March 27, 2020. https://www.nytimes.com/2020/03/27/us/politics/coronavirus-house-voting.html.

Cohen, Jon. "The United States Badly Bungled Coronavirus Testing, but Things May Soon Improve." *Science*, February, 2020. https://www.sciencemag.org/news/2020/02/united-states-badly-bungled-coronavirus-testing-things-may-soon-improve.

Cohen, Rachel, "Why Education Isn't a Key to a Good Income." *The Atlantic*, September 26, 2017. https://www.theatlantic.com/education/archive/2017/09/education-and-economic-mobility/541041/.

Colby, Glen T., and C. Fowler. *The Annual Report of the Economic Status of the Profession, 2019–2020*. American Association of University Professors. May, 2020. https://www.aaup.org/sites/default/files/2019-20_ARES.pdf.

Cole, Gene, and R. S. Smith. "Using Results of the NCEE Literacy Test to Assess and Improve Economic Instruction." *Journal of Business Administration Online* 1.1 (2002) 1–9.

Coleman, James, E. Q. Campbell, C. J. Hobson, J. McPartland, A. M. Mood, F. D Weinfeld, and R. L. York. *Equality of Educational Opportunity*. Washington, DC: U.S Department of Health, Education and Welfare, 1966.

Coleman, Justine. "Nearly 6 in 10 Concerned about US Opening too quickly." *The Hill*, April 19, 2020. https://thehill.com/policy/healthcare/public-global-health/493556-poll-almost-6-in-10-concerned-about-us-reopening-too.

Collman, Ashley. "In 2017, Obama Officials Briefed Trump's Team on Dealing with a Pandemic Like the Coronavirus. One Cabinet member Reportedly Fell Asleep, and Others Didn't Want to Be There." *Business Insider*, March 17, 2020. https://www.businessinsider.com/trump-appointees-trained-pandemic-response-in-2016-2020-3.

Complete College America. *Remediation. Higher Education's Bridge to Nowhere*. Washington, DC: Complete College America, 2012. https://postsecondary.gatesfoundation.org/wp-content/uploads/2014/10/CCA-Remediation-Bridge-to-No-Where.pdf.

Council on Foreign Relations and National Geographic. *What College-Aged Student Know about the World. A Survey of Geographic Literacy*. New York: Council on Foreign Relations, 2016. https://drive.google.com/file/d/0B2AUpoucQL4jQXhzOWt4QjBfMFk/view.

Czelusniak, Sandra. "The Crisis of Economic Literacy." ATCA in the News, Spring/Summer, 2009. Washington, DC: American Council of Trustee and Alumni. https://www.goacta.org/news/the_crisis_of_economic_illiteracy.

Daniels, Mitch. *Keeping the Republic: Saving America by Trusting Americans*. New York: Penguin, 2011.

"David J. Skorton to Deborah Birx." [Private correspondence] April 13, 2020. Association of American Medical Colleges. https://www.aamc.org/system/files/2020-04/ocomm-ogr-skorton-letter-diagnostic-testing.pdf.

Del Faltore, Joan. *What Johnny Shouldn't Read: Textbook Censorship in America*. New Have, CT: Yale University Press, 1992.

Democracy Now! "'Nobody Wants to do This:' Georgia Reopens Nonessential Businesses Despite Public health Warnings." Democracy Now! Transcript, April 24, 2020. https://www.democracynow.org/2020/4/24/georgia_lifts_lockdown_coronavirus.

Department of the Treasury. *The Economics of Higher Education*. Washington, DC: United States Department of Treasury, 2012. https://www.treasury.gov/connect/blog/documents/20121212_economics%20of%20higher%20ed_vfinal.pdf.

Dickenson, Tim. "The Four Men Responsible for America's COVID-19 Test Disaster." *Rolling Stone*, May 10, 2020. https://www.rollingstone.com/politics/politics-features/covid-19-test-trump-admin-failed-disaster-995930/.

Diehm, Jay, S. Petulla, and Z. Wolf. "Who has Left Trump's Administration and Orbit?" CNN, October 21, 2019. https://www.cnn.com/interactive/2017/08/politics/trump-admin-departures-trnd/.

Desa, Geoffrey, P. Howard, M. Gorzycki, and D. Allen. "Essential but Invisible: Collegiate Academic Reading Explored from the Faculty Perspective." *College Teaching* 68.3 (2020) 126–37.

Domina, Thurston. "Coronavirus School Closures Threaten America's Poorest Children." *U.S. News and World Report*, March 13, 2020. https://www.usnews.com/news/healthiest-communities/articles/2020–03-13/coronavirus-school-closings-threaten-americas-poorest-children.

Dunning, David. "The Dunning–Kruger Effect: On Being Ignorant of One's Own Ignorance." In *Advances in Experimental Social Psychology*, vol. 44, pp. 247–96. Academic Press, 2011.

Durkin, Erin. "Mass Burials Surge as New York City Set to Hit 100,000 Coronavirus Cases." *Politico New York*, April 10, 2020. https://www.politico.com/states/new-york/albany/story/2020/04/10/mass-burials-surge-as-new-york-city-set-to-hit-100-000-coronavirus-cases-1274835.

———. "NYC Death Toll Jumps by 37,000 After Uncounted Fatalities are Added." *Politico New York*, April 14, 2020. https://www.politico.com/states/new-york/albany/story/2020/04/14/new-york-city-coronavirus-death-toll-jumps-by-3-700-after-uncounted-fatalities-are-added-1275931.

Education Week. "Date: Breaking Down the Where and why of K-12 Spending." *Education Week*, September 24, 2019. https://www.edweek.org/ew/section/multimedia/the-where-and-why-of-k-12-spending.html.

Egalite, Anna J. "How Family Background Influences Student Achievement." *Education Next* (Spring 2016) 70–78. https://www.educationnext.org/files/ednext_XVI_2_egalite.pdf.

Egan, Laura. "Trump Calls Coronavirus Democrats 'New Hoax.'" NBC New, Feb. 28, 2020. https://www.nbcnews.com/politics/donald-trump/trump-calls-coronavirus -democrats-new-hoax-n1145721.

Elliot, Charles William. "Inaugural Address." In *Addresses at the Inauguration of Charles William Elliot as President of Harvard College, October 19, 1869.* Cambridge, MA: Sever and Francis, 1869.

Engstrom, Cathy, and V. Tinto. "Access without Support is not Opportunity." *Change: The Magazine of Higher Learning* 40.1 (2008) 46–50.

Etzkowitz, Henry, E. Schuler, Jr., and N. Gulbrandsen. "The Evolution of the Entrepreneurial University." In Merle Jacob and Tomas Hellström (Eds.), *The Future of Knowledge Production in the Academy*, pp. 40–60. Buckingham, UK: SRHE and Open University Press, 2000.

FAIR. "Interlocking Directorates." Fairness and Accuracy in Reporting, 2020. https://fair.org/interlocking-directorates/.

Fazey, Ioan. "Resilience and Higher Order Thinking." *Ecology and Society* 15.3 (2010).

Federal Emergency Management Agency. *2019 National Threat and Hazard Identification and Risk Assessment (THIRA).* U.S. Department of Homeland Security, July 25, 2019. https://www.fema.gov/media-library-data/1563998211160-f5da0c6offeb23 9845d2e577c953f136/2019NTHIRA_20190725_508c.pdf.

Feng, Emily. "Critics Say China has Suppressed and Censored Information in Coronavirus Outbreak." NPR, February 8, 2020. https://www.npr.org/sections/goatsandsoda/2020/02/08/803766743/critics-say-china-has-suppressed-and-censored-information-in-coronavirus-outbrea.

Fields, Zach. "Student Loan Debt Statistics in 2020: A Record $1.6 Trillion." *Forbes*, February 3, 2020. https://www.forbes.com/sites/zackfriedman/2020/02/03/student -loan-debt-statistics/#707ba9a6281f.

Finkelstein, James, and J. Wilde. "Bonuses and Benefits." *Inside Higher Education*, May 25, 2017. https://www.insidehighered.com/advice/2017/05/25/examination-growing-number-perks-and-bonuses-college-presidents-essay.

Fishel, Justin, E. Thomas, and L. Lantry. "Fact Check: Trump's Coronavirus Response Plagued with Misstatements." ABC News, March 16, 2020. https://abcnews.go.com/Politics/fact-check-friday-trumps-coronavirus-response-plagued-misstatements/story?id=69590582.

Fishman, Ethan M. "Counteracting Misconceptions about the Socratic Method." *College Teaching* 33.4 (1985) 185–88.

Forgey, Quint. "'We're Not a Shipping Clerk': Trump Tells Governors to Step Up Efforts to Get Medical Supplies. *Politico*, March 19, 2020. https://www.politico.com/news/2020/03/19/trump-governors-coronavirus-medical-supplies-137658.

Fottrell, Quentin. "Trump Floats Idea of Disinfectant for Coronavirus 'By Injection Inside or almost a Cleaning'—Later Says He was Speaking 'Sarcastically.'" *Market Watch*, April 24, 2020. https://www.marketwatch.com/story/trump-suggests-disinfectant

-as-treatment-for-coronavirus-by-injection-inside-or-almost-a-cleaning-doctors-call-the-idea-dangerous-2020–04-24?mod=article_inline.

Frank, Robert. "States with the Most Millionaires per Capita." CNBC, February 7, 2018. https://www.cnbc.com/2018/02/07/states-with-the-most-millionaires-per-capita.html.

Freire, Paulo. *Pedagogy of the Oppressed.* Transl. by Myra Berman Ramos. First published in 1968. New York: Bloomsbury, 2014.

Friedersdorf, Conor. "Firing Bad Teachers: A Superintendent and a Teacher's Union Official Debate." *The Atlantic Monthly*, June 29, 2014. https://www.theatlantic.com/education/archive/2014/06/firing-bad-teachers-a-superintendent-and-a-teachers-union-official-debate/373651/.

Fessenden, Tracy. "The Nineteenth Century Bible Wars and the Separation of Church and State." *Church History* 74.4 (2005) 784–811.

G, Deyan. "How Much time do People Spend on Social Media in 2020?" *Techjury*, June 15, 2020. https://techjury.net/blog/time-spent-on-social-media/#gref.

Garcia, Emma, and E. Weiss. *Reducing and Averting Achievement Gaps. Key Findings from the report 'Education Inequalities at the School Starting Gate' and Comprehensive Strategies to Mitigate Early Skills Gaps.* Washington, DC: Economic Policy Institute, September 27, 2017. https://files.epi.org/pdf/130888.pdf.

Garrett, R., D. and R. Legon. *CHOLE 4: Navigating the Mainstream, the Changing Landscape of Online Education*, 2020. https://www.qualitymatters.org/sites/default/files/research-docs-pdfs/CHLOE-4-Report-2020-Navigating-the-Mainstream.pdf.

Gaviria, Marcela, and M. Smith. "The Virus: What Went Wrong?" [Transcript] Frontline, PBS, June 2020. https://www.pbs.org/wgbh/frontline/film/the-virus/transcript/.

Gearan, Anne, M. DeBonis, and B. Dennis. "Trump Says Testing 'Isn't Necessary' as U.S. Falls short of Benchmarks." *Anchorage Daily News*, May 9, 2020. https://www.adn.com/nation-world/2020/05/08/trump-says-testing-isnt-necessary-as-us-falls-short-of-benchmarks/.

Geisler, Cheryl. "Academic Literacy and the Nature of Expertise: Reading, Writing, and Knowing." In *Academic Philosophy*, pp. 81–98. Hillsdale, NJ: Lawrence Erlbaum Associates Publishing, 1994.

Gillespie, Claire. "This is How Many People Die from the Flu Each Year, According to the CDC." *Health*, March 26, 2020. https://www.health.com/condition/cold-flu-sinus/how-many-people-die-of-the-flu-every-year.

Gindler, Jacqueline, S. Tinker, L. Markowitz, and W. Atkinson. "Acute Measles Morality in the United States, 1987–2002." *Journal of Infectious Diseases* 221.8 (2004) 69–77.

Ginsberg, Benjamin. *The Fall of the Faculty. The Rise of the All-Administrative University and Why it Matters.* New York: Oxford University Press, 2011.

Global Biodefense. "CDC Update: Failed Roll-Out of Diagnostic Due to Faulty Reagent; Sample Prioritization Mishap Delayed COVID-19 Diagnosis. Global Biodefense, February 13, 2020. https://globalbiodefense.com/2020/02/13/cdc-update-bumpy-roll-out-of-diagnostic-kits-due-to-faulty-reagent-sample-prioritization-mishap-delayed-covid-19-diagnosis/.

———. "German Researchers Develop 1st Test for New Coronavirus." Global Biodefense, January 17, 2020. https://globalbiodefense.com/newswire/german-researchers-develop-1st-test-for-new-coronavirus/.

Goldstein, Dana, A. Popescu, and N. Hannah-Jones. "As Schools Move Online, Many Students Logged Out." *New York Times*, April 8, 2020. https://www.nytimes.com/2020/04/06/us/coronavirus-schools-attendance-absent.html.

Gorzycki, Meg, G. Desa, P. Howard, and D. Allen. "Reading Is Important," but "I Don't Read": Undergraduates' Experiences With Academic Reading." *Journal of Adolescent & Adult Literacy* (2020).

Gorzycki, Meg, P. Howard, G. Desa, D. Allen and E. Rosegard. "An Exploration of Academic Reading Proficiency at the University Level: A Cross-sectional Study of 848 Undergraduates." *Literacy Research and Instruction* 55.2 (2016) 142–62.

Grabar, Mary. "The Ugly Truth behind a College's 'Diversity' Requirement." The James G. Martin Center for Academic Renewal, July 22, 2016. https://www.jamesgmartin.center/2016/07/ugly-truth-behind-colleges-diversity-requirement/.

Gray, Peter. "Declining Student Resilience: A Serious Problem for Colleges." *Psychology Today* 22 (2015) 9–15. https://www.psychologytoday.com/us/blog/freedom-learn/201509/declining-student-resilience-serious-problem-colleges.

Green, Francis, and D. Kynaston. *Engines of Privilege. Britain's Private School Problem.* London: Bloomsbury, 2019.

Greenstone, Michale, A. Looney, J. Pasternik, and M. Yu. "Thirteen Economic Facts about Social Mobility and the Role of Education." Brookings, June 26, 2013. https://www.brookings.edu/research/thirteen-economic-facts-about-social-mobility-and-the-role-of-education/.

Guzman-Lopez, Adolfo. "More Than a Third of Cal-State Freshmen Ill-Prepared for College Level Math, English." KPCC, April 19, 2014. https://www.scpr.org/blogs/education/2014/02/19/15882/more-than-a-third-of-cal-state-freshman-ill-prepar/.

Halpern, Diane F., and M. D. Hakel. "Applying the Science of Learning to the University and Beyond: Teaching for Long-Term Retention and Transfer." *Change* 35.4 (2003) 36–41.

Hanushek, Eric A., L. Talpey, P. E. Peterson, and L. Woessmann. "The Achievement Gap Fails to Close." *Education Next* 19.3. (Summer, 2019). https://www.educationnext.org/achievement-gap-fails-close-half-century-testing-shows-persistent-divide/.

Harris, Colleen S. "The Case for Partnering Doctoral Students with Librarians: A Synthesis of the Literatures." *Library Review* 60.7 (2011) 599–620.

Hart, C. "Factors Associated with Student Persistence in an Online Program of Study: A Review of the Literature. *Journal of Interactive Online Learning*, 11.1 (2012) http://itecideas.pbworks.com/w/file/fetch/58620369/Factors%20Associated%20With%20Student%20Persistence%20in%20an%20Online%20Program%20of%20Study.pdf.

Hart Research Associates. *Fulfilling the American Dream: Liberal Education and the Future of Work.* Washington, DC: Hart Research Associates, 2018. https://www.aacu.org/sites/default/files/files/LEAP/2018EmployerResearchReport.pdf.

Hartman, Katherine B., and J. B. Hunt. "What RateMyProfessors. com Reveals about How and Why Students Evaluate Their Professors: A Glimpse into the Student Mind-Set." *Marketing Education Review* 23.2 (2013) 151–62.

Hastings, Justin S., B. C. Madrian, and W. L. Skimmyhorn. "Financial Literacy, Financial Education, and Economic Outcomes." NEBR Working Paper Series. Cambridge, MA: National Bureau of Economic Research. (2012).

Heck, Patrick R., D. Simons, and C. F. Chabris. "65% of Americans Believe They are Above Average in Intelligence Results of Two Nationally Representative Surveys." *PLoS One* 13.7 (2018). https://www.ncbi.nlm.nih.gov/pmc/articles/PMC6029792/.

Hellerstein, Erica. "Income Inequality on the Rise in California. In Some Counties, the Disparities are Extreme." *Cal Matters*, October 7, 2019. https://calmatters.org/california-divide/2019/10/income-inequality-is-on-the-rise-in-california-in-some-counties-the-disparities-are-extreme/.

Herman, Edward S. and N. Chomsky. *Manufacturing Consent. The Political Economy of Mass Media*. New York: Pantheon, 2008.

Herman, Peter. "Opinion: There's No End—and No Accounting—to CSU's Administrative Bloat." *Times of San Diego*, April 25, 2017. https://timesofsandiego.com/opinion/2017/04/25/theres-no-end-and-no-accounting-to-csus-administrative-bloat/.

Herscowitz, Eva. "Timeline: Pritzker's Feud with Trump over COVID-19 Response." *The Daily Northwestern*, May 4, 2020. https://dailynorthwestern.com/2020/05/04/city/timeline-pritzkers-feud-with-trump-over-covid-19-response/.

Hess, Abigale. "Here's How Much Colleges Cost When You Were Born. CNBC Make It, September 4, 2019. https://www.cnbc.com/2019/09/04/heres-how-much-college-cost-the-year-you-were-born.html.

———. "Some Students are Considering Dropping Out of College because of the Coronavirus." CNBC, April 29, 2020. https://www.cnbc.com/2020/04/28/students-are-dropping-out-of-college-because-of-coronavirus.html.

Hibbs, Janet, and A. Rostain. "Rising Rates of College Mental health Services Demand." *Psychology Today*, January 13, 2019. https://www.psychologytoday.com/us/blog/the-stressed-years-their-lives/201901/rising-rates-college-mental-health-services-utilization.

Hiltonsmith, Robert. "Pulling Up the Higher-Ed Ladder: The Myth and Reality of the Crisis in College Affordability." Demos, 2015. https://www.demos.org/sites/default/files/publications/Robbie%20admin-bloat.pdf.

Hirsch, Lauren. "Trump Says, 'Anybody Who Wants a Test Gets a Test' After Pence Says US Can't Meet Coronavirus Testing Demand." CNBC, March 6, 2020. https://www.cnbc.com/2020/03/06/trump-anybody-who-wants-a-test-gets-a-test-amid-shortage-for-coronavirus.html.

Hoeft, Mary E. "Why University Students Don't Read: What Professors Can Do To Increase Compliance." *International Journal for the Scholarship of Teaching and Learning* 6.2 (2012) n2.

Hofer, Barbara K. "Personal Epistemology Research: Implications for Learning and Teaching." *Educational Psychology Review* 13.4 (2001) 353–83.

Hofstadter, Richard. *Anti-Intellectualism in American Life*. New York: Knopf, 1963.

Holman, Myra, E. Key, and R. Kreitzer. "Evidence of Bias in Standard Evaluations of Teaching." https://docs.google.com/document/d/14JiF-fT—F3Qaefjv2jMRFRWUS8TaaT9JjbYke1fgxE/edit.

Holland, Steve. "Exclusive: Trump Says China Wants Him to Lose Re-Election Bid. Reuters, April 29, 2020. https://www.reuters.com/article/us-usa-trump-china-exclusive/exclusive-trump-says-china-wants-him-to-lose-his-bid-for-re-election-idUSKBN22C01F.

House Appropriations Committee. "Lowey, DeLauro Urge Administration to Request Emergency Funding for Coronavirus Response." United States House of Representatives, February 4, 2020. https://appropriations.house.gov/news/press-releases/lowey-delauro-urge-administration-to-request-emergency-funding-for-coronavirus.

How Colleges Spend Money. "Find a College." American Council of Trustees and Alumni, 2020. https://www.howcollegesspendmoney.com/.

Howard, Pamela. J., M. Gorzycki, G. Desa, and D. Allen. "Academic Reading: Comparing Students' and Faculty Perceptions of Its Value, Practice, and Pedagogy." *Journal of College Reading and Learning* 48, no.3 (2018) 189–209.

Humphreys, Debra. *Making the Case for Liberal Education. Responding to Challenges.* Washington, DC: Association of American Colleges and Universities, 2006. https://secure.aacu.org/AACU/PDF/LEAP_MakingtheCase_Final.pdf.

Ihara, Rachel, and A. Del Principe. "'I Bought the Book and I Didn't Need It': What Reading Looks like at an Urban Community College." CUNY Academic Works. (2016). https://academicworks.cuny.edu/cgi/viewcontent.cgi?article=1111&context=kb_pubs.

Inequality. "Global Inequality." Institute for Policy Studies, 2020. https://inequality.org/facts/global-inequality/#us-wealth-concentration.

Ingram, LaDrea, and B. Wallace. "'It Creates Fear and Divides Us': Minority College Students' Experience of Stress from Racism, Coping Responses, and Recommendations for Colleges." *Journal of Health Disparities Research and Practice* 12.1 (Spring 2019) 80–112.

Intercollegiate Studies Institute's National Civic Literacy Board. *Our Fading Heritage: Americans Fail a Basic test on Their History and Institutions.* Wilmington, DE: Intercollegiate Studies Institutes, 2008. http://static1.1.sqspcdn.com/static/f/307420/2544285/1235086147343/ISI+Civic+Literacy+Report+08–09.pdf?token=v%2FOWE474sZgvC9uqNhZTew4LdEA%3D.

International Institute for Applied Systems Analysis. "Negotiating with Terrorists: A Mediator's Guide." Laxenburg, Austria. International Institute for Applied systems Analysis. March, 2009. https://www.jstor.org/stable/pdf/resrep24552.pdf?refreqid=excelsior%3Af3f7b7eb9ea612440e96c4d2d6fc75.

Intersegmental Committee of the Academic Senates of the California Community Colleges, the California State University, and the University of California. *Academic Literacy: A Statement of Competencies of Students Entering California's Public Colleges and Universities.* Sacramento, CA: Academic Senate for California Community Colleges, 1002.

Jack, Zachary Michael. "Gen-Ed Revision Could be Gen-Ed Reduction." *Inside Higher Education,* April 5, 2018. https://www.insidehighered.com/views/2018/04/05/colleges-should-consider-halving-gen-ed-curriculum-requirements-opinion.

Jacobs, Ken. "The High Cost of Furloughs." The Berkeley Center for Labor Research and Education. Policy Brief, October, 2009. Berkeley, CA: Berkeley Labor Center, 1009. http://laborcenter.berkeley.edu/pdf/2009/furloughs09.pdf.

Jaschik, Scott, and D. Lederman. "2019 Faculty Survey of Faculty Attitudes on Technology. A Study by Higher Ed and Gallup." Washington, DC: Inside Higher Ed, 2019. https://www.insidehighered.com/system/files/media/IHE_2019_Faculty_Tech_Survey_20191030.pdf.

Jensen, Eric. *Brain-Based Learning.* Thousand Oaks, CA: Corwin. 2008.

Johnson, Kevin, W. Cummings, and J. Fritze. "Trump Says He'll Speak to All 50 Governors and Will Be 'Authorizing' Reopenings. States Disagree on His Role." *USA*

Today, April 14, 2020. https://www.usatoday.com/story/news/politics/2020/04/14/coronavirus-governors-not-trump-have-total-authority-re-open/2989205001/.

Johnson, Sydney. "California Moves to Close Digital Divide as Schools Shift Online." *Ed Source*, April 16, 2020. https://edsource.org/2020/california-moves-to-close-digital-divide-as-schools-shift-online/629281.

Jones, Paula, M. Kolloff, and F. Kolloff. "Students' Perspectives on Humanizing and Establishing Teacher Presence in an Online Course." In *Society for Information Technology & Teacher Education International Conference*, pp. 460–65. Association for the Advancement of Computing in Education (AACE), 2008.

Jowett, Garth S., and V. O'Donnell. *Propaganda and Persuasion*, 6th ed. Thousand Oaks, CA: Sage, 2015.

Judin, Nick. "Governor Rejects State Lockdown for COVID-19: 'Mississippi is Never Going to be China.'" *Jackson Free Press*, March 23, 2020. https://www.jacksonfreepress.com/news/2020/mar/23/governor-rejects-state-lockdown-covid-19-mississip/.

Kadison, Richard, and T. F. DiGeronimo. *College of the Overwhelmed: The Campus Mental Health Crisis and What to Do about It*. San Francisco, CA: Jossey-Bass, 1004.

Kagan, Julie, "How Much Income Puts you in the Top 1%, 5%, 10%?" *Investopia*, November 21, 2019. https://www.investopedia.com/personal-finance/how-much-income-puts-you-top-1-5-10/.

Kamenetz, Anya. "4 in 10 U.S. Teens Say They Haven't Done Online Learning since Schools Closed." NPR, April 8, 2020. https://www.npr.org/sections/coronavirus-live-updates/2020/04/08/829618124/4-in-10-u-s-teens-say-they-havent-done-online-learning-since-schools-closed.

Kaplan, Ivy. "Breaking Down Administrative Bloat." *The College Post*, April 24, 2019. https://thecollegepost.com/breaking-down-administrative-bloat/.

Kauffman, Heather. "A Review of Predictive Factors of Student Success in and Satisfaction with Online Learning." *Research in Learning Technology* 23 (2015) 1–13.

Kenen, Joanne. "How Testing Failures Allow coronavirus to Sweep the U.S." *Politico*, March 6, 2020. https://www.politico.com/news/2020/03/06/coronavirus-testing-failure-123166.

Kennedy, Brian, and M. Hefferon. "What Americans Know about Science." Pew Research Center, March 28, 2019. https://www.pewresearch.org/science/2019/03/28/what-americans-know-about-science/.

Kerr, Clark. *The Uses of the University*. Cambridge, MA: Harvard University Press, 1963.

Kerr, Emma. "What You'll Pay for an Online Bachelor's Degree." *U.S. News & World Report*, January 14, 2020. https://www.usnews.com/higher-education/online-education/articles/what-youll-pay-for-an-online-bachelors-degree.

Kerr, Marcel S., K. Rynearson, and M. C. Kerr. "Student Characteristics for Online Learning Success." *The Internet and Higher Education* 9.2 (2006) 91–105.

Kezar, Adrianna. "Curing Programitis to Create Divers Success." *Inside Higher Education*, January 29, 2020. https://www.insidehighered.com/views/2020/01/29/transformational-change-needed-campuses-adequately-serve-diverse-new-student-body.

Kline, Joel. "The Failure of American Schools." *The Atlantic*, June (2011). https://www.theatlantic.com/magazine/archive/2011/06/the-failure-of-american-schools/308497/.

Klein, Naomi. "Screen New Deal." *The Intercept*, May 8, 2020. https://theintercept.com/2020/05/08/andrew-cuomo-eric-schmidt-coronavirus-tech-shock-doctrine/.

Kremer, Rich. "Administration Within UW System Grew While Faculty Numbers Decline." *WPR News*, September 11, 2019. https://www.wpr.org/administration-within-uw-system-grew-while-faculty-numbers-declined.

Kronman, Anthony T. *Education's End. Why Our Colleges and Universities have Given Up on the Meaning of Life*. New Haven, CY: Yale University Press, 2007.

Koseff, Alexi, "California Coronavirus Budget is Grim: Deficits Top $54 Billion. *San Francisco Chronicle*, May 7, 2020. https://www.sfchronicle.com/politics/article/California-coronavirus-budget-is-grim-Deficit-15253695.php.

———. "CSU Eliminates Remedial Classes in Push to Improve Graduation Rates." *The Sacramento Bee*, August 3, 2017. https://www.sacbee.com/news/politics-government/capitol-alert/article165342632.html.

Krisberg, Kim. "President's Budget would Hinder U.S. Public Health Progress: Huge Cuts Proposed." *The Nation's Health* 49, 3: 1–14. (May, 2019). http://thenationshealth.aphapublications.org/content/49/3/1.2.

Kupferschmidt, Kai. "Study Claiming New Coronavirus Can Be Transmitted by People Without Symptoms Was Flawed." *Science*, February 3, 2020. https://www.sciencemag.org/news/2020/02/paper-non-symptomatic-patient-transmitting-coronavirus-wrong.

Kuruvilla, Carol. "Amid the COVID-19 Spread, D.C. Pastor says 'God's Wrath' Caused by LGBTQ People. *Huffington Post*, March 27, 2020. https://www.huffpost.com/entry/ralph-drollinger-coronavirus-lgbtq-evangelical-christian_n_5e7cc7cdc5b6cb08a92964e1.

Legal Information Institute. "Freedom of Expression—Speech and Press." Cornell Law School, 2020. https://www.law.cornell.edu/constitution-conan/amendment-1/freedom-of-expression-speech-and-press.

Learner, Sharon. "Trumps Deadly Mistake in Comparing Coronavirus to Flu. *The Intercept*, March 25, 2020. https://theintercept.com/2020/03/25/coronavirus-flu-comparison-trump/.

Lee, Bandy X. *The Dangerous Case of Donald Trump. 37 Psychiatrists and Mental Health Experts Assess a President*. New York: St. Martin's, 2019.

Leef, George. "What Do College 'Chief Diversity Officers' Accomplish?" James G. Martin Center for Academic Renewal. October 26, 2018. https://www.jamesgmartin.center/2018/10/what-do-college-chief-diversity-officers-accomplish/.

Lei, Simon A., K. A. Bartlett, S. E. Gorney, and T. R. Herschbach. "Resistance to Reading Compliance among College Students: Instructors' Perspectives." *College Student Journal* 44.2 (2010) 219–29.

Lenthang, Marlene. "Protestors Waving MAGA Flags Defy Social Distancing and Swarm the Steps of Michigan's State Capitol to Demand Gov. Gretchen Whitmer End Her Strict Stay-At-Home Orders Because 'They Restrict Freedom and Are Against the Constitution.'" *The Daily Mail*, April 15, 2020. https://www.dailymail.co.uk/news/article-8223017/Thousands-protest-Michigan-state-Capitol-against-states-stay-home-orders.html.

Levi, Kenneth J. *Violence and Religious Commitment: Implications of Jim Jones' Peoples' Temple Movement*. University Park, PA: Penn State University Press, 1990.

Levin, Bess. "Lysol Manufacturer Warns Trump is a Dangerous Moron. 'Under No Circumstance' Should Disinfectant be Injected in Body." *Vanity Fair*, April 24,

2020. https://www.vanityfair.com/news/2020/04/donald-trump-lysol-coronavirus-warning.

———. "Of Course Jared Kushner Told Trump the Coronavirus was Fake News." *Vanity Fair*, March 17, 2020. https://www.vanityfair.com/news/2020/03/jared-kushner-coronavirus-fake-news.

———. "Trump Claims Coronavirus Will 'Miraculously' Go Away by April." *Vanity Fair*, February 11, 2020. https://www.vanityfair.com/news/2020/02/donald-trump-coronavirus-warm-weather.

Lewis, Harry R. *Excellence without a Soul. How a Great University forget Education.* New York: Public Affairs, 2006.

Lizotte, Brian L. "The Diversity Rationale: Unprovable, Uncompelling." *Michigan Journal of Race and Law* 11, (2006) 625–99.

Lynch, Matthew. "Top 3 Reasons Why the US Should Switch to Year-Round Schooling." *The Advocate*, August 13, 2018. https://www.theedadvocate.org/top-3-reasons-the-us-should-switch-to-year-round-schooling/.

———. "Year-Round Schools: 10 Things that You Should Know." *The Advocate*, April 15, 2017. https://www.theedadvocate.org/10-things-know-year-round-schools/.

Ma, Josephine. "Coronavirus: China's First Confirmed COVID-19 Case Traced Back to November 17." *South China Morning Post*, March 13, 2020. https://www.scmp.com/news/china/society/article/3074991/coronavirus-chinas-first-confirmed-covid-19-case-traced-back.

Maggioni, L., and M. Parkinson. "The Role of Teacher Epistemic Cognition, Epistemic Beliefs, and Calibration in Instruction." *Educational Psychology Review* 20.4 (2008) 445–61.

Magolda, Marcia B. Baxter. "Students' Epistemologies and Academic Experiences: Implications for Pedagogy." In Karen D. Arnold and Ida Carreiro King (Eds.), *College Student Development and Academic Life: Psychological, Intellectual, Social, and Moral Issues*, pp. 117–40. New York: Routledge, 2013.

Makunda, Gautam. "Why Staff Turnover in the White House is such a Bad Thing—Especially for Trump." *Harvard Business Review, April 6, 2018.* https://hbr.org/2018/04/why-staff-turnover-in-the-white-house-is-such-a-bad-thing-especially-for-president-trump.

Manarin, Karen. "Reading Value: Student Choice in Reading Strategies." *Pedagogy* 12.2. (2012) 281–97.

Manarin, Karen, M. Carey, M. Rathbun, and G. Ryland. *Critical Reading in Higher Education. Academic Goals and Social Engagement.* Bloomington, IN: Indiana University Press, 2015.

Maragakis, Lisa Lockerd. "Coronavirus 2019 vs. the Flu." Health. Johns Hopkins University, 2020. https://www.hopkinsmedicine.org/health/conditions-and-diseases/coronavirus/coronavirus-disease-2019-vs-the-flu.

Mark, Michelle. "Trump Learned of a Memo in January Warning 'Half a Million American Souls' Could Die of Coronavirus, and He was Displeased His Advisor put it in Writing." *Business Insider*, April 11, 2020. https://www.businessinsider.com/trump-peter-navarro-january-memo-coronavirus-deaths-2020-4.

Maxouris, Christine. "Some Americans Take a Holiday from Social Distancing and Officials Fear Spike in Coronavirus Cases." CNN, May 25, 2020. https://www.cnn.com/2020/05/25/health/us-coronavirus-memorial-day/index.html.

Maxouris, Christine, H. Yan, and R. Ellis. "Cities Extend Curfews for Another Night in an Attempt to Avoid Violent Protest over George Floyd's Death." CNN, May 31, 2020. https://www.cnn.com/2020/05/31/us/george-floyd-protests-sunday/index.html.

McCardle, Mairead. "Markets Suffer Worst Day of COVID-19 Crisis as Stocks Nosedive." National Review, March 16, 2020. https://www.nationalreview.com/news/corona virus-outbreak-markets-suffer-worst-day-of-crisis-as-stocks-nosedive/.

McClellan, B. Edward. Moral Education in America: Schools and the Shaping of Character from Colonial Times to the Present. New York: Teachers College, Columbia University, 1999.

McKeachie, Wilbert J. "Research on College Teaching: The Background." Journal of Educational Psychology 82.2 (1990) 189–200.

McMurthie, Beth. "Students Without Laptops, Instructors Without Internet: How Struggling Colleges Move Online During COVID-19." Chronicle of Higher Education, April 6, 2020.

Melia, Michael, J. Amy, and L. Fenn. "AP: 3 Million US Students Don't Have Home Internet." AP, June 10, 2019. https://apnews.com/7f263b8f7d3a43d6be014f860d 5e4132.

Merrill, Dave, and E. Dey. "What the Dow's 28% Crash Tells us about the Economy." Bloomberg, March 18, 2020. https://www.bloomberg.com/graphics/2020-stock-market-recover-dow-industrial-decline/.

Miller, Michelle D. "5 Takeaways from My Covid-19 Remote Teaching." Chronicle Vitae, May 6, 2020. https://chroniclevitae.com/news/2348–5-takeaways-from-my-covid-19-remote-teaching?cid=VTEVPMSED1.

Milman, Oliver. Trump Administration Cut Pandemic Early Warning system in September. The Guardian, April 3, 2020. https://www.theguardian.com/world /2020/apr/03/trump-scrapped-pandemic-early-warning-program-system-before -coronaviru.

Minnesota Department of Education. Minnesota K-12 Academic Standards, Social Studies, 2011. St. Paul, MN: Minnesota Department of Education, 2013.

Monmaney, Terrence. "How Much Do Americans Know about Science?" The Smithsonian, May, 2013. https://www.smithsonianmag.com/innovation/how-much-do-americans-know-about-science-27747364/.

Moore, Rebecca. Understanding Jonestown and the People's Temple. Santa Barbara, CA: Praeger, 2009.

Moore, Raeal, D. Vitale, and N. Stanwinoga. The Digital Divide and Educational Equity. A Look at Students with Very Limited Access to Technology at Home. ACT Center for Educational Equity, August, 2018. https://www.act.org/content/dam/act/ unsecured/documents/R1698-digital-divide-2018–08.pdf.

Moreno, J. Edward. "Government Health Agency Official: Coronavirus 'Isn't Something the American Public Need to Worry About." The Hill, January 26, 2020. https:// thehill.com/homenews/sunday-talk-shows/479939-government-health-agency-official-corona-virus-isnt-something-the.

———. "Trump Threatened to Fire CDC's Chief of Respiratory Diseases in February: Report." The Hill, April 22, 2020. https://thehill.com/homenews/administration /494187-trump-threatened-to-fire-cdcs-chief-of-respiratory-diseases-in.

Mossburg, Cheri, R. Ellis, A. Watts, and S. Almasy. "US Sees a Record Number of New Coronavirus Cases Reported in a Single Day." CNN, July 1, 2020. https://www.cnn.com/2020/07/01/health/us-coronavirus-wednesday/index.html.

Mower, Lawrence. "No Statewide Shutdown for Florida, DeSantis Says, Because White House Hasn't Advised It." *Miami Herald*, March 31, 2020. https://www.miamiherald.com/news/politics-government/state-politics/article241660601.html.

Murphy, Paul. "Why Districts are Reluctant to Let Even Struggling Teachers Go." *Teacher Habits*, December 3, 2019. http://teacherhabits.com/why-districts-are-reluctant-to-let-even-struggling-teachers-go/.

Nair, Arathy S. "DuPont Settles Lawsuits over Leak of Chemical used to Make Teflon." Reuters, February 13, 2017. https://www.reuters.com/article/us-du-pont-lawsuit-west-virginia/dupont-settles-lawsuits-over-leak-of-chemical-used-to-make-teflon-idUSKBN15S18U.

National Center for Educational Statistics. "Economics 2012. National Assessment of Educational Progress at Grade 12." Washington, DC: U.S. Department of education, 2012. https://www.nces.ed.gov/nationsreportcard/subject/publications/main2012/pdf/2013453.pdf.

———. *Reading, 2011*. The Nation's Report Card. Washington, DC: U.S. Department of Education, 2011. https://nces.ed.gov/nationsreportcard/pdf/main2011/2012457.pdf.

———. Results from the 2019 Mathematics and Reading Assessments. The Nation's Report Card. [Infographic]. United States Department of Education, 2019. https://www.nationsreportcard.gov/mathematics/supportive_files/2019_infographic.pdf.

National Commission on Excellence in Education. *A Nation at Risk: the Imperative for Educational Reform*. Washington, DC: United States Printing Office, 1983. https://www.edreform.com/wp-content/uploads/2013/02/A_Nation_At_Risk_1983.pdf.

National Institutes for Research. *The Literacy of America's College Students*. National Institutes for Research, 2009. https://www.air.org/sites/default/files/downloads/report/The%20Literacy%20of%20Americas%20College%20Students_final%20report_0.pdf.

Newman, Omarosa Manigault. *Unhinged: An Insider's Account of the Trump White House*. New York: Gallery, 2018.

New York State. "Amid Ongoing COVID-19 Pandemic, Governor Cuomo Calls for Federal Coordination of Supply Chain to Bring Testing to Scale." April 18, 2020. https://www.governor.ny.gov/news/amid-ongoing-covid-19-pandemic-governor-cuomo-calls-federal-coordination-supply-chain-bring.

Nixon, Richard. "Transcripts of David Frost's Interview with Richard Nixon." 1977. Teaching American History. https://docs.house.gov/meetings/JU/JU00/20191211/110331/HMKP-116-JU00-20191211-SD408.pdf.

Obama, Barack. "Remarks by President on Research for Potential Ebola Vaccines." Speech, Washington, DC, December 2, 2014. The White House. https://obamawhitehouse.archives.gov/the-press-office/2014/12/02/remarks-president-research-potential-ebola-vaccines.

———. "Remarks to the United States Hispanic Chamber of Commerce" [Speech, Washington, DC, March 10, 2009]. The American Presidency Project, University of California, Santa Barbara. https://www.presidency.ucsb.edu/documents/remarks-the-united-states-hispanic-chamber-commerce-1.

O'Banion, Terry. "A Brief History of General Education." *Community College Journal of Research and Practice* 40.4 (2016) 327–34.

Ollstein, Alice Miranda. "Trump Halts funding to world Health Organization." *Politico,* April 14, 2020. https://www.politico.com/news/2020/04/14/trump-world-health-organization-funding-186786.

Oprysko, Catlin, and S. Luthi. "Trump Labels Himself "A Wartime President" combating Coronavirus." *Politico,* March 18, 2020. https://www.politico.com/news/2020/03/18/trump-administration-self-swab-coronavirus-tests-135590.

Ordonez, Victor. "Pending Applications for Unemployment Benefits Mark a Month without Income for Many in COVUD Pandemic." ABC News, April 17, 2020. https://abcnews.go.com/Business/pending-unemployment-applications-mark-month-income-covid-pandemic/story?id=70189883.

Osnos, Evan. "'An Abuse of Sacred Symbols': Trump, A Bible, and A Sanctuary." *The New Yorker,* June 2, 2020. https://www.newyorker.com/news/daily-comment/an-abuse-of-sacred-symbols-trump-a-bible-and-a-sanctuary.

O'Sullivan, Joseph. "President Trump Calls Inslee a 'Snake' after Governor and Pence Meet on Coronavirus." *Seattle Times,* March 6, 2020. https://www.seattletimes.com/seattle-news/politics/president-trump-calls-inslee-a-snake-after-governor-and-vice-presidents-bipartisan-meeting-on-coronavirus/.

Owings, William A., L. S. Kaplan, J. Nunnery, D. Blackburn, and S. Myran. "Teacher Quality and Troops to Teachers: A National Study with Implications for Principals." *NASSP Bulletin* 90.2 (2006) 102–31.

Parker, Kim. "The Growing Partisan Divide in Views of Higher Education," Pew Research Center, February 19, 2019. https://www.pewsocialtrends.org/essay/the-growing-partisan-divide-in-views-of-higher-education/.

Parker, Kim, et al. *The Digital Revolution in Higher Education.* Pew Research Center, August 28, 2011. https://files.eric.ed.gov/fulltext/ED524306.pdf.

Paul, Richard, and L. Elder. *How to Read a Paragraph.* Dillion Beach, CA: Foundation for Critical Thinking, 2003.

Perper, Rosie, A. Al-Arshani, and H. Secon. "More Than Half of the US Population is Under Orders to Stay at Home—Here's a List of Coronavirus Lockdowns." *Business Insider,* March 31, 2020. https://www.businessinsider.com/states-cities-shutting-down-bars-restaurants-concerts-curfew-2020-3.

Perrett, Connor. "The U.S. Surgeon General Once Warned against Wearing Face Masks for the Coronavirus but Now the CDC Recommends It." *Business Insider,* March 2, 2020. https://www.businessinsider.com/americans-dont-need-masks-pence-says-as-demand-increases-2020-2.

Perry, William. *Forms of Intellectual and Ethical Development in the College Years.* San Francisco, CA: Jossey-Bass, 1999.

Pew Research Center. "US Public Sees Multiple Treats from Coronavirus—And Concerns are Growing." March 18, 2020. https://www.people-press.org/2020/03/18/u-s-public-sees-multiple-threats-from-the-coronavirus-and-concerns-are-growing/.

———. "What Americans Know about Religion." Pew Research Center, Religion and Public Life, July 23, 2019. https://www.pewforum.org/2019/07/23/what-americans-know-about-religion/.

Phillips, Elizabeth D. Capaldi, and M. B. Poliakoff. *The Cost of Chaos in the Curriculum. Perspectives on Education.* Washington, DC: American Council of Trustees and Alumni, 2015. https://www.goacta.org/images/download/The_Cost_of_Chaos_in_the_Curriculum.pdf.

Porter, Tom. "Jared Kushner, Who's Operating a 'Shadow' Coronavirus Task Force, Appears Not to Know Why Stockpiles Exist." *Business Insider*, April 3, 2020. https://www.businessinsider.com/jared-kushner-coronavirus-briefing-federal-stockpiles-blames-states-ventilator-shortages-2020–4.

President's Commission on Higher Education. *Higher Education for American Democracy, Vol. I.* Washington, DC: Government Printing Office, 1947.

Prothero, Stephen. *Religious Literacy: What Every American Needs to Know—and Doesn't.* New York: HarperCollins, 2007.

Raikes, Jeff, and L. Darling-Hammond. "Why Our Education Funding Systems are De-Railing the American Dream." Palo Alto, CA: Learning Policy Institute. https://learningpolicyinstitute.org/blog/why-our-education-funding-systems-are-derailing-american-dream.

Rainey, James and E. Baumgaertner. "Trump, Congress Scramble to Revive virus Hunting Agency That was Marked for Cuts." *Philadelphia Enquirer*, April 12, 2020. https://www.inquirer.com/health/coronavirus/coronavirus-covid-usaid-global-health-bureau-pandemic-response-funding-20200412.html.

Range, Bret G.,H. E. Duncan, S. D. Scherz, and C. A. Haines. "School Leaders' Perceptions about Incompetent Teachers and Implications for Supervision and Evaluation." *NSSAP Bulletin* 96.4 (2012) 302–22.

Ranney, Megan L., V. Griffeth, and A. K. Jha. "Critical Supply Shortages—The Need for Ventilators and Personal Protective Equipment during the Covid-19 Pandemic." *New England Journal of Medicine* (2020). https://www.nejm.org/doi/full/10.1056/NEJMp2006141.

Rascoe, Ayesha, and T. Keith. "Trump Defends 'Law and Order' Symbolism of Photo-Op." NPR, KQED, June 3, 2020. https://www.npr.org/2020/06/03/868779265/trump-defends-symbolism-of-photo-op-at-st-johns-church.

Ravitch, Diane. "Why Teacher Unions are Good for Teachers—and the Public." *American Educator*, Winter (2006–2007). American Federation of Techers. https://www.aft.org/periodical/american-educator/winter-2006–2007/why-teacher-unions-are-good-teachers-and.

Raymond, Adam K. "The Rapid Increase of Coronavirus Deaths in One Chilling Graphic. *New York Intelligencer*, April 8, 2020. https://nymag.com/intelligencer/2020/04/the-rapid-increase-of-u-s-coronavirus-deaths-in-one-graphic.html.

Reich, Robert. *The System: Who Rigged It and How We Fix It.* New York: Alfred A. Knopf, 2020.

Renzulli, Kerri Anne, and C. Connley. "Here's What the Average NFL Player Makes in a Season. MSNBC, February 1, 2019. https://www.cnbc.com/2019/02/01/heres-what-the-average-nfl-players-makes-in-a-season.html.

Rettner, Rachael, "How does the New Coronavirus Compare with the Flu?" *Live Science*, May 14, 2020. https://www.livescience.com/new-coronavirus-compare-with-flu.html.

Richter, Felix. "The Generation Gap in TV Consumption." Statistia, August 19, 2019. https://www.statista.com/chart/15224/daily-tv-consumption-by-us-adults/.

Ricketts, Glenn, P. W. Wood, S. H. Balch, and A. Thorne. *The Vanishing West, 1964–2010: The Disappearance of Western Civilization from Undergraduate Education.* Princeton, NJ: National Association of Scholars, 2011. https://www.nas.org/storage/app/media/images/documents/TheVanishingWest.pdf.

Ring, Edward. "Why Teachers' Unions are the Worst of the Worst." California Policy Center. August 1, 2018. https://californiapolicycenter.org/why-teachers-unions-are-the-worst-of-the-worst/.

Robbins, A., A. Kaye, and J. C. Catling. "Predictors of Student Resilience in Higher Education." *Psychology Teaching Review* 24.1 (2018) 44–52.

Rollwage, Max, R. J. Dolan and S. M. Fleming. "Metacognitive Failure as a Feature of Those Holding Radical Beliefs." *Current Biology* 28, 4014–4021. (2018). https://www.cell.com/action/showPdf?pii=S0960-9822%2818%2931420-9.

Ronayne, Kathleen, and J. Lemire. "Flatter or Fight? Governors Seeking Help Must Navigate Trump." *AP News*, March 26, 2020. https://apnews.com/f9fb8c41b7f8acc215e3ec78ca32210a.

Rose, Joel. "A War for Medical Supplies: States Say FEMA Wins by Poaching Orders." NPR KQED, April 15, 2020. https://www.npr.org/2020/04/15/835308133/governors-say-fema-is-outbidding-redirecting-or-poaching-their-medical-supply-or.

Rosen, David. "God's Vengeance: The Christian Right and the Coronavirus." *Counterpunch*, March 27, 2020. https://www.counterpunch.org/2020/03/27/gods-vengeance-the-christian-right-and-the-coronavirus/.

Roser, Max, E. Ortiz-Espina, H. Richie, J. Hasell, C. Giattino, and R. McDonald. "Mortality Risk of COVID-19." Our World in Data. University of Oxford. June4, 2020. https://ourworldindata.org/mortality-risk-covid#the-case-fatality-rate.

Ross, Terris, G. Kena, A. Rathburn, A. K. Ramani, J. Zhang, P. Kristapovich, and E. Manning. *Higher Education: Gaps in Access and Persistence Study*. National Center for educational Statistics. Washington, DC: U.S. Department of Education. August, 20212. https://nces.ed.gov/pubs2012/2012046.pdf.

Rupar, Aaron. "Trump is Blaming Obama for Leaving Him with 'Broken Tests' for a Virus That didn't Exist. Yes, Really." Vox, April 30, 2020. https://www.vox.com/2020/4/30/21243117/trump-blames-obama-coronavirus-broken-tests-jim-acosta.

Ryan, Simon. "Critical Reading, Metacognition and Relevance in the Humanities." *International Journal of Learning*, 18.2 (2011) 159–65.

Ryan, T. E. "Motivating Novice Students to Read Their Textbooks." *Journal of Instructional Psychology* 33.2 (2006) 135–40.

Samms, Grant. "As Cities FaceCOVID-19, the Digital Divide Becomes More Acute. *Forbes*, April 2, 2020. https://www.forbes.com/sites/pikeresearch/2020/04/02/as-cities-face-covid-19-the-digital-divide-becomes-more-acute/#31f2a20458c5.

Samuels, Brett. "Trump Decries IG Report as 'Another Fake Dossier.'" *The Hill*, April 7, 2020. https://thehill.com/homenews/administration/491561-trump-decries-ig-report-on-hospital-shortages-as-another-fake-dossier.

Sarzyncki, Sarah. *Revolution in the Terra Do Sol: The Cold War in Brazil*. Stanford, CA: Stanford University Press, 2018.

Schumaker, Erin. "Timeline: How Coronavirus Got Started. *ABC News*, April 9, 2020. https://abcnews.go.com/Health/timeline-coronavirus-started/story?id=69435165.

Schuhmann, Peter W., K. M. Goldrick, and R. T. Burrus. "Student Quantitative Literacy: Importance, Measurement, and Correlation with Economic Literacy." *The American Economist* 49.1 (2005) 49–65.

Schultz, David. *American Politics in the Age of Ignorance. Why Lawmakers Choose Belief Over Research*. New York: Palgrave, 2013.

———. "The Anatomy of a Failing University." *CounterPunch*, May 4, 2020. https://www.counterpunch.org/2020/05/04/the-anatomy-of-a-failing-university/.

Schuster, Adam. "Illinois K-12 Districts Loosing Students, Gaining Administrators." Illinois Policy Center. August 27, 2019. https://www.illinoispolicy.org/illinois-k-12-school-districts-losing-students-gaining-administrators/.

Schwartz, Ian. "Limbaugh: I Hope Some Governor Grows so Fed Up With This Shutdown and Reopens Their State." *Real Clear Politics*, April 15, 2020. https://www.realclearpolitics.com/video/2020/04/15/limbaugh_i_hope_some_governor_grows_so_fed_up_with_this_shutdown_and_reopens_their_state.html.

———. "Trump on Coronavirus: 'Nobody Could have Predicted Something Like This.'" Real Clear Politics, March 30, 2020. https://www.realclearpolitics.com/video/2020/03/30/trump_on_coronavirus_nobody_could_have_predicted_something_like_this.html.

Semuels, Alana. "Good School, Rich School; Bad School, Poor School." *The Atlantic*, Aug. 25, 2016. https://www.theatlantic.com/business/archive/2016/08/property-taxes-and-unequal-schools/497333/.

Shanahan, Timothy, and C. Shanahan. "What is Disciplinary Literacy and Why Does it Matter?" *Topics in Language Disorders* 32, no.1 (2012) 7–18.

Shapiro, Harold. *A Larger Sense of Purpose: Higher Education and Society*. Princeton, NJ: Princeton University Press, 2005.

Shapiro, Sarah, and C. Brown. "A Look at Civics Education in the United States." American Educators, Summer 2018. https://www.aft.org/ae/summer2018/shapiro_brown.

———. "The State of Civics Education." Center for American Progress, February 21, 2018. https://www.americanprogress.org/issues/education-k-12/reports/2018/02/21/446857/state-civics-education/.

Shaw, Emily. "Researching the Educational Benefits of Diversity." Research Report No. 2005-4. New York: College Board, 2005. https://files.eric.ed.gov/fulltext/ED562839.pdf.

Shepard, Steven. "Poll: Don't Stop Social Distancing if Coronavirus Will Spread." *Politico*, April 15, 2020. https://www.politico.com/news/2020/04/15/poll-dont-stop-social-distancing-coronavirus-spread-187290.

Sidhu, Preety, and V. J. Calderon. "Many Business Leaders Doubt U.S. Colleges Prepare Students." Gallup, February 26, 2017. https://news.gallup.com/poll/167630/business-leaders-doubt-colleges-prepare-students.aspx.

Simon, Caroline. "Bureaucrats and Buildings: The Case for Why Colleges are So Expensive." *Forbes*, September 5, 2017. https://www.forbes.com/sites/carolinesimon/2017/09/05/bureaucrats-and-buildings-the-case-for-why-college-is-so-expensive/#1d92b001456a.

Simon, Morgan. "What the Stimulus Package Means for Everyday People, Not Corporations." *Forbes*, April 1, 2020. https://www.forbes.com/sites/morgansimon/2020/04/01/what-the-stimulus-package-means-for-everyday-people-not-corporations/#3f357a3371ff.

Skinner, Rebecca. *Year-Round Schools: In Brief*. Washington, DC: Congressional Research Service, June 9, 2014. https://fas.org/sgp/crs/misc/R43588.pdf.

Slisco, Aila. "Conservative Pastor Says Spreading of Coronavirus in Synagogues is God's Punishment to Jews for 'Opposing' Jesus Christ. *Newsweek*, March 26, 2020. https://www.newsweek.com/conservative-pastor-says-coronavirus-spreading-synagogues-gods-punishment-jews-opposing-1494578.

Smith, Ashely A. "Study Finds More Low-Income Students Attending College." *Inside Higher Education*, May 23, 2019. https://www.insidehighered.com/news/2019/05/23/pew-study-finds-more-poor-students-attending-college.

Smith, Christian. "Higher Education is Drowning in BS." *The Chronicle of Higher Education*, January 9, 2018. https://www.chronicle.com/article/Higher-Education-Is-Drowning/242195.

Smith, Joseph. *Brazil and the United States: Convergence and Divergence*. Series: United States and the Americas, ed. Lester D. Langley. Washington, DC: University of Georgetown Press, 2010.

Smith, Wilson, and T. Bender. "Introduction." In W. Smith and T. Bender, *American Higher Education Transformed* 1940–2005, pp. 1–11. Baltimore, MD: Johns Hopkins University Press, 2008.

Snyder, Thomas, ed. *120 Years of American Education: A Statistical Portrait*. Washington, DC: U.S. Department of Education, 1993. https://nces.ed.gov/pubs93/93442.pdf.

St. Clair-Thompson, Helen, A. Graham, and S. Marsham. "Exploring the Reading Practices of Undergraduate Students." *Education Inquiry* 9.3 (2018) 284–98.

Staddon, John. "Administrative Bloat: Where does it come From and What is it Doing?" The James G. Martin Center for Academic Renewal, July 19, 2019. https://www.jamesgmartin.center/2019/06/administrative-bloat-where-does-it-come-from-and-what-is-it-doing/.

Steinberg, Brian. "TV Ratings: Cable News Views Soar during Pandemic." *Variety*, April 28, 2020. https://variety.com/2020/tv/news/tv-ratings-cable-news-cnn-fox-news-msnbc-coronavirus-1234592202/.

Stout, Rebecca, C. Archie, D. Cross, and C. A. Carman. "The Relationship between Faculty Diversity and Graduation Rates in Higher Education." *Intercultural Education* 29.3 (2018) 399–417.

Strayhorn, Terell L. *College Students' Sense of Belonging: A Key to Educational Success for All Students*. New York: Routledge, 2019.

Stoddard, Hugh A., and D. V. O'Dell. "Would Socrates have used the 'Socratic Method' in Clinical Teaching?" *Journal of Internal Medicine* 31.9 (2016) 1092–96. https://www.ncbi.nlm.nih.gov/pmc/articles/PMC4978680/.

Subramanian, Courtney, N. Wu, and D. Jackson. "Trump Uses China as Foil When Talking Coronavirus, Distancing Himself from Criticism. *USA Today*, March 21, 2020. https://www.usatoday.com/story/news/politics/2020/03/20/coronavirus-trump-blames-china-distancing-himself-fallout/2876983001/.

Subramaniam, Tara, and H. Lybrand. "Fact Check: U.S. has Done More Coronavirus Tests than South Korea, but Not Per Person." CNN Politics, March 25, 2020. https://www.cnn.com/2020/03/25/politics/coronavirus-testing-trump-south-korea-fact-check/index.html.

Swasey, Benjamin. "Federal Scientist Says He Was Removed for Resisting Unproven Coronavirus Treatments." NPR, April 23, 2020. https://www.npr.org/sections/coronavirus-live-updates/2020/04/22/842013672/federal-doctor-says-he-was-removed-for-resisting-unproven-coronavirus-treatments.

Tabachnik, Sam. "'Either Be In or Out': Feds Swooped in on Colorado's Ventilator Order, Polis Says." *Denver Post*, April 4, 2020. https://www.denverpost.com/2020/04/04/coronavirus-colorado-polis-ventilators-fema/.

Tenpas, Kathryn Dunn. "Tracking Turnover in the Trump Administration. Brookings Institute, May 2020. https://www.brookings.edu/research/tracking-turnover-in-the-trump-administration/.

Thomas, Nancy L. "Teaching for a Strong, Deliberative Democracy." *Learning and Teaching* 2.3 (2009) 74–97.

Thorne, Ashley. "5 Consequences of Administrative Bloat." National Association of Scholars, August 10, 2010. https://www.nas.org/blogs/article/5_consequences_of_administrative_bloat.

Tinto, Vincent. "Dropout from Higher Education: A Theoretical Synthesis of Recent Research." *Review of Educational Research* 45.1 (1975) 89–125.

Towler, Luke. "Districts Weigh Pros and Cons of Year-Round Schools." *NEA Today*, September 4, 2014. http://neatoday.org/2014/09/04/districts-weigh-pros-and-cons-of-year-round-schools-2/.

Tribal Colleges and Universities. "Tribal Colleges Need Immediate Funding for COVID-19 Challenges." *Tribal Colleges. Journal of American Indians Higher Education*, March 24, 2020. https://tribalcollegejournal.org/tribal-colleges-need-immediate-funding-to-confront-covid-19-challenges/.

Trump, Donald. "Remarks by President Trump at Signing of the Coronavirus Preparedness and Response Supplemental Funding Act, 2020." White House, March 6, 2020. https://www.whitehouse.gov/briefings-statements/remarks-president-trump-signing-coronavirus-preparedness-response-supplemental-appropriations-act-2020/.

———. "Remarks by President Trump, Vice President Pence, and Members of the Coronavirus Task Force." White House, March 19, 2020. https://www.whitehouse.gov/briefings-statements/remarks-president-trump-vice-president-pence-members-coronavirus-task-force-press-briefing-6/.

Tucker, Pete. "Gov. Hogan's Purchase of Korean Covid Tests Looks Like a PR Stunt—and the Media Fell for It." *Extra! FAIR Magazine*, May 8, 2020. https://fair.org/home/gov-hogans-purchase-of-korean-covid-tests-looks-like-a-pr-stunt-and-media-fell-for-it/.

Turse, Nick. *The Complex. How the Military Invades Our Everyday Lives*. New York: Metropolitan, 2008.

United States. Executive Office of the President. *National Biodefense Strategy*, 2018. Washington, DC. https://www.hsdl.org/?view&did=815921

USA Facts. "More Than 9 Million Children Lack Internet Access at Home for Online Learning." USA Facts, 2020. https://usafacts.org/articles/internet-access-students-at-home/.

USAID. *Predict*. United States Agency for International Development. https://www.usaid.gov/sites/default/files/documents/1864/predict-global-flyer-508.pdf.

USAID Press Office. "USAID Launches Pandemic Threats Program." [Press release October 21, 2009]. Washington, D. C.: United States Agency for International Development. https://2012-2017.usaid.gov/news-information/press-releases/usaid-launches-emerging-pandemic-threats-program.

U.S. Department of Education. *America's Teachers: Profile of a Profession*. Washington, DC: U.S Department of Education, 1993. http://nces.ed.gov/pubs93/93025.pdf.

———. National Center for Education Statistics. Schools and Staffing Survey (SASS), Public School District Data File, 2007–08, Table 8. In Patrick McGuinn, "Ringing the Bell for K-12 Teacher Tenure Reform" (Washington: Center for American Progress, 2010).

Vaccaro, A. "What Lies Beneath Seemingly Positive Campus climate Results: Institutional Sexism, Racism, and Male Hostility toward Equity Initiatives and Liberal Bias." *Equity and Excellence in Education* 43.2 (2010) 202–15.

Vacchiano, Andrea. "College Pay Diversity Officers More than Professors, Staff." *The Daily Signal*, July 14, 2017. https://www.dailysignal.com/2017/07/14/colleges-pay-diversity-officers-more-than-professors-staff/.

Vafeas, Mario. "Attitudes Toward, and Use of, Textbooks among Undergraduates: An Exploratory Study. *Journal of Marketing Education* 35.3 (2013) 245–58.

Valverde, Miriam. "Donald Trump's Wrong Claim that 'Anybody' Can Get Tested for Coronavirus." Politifact. The Poynter Institute. March 6, 2020. https://www.politifact.com/factchecks/2020/mar/11/donald-trump/donald-trumps-wrong-claim-anybody-can-get-tested-c/.

Van Der Ark, Tom. "Learning for a Reason: 4 Levels of Engagement." Getting Smart, April 17, 2015. https://www.gettingsmart.com/2015/08/learning-for-a-reason-4-levels-of-engagement/.

Vanderwicken, Peter. "Why the News is Not the Truth." *Harvard Business Review*, May-June, 1995. https://hbr.org/1995/05/why-the-news-is-not-the-truth.

Vasquez, Meagan, and K. Homes. "Trump Targets Holmes in Attempt to Flip Testing Criticism Back on Governors." CNN Politics, April 20, 2020. https://www.cnn.com/2020/04/20/politics/mike-pence-governors-call-coronavirus-testing-supplies/index.htm.

Vedder, Richard. "Diversity and Other Monstrosities: The Case of the University of Michigan." *Forbes*, July 23, 2018. https://www.forbes.com/sites/richardvedder/2018/07/23/diversity-and-other-administrative-monstrousities-the-case-of-the-university-of-michigan/#221681d468ec.

Vianden, Jörg. "In All Honest, You Don't Learn Much: White College Men's Perceptions of Diversity Courses." *International Journal of Teaching and Learning in Higher Education* 30.3 (2018) 465–76.

Vinton, Kate. "These 15 Billionaires Own America's News Media Companies. *Forbes*, June 1, 2016. https://www.forbes.com/sites/katevinton/2016/06/01/these-15-billionaires-own-americas-news-media-companies/#4552402d660a.

Vygotsky, Lev. *Mind in Society. The Development of Higher Psychological Processes.* Cambridge, MA: Fellows of Harvard College, 1978.

Wadsworth, Barry J. *Piaget's Theory of Cognitive and Affective Development.* London: Pearson, 2003.

Walker, Theresa M., and E. Schor. "Pandemic Provokes Spike in Demand for Food Pantries in the US." AP News, April 19, 2020. https://apnews.com/0667573c06ffd15bcebb58f656b1630d.

Wallace-Wells, David. "We Still Don't Know How the Coronavirus is Killing Us." New York Intelligencer, April 26, 2020. https://nymag.com/intelligencer/2020/04/we-still-dont-know-how-the-coronavirus-is-killing-us.html.

Ward, Janie Victoria. "Lessons in Resistance and Resilience," *Diversity and Democracy* 21.1 (2018). https://www.aacu.org/diversitydemocracy/2018/winter/ward.

Warwick, Claire, J. Rimmer, A. Blandford, J. Gow, and G. Buchanan. "Cognitive Economy and Satisficing in Information Seeking: A Longitudinal Study of Undergraduate Information Behavior." *Journal of the American Society for Information Science and Technology* 60.12 (2009) 2402–15.

Washington, George. "Farewell Address, 1796." The Avalon Project. Yale University. https://avalon.law.yale.edu/18th_century/washing.asp.

Weir, Melanie. "10 Alarming Facts about Teacher Salaries in the U.S." *Business Insider*, October 4, 2019. https://www.businessinsider.com/10-alarming-facts-about-teacher-pay-in-the-united-states-2019-10.

Weisberg, Daniel, S. Sexton, J. Mulhern, and D. Keeling. *The Widget Effect*, 2nd ed. The New Teacher Project. New York, 2009. https://tntp.org/assets/documents/TheWidgetEffect_2nd_ed.pdf.

Welna, David. "Navy Not Ruling Out Reinstating USS Roosevelt Skipper Who Complained about Coronavirus. NPR. KQED, April 16, 2020. https://www.npr.org/2020/04/16/836518097/navy-not-ruling-out-reinstating-uss-roosevelt-skipper-who-complained-about-coron.

Wessinger, Catherine. "The Deaths of 76 Branch Davidians in April 1993 Could Have Been Avoided—So Why Didn't anyone Care?" *The Conversation*, April 13, 2018. https://theconversation.com/the-deaths-of-76-branch-davidians-in-april-1993-could-have-been-avoided-so-why-didnt-anyone-care-90816.

White House Press Secretary. "Statement from the Press Secretary Regarding the President's Coronavirus Task Force." [Speech, Washington, D. C. January 29, 2020]. https://www.whitehouse.gov/briefings-statements/statement-press-secretary-regarding-presidents-coronavirus-task-force/.

Whitmire, Ethelene. "Epistemological Beliefs and the Information-seeking Behavior of Undergraduates." *Library & Information Science Research* 25.2 (2003) 127–42.

Wigfall, Catrin. "Teachers Agree: Teachers' Unions Make it Harder to Fire Bad Teachers." Center of the American Experiment, May 17, 2018. https://www.americanexperiment.org/2018/05/teachers-agree-teachers-union-makes-harder-fire-bad-teachers/.

Wilson, Jason. "The Rightwing Christian Preachers in Deep Denial over COVID-19's Danger. *The Guardian*, April 4, 2020. https://www.theguardian.com/us-news/2020/apr/04/america-rightwing-christian-preachers-virus-hoax.

"WHO Urges Nations to Pull 'Out All the Stops' in the Coronavirus fight: 'This is not a Drill." CBS News, March 8, 2020, para 3–4. https://www.cbsnews.com/live-updates/coronavirus-outbreak-death-toll-us-infections-latest-news-updates-2020–03-05/.

Wilke, Christina, and D. Mangan. "Trump Blames Obama for Lack of Coronavirus Tests, 'I Don't' Take Responsibility at All.'" CNBC, March 13, 2020. https://www.cnbc.com/2020/03/13/coronavirus-trump-says-i-dont-take-responsibility-at-all-for-lack-of-tests.html.

Wilson, Jason. "The Rightwing Christian Preachers in Deep Denial of Covid-19 Danger." *The Guardian*, April 4, 2020. https://www.theguardian.com/us-news/2020/apr/04/america-rightwing-christian-preachers-virus-hoax.

Wilson, Steve. "School Administrative Costs Balloon." Mississippi Center for Public Policy, April 17, 2019. https://mspolicy.org/school-administrative-costs-balloon/

Wolf, Michael. *Fire and Fury: Inside the Trump White House*. New York: Henry Holt, 2018.

Wooden, Cindy. "COVID-19 is not God's Judgment, but Call to Live Differently, Pope Says." *National Catholic Reporter*, March 27, 2020. https://www.ncronline.org/news/vatican/covid-19-not-gods-judgment-call-live-differently-pope-says.

Woodward, Bob. *Fear: Trump in the White House*. New York, 2018.

World Health Organization. "Shortage of Personal Protective Equipment Endangering Health Workers Worldwide." Geneva, World Health Organization, March 3, 2020. https://www.who.int/news-room/detail/03-03-2020-shortage-of-personal-protective-equipment-endangering-health-workers-worldwide.

Worldometer. "Coronavirus. South Korea." Chart "Total Coronavirus Deaths in the United States," 2020. https://www.worldometers.info/coronavirus/country/south-korea/.

Worldometer. "Coronavirus. United States." Chart "Total Coronavirus Deaths in the United States," 2020. https://www.worldometers.info/coronavirus/country/us/.

Yariv, Eliezer. "'Challenging' Teachers." *Educational Management Administration Quarterly*, 32 (2004) 149–69.

Yoo, John. "No, Trump Can't Force States to Open." *National Review*, April 13, 2020. https://www.nationalreview.com/2020/04/no-trump-cant-force-states-to-reopen/.

Zachary, G. Pascal. *Endless Frontier: Vannevar Bush Engineer of the American Century.* Cambridge: MA MIT Press, 1999.

Zamoyski, Adam. *Moscow 1812: Napoleon's Fatal March on Moscow.* London: Harper, 2004.

Zivin, Kara, D. Eisenberg, S. E. Gollust, and E. Golberstein. "Persistence of Mental Health Problems and Needs in a College Student Population." *Journal of affective disorders* 117.3 (2009) 180–85.

Index

www.ingramcontent.com/pod-product-compliance
Lightning Source LLC
Chambersburg PA
CBHW061734270326
41928CB00011B/2236